The Beats

'*The Beats: Authorships, Legacies* provides a complex view of the Beat Generation from its origins to its on-going influence. A. Robert Lee packs his study with details on core Beat texts and key figures as well as esoteric works and peripheral figures. He makes visible the intricate web of works and associations so that readers can assemble for themselves the meaning and impact of "Beat". Lee taps his long, productive career in American literary studies to unleash a torrent of insight, biography, and criticism in his meticulously organized and widely inclusive book.'

Matt Theado, Editor of *The Beats: A Literary Reference*

'One of the striking features of A. Robert Lee's scholarship has been his persistent reminder that the Beat Generation was about far more than its architects – Jack Kerouac, Allen Ginsberg and William Burroughs. Lee has produced an important revision of Beat lore, which now includes the critically neglected contributions of African American authors (Ted Joans, Bob Kaufman), as well as female Beats (Diane di Prima, Anne Waldman). Written with brio and authority, this is a tremendous contribution to Beat Studies.'

Douglas Field, University of Manchester

'An impressive and panoramic cartography of Beat creativity. A. Robert Lee charts both iconic texts and their far lesser known (post-) Beat ramifications. Written with an infectious zest and energy, this inclusive survey of an *extended* Beat Generation offers Whitmanesque multitudes!'

Franca Bellarsi, Université libre de Bruxelles

The Beats

Authorships, Legacies

A. ROBERT LEE

EDINBURGH
University Press

Edinburgh University Press is one of the leading university presses in the UK. We publish academic books and journals in our selected subject areas across the humanities and social sciences, combining cutting-edge scholarship with high editorial and production values to produce academic works of lasting importance. For more information visit our website: edinburghuniversitypress.com

Edinburgh University Press Ltd
The Tun – Holyrood Road
12(2f) Jackson's Entry
Edinburgh EH8 8PJ

Typeset in 10/12 Adobe Sabon by
IDSUK (DataConnection) Ltd, and
printed and bound in Great Britain.

A CIP record for this book is available from the British Library

ISBN 978 1 4744 0396 2 (hardback)
ISBN 978 1 4744 0398 6 (webready PDF)
ISBN 978 1 4744 0397 9 (paperback)
ISBN 978 1 4744 0400 6 (epub)

Contents

Acknowledgements

My debts in writing this volume are many, first to writers within the Beat tradition who have given me the benefits of close encounter. Foremost has to be Anne Waldman with whom I have shared panels in Boulder, Tokyo and Brussels and who has been a fount of information backed by her customary energy of spirit. I also have cause to remember with great fondness the late Ted Joans, Lorenzo Thomas, Ron Loewinsohn, Bill Butler and Anselm Hollo. Latterly there have been exchanges with Steve Dalachinsky, Yuko Otomo and Clive Matson. To these I should add Bobbie Louise Hawkins, Ann Charters and Kazuko Shiraishi.

Fellow scholar-critics much come into the frame. Eric Mottram in the 1960s of my students years in London was early to deliver news of the Beats. It now seems a historic landmark to have attended the 1965 Royal Albert Hall 'Wholly Communion' gathering. Contributors to both my time-ago and recent Beat essay collections, *The Beat Generation Writers* (1996) and *The Routledge Handbook of International Beat Literature* (2018), have been mainstays as have those who encouraged the work behind *Modern American Counter Writing: Beats, Outriders, Ethnics* (2010). Over this span I have also had the bonus of much shared Beat correspondence with Jennie Skerl, Nancy M. Grace and Steven Belletto.

Matt Theado, Douglas Field and Franca Bellarsi were good enough to read portions of the manuscript. Their keen eye and sharp suggestions have been invaluable. Thank you. For the ongoing benefit of exchange in ideas I have gained greatly from fellow members of the European Beat Studies Network (EBSN) at whose 2nd Annual Meeting in Denmark in 2013 I was privileged to give the keynote address: 'Beat Compass: Literary Widths and Circles'. It is a true advantage to have the friendship of Jaap van der Bent, Erik Mortensen, Polina McKay, Bent Sørensen, Frida Forsgren, Lars

Movin, Simon Warner, Kurt Hemmer, Thomas Antonic, Benjamin Heal and Peggy Pacini.

I also need to acknowledge Lisa Yinwen Yu at the University of Arizona and Estíbaliz Encarnación-Pinedo at the University of Murcia for their help with book borrowing and reference. Both are owed my great thanks.

A hurrah to Michelle Houston as Commissioning Editor at the University of Edinburgh Press for all her support. Equally my great thanks to Martin Halliwell as Academic Editor for this BAAS series for his conscientious scrutiny of the text.

As always, the singular debt I owe to Josefa Vivancos Hernández un-diminishes. *Mil gracias.*

BAAS Paperbacks

Published titles

African American Visual Arts
Celeste-Marie Bernier
The American Short Story since 1950
Kasia Boddy
American Imperialism: The Territorial Expansion of the United States, 1783–2013
Adam Burns
The Cultures of the American New West
Neil Campbell
The Open Door Era: United States Foreign Policy in the Twentieth Century
Michael Patrick Cullinane and Alex Goodall
Gender, Ethnicity and Sexuality in Contemporary American Film
Jude Davies and Carol R. Smith
The United States and World War II: The Awakening Giant
Martin Folly
The Sixties in America: History, Politics and Protest
M. J. Heale
Religion, Culture and Politics in the Twentieth-Century United States
Mark Hulsether
The Civil War in American Culture
Will Kaufman
The United States and European Reconstruction, 1945–1960
John Killick
American Exceptionalism
Deborah L. Madsen
American Autobiography
Rachael McLennan
The American Landscape
Stephen F. Mills
Slavery and Servitude in North America, 1607–1800
Kenneth Morgan
The Civil Rights Movement
Mark Newman
The Twenties in America: Politics and History
Niall Palmer

American Theatre
Theresa Saxon
The Vietnam War in History, Literature and Film
Mark Taylor
Contemporary Native American Literature
Rebecca Tillett
Jazz in American Culture
Peter Townsend
The New Deal
Fiona Venn
Animation and America
Paul Wells
Political Scandals in the USA
Robert Williams
Black Nationalism in American History: From the Nineteenth Century to the Million Man March
Mark Newman
The American Photo-Text, 1930–1960
Caroline Blinder
The Beats: Authorships, Legacies
A. Robert Lee

Forthcoming titles
American Detective Fiction
Ruth Hawthorn
Staging Transatlantic Relations, 1776–1917
Theresa Saxon
American Poetry since 1900
Nick Selby
The US Graphic Novel
Paul Williams
The Classical Tradition and Modern American Fiction
Tessa Roynon
The Canada US Border: Culture and Theory
Jeffrey Orr and David Stirrup

www.edinburghuniversitypress.com/series/BAAS

Introduction

my poetry is Angelic Ravings.

Allen Ginsberg, 'Notes Written on Finally Recording
"Howl"' (1959)[1]

Write for the world to read and see yr exact pictures of it.

Jack Kerouac, 'Belief & Technique for Modern Prose:
List of Essentials' (1958)[2]

I want the flare & counterpoints of words
& I want the non-verbal – what never can be spoken
as a foundation.

Diane di Prima, 'The Poetry Deal' (2014)[3]

FOR YOU
I OFFER
THIS poem
FOR YOU
ARE IN
DEED
IN NEED
OF A
   black poem

Ted Joans, *Black Pow-Wow* (1969)[4]

The Beats. The Beat Generation. 'Howl', *On the Road, Naked Lunch*. The bow made in America's 1940s–50s, with a follow-through into the fabled 1960s, has long taken on the status of period myth, the energising thrust of mid-twentieth century dissent, the show-and-tell of counterculture. Beat's legendary names, moreover, continue to resonate: Allen Ginsberg, Jack Kerouac, William

I

Burroughs, with Gregory Corso and Lawrence Ferlinghetti in the frame. Their literary insignia remains foundational, that of 'alternative' path-makers. Invocation of Diane di Prima alongside underlines that, however belated the recognition, Beat possesses its formidable range of women writers for whom di Prima serves as pioneer main strength. Ted Joans, likewise, underlines that Afro-America, its own writers and those of other birthright drawn to its jazz and style, holds a premier role in the formation of Beat. Even so, and for all that they offer necessary points of departure, the reputational figures as those more situated at the margins still do not wholly tell the story of Beat authorship or of its different legacies.

For Beat writings have actually always been the wider consortium. The manifestations span the East and West Coast (sometimes called the Left Coast), male and female, straight and gay, white and black, countercultural and best-selling, Judaeo-Christian and Buddhist, national and international, and, in historical perspective, from the immediate post-World War II right through to the twenty-first century. Beat, too, has its overlap with America's contending post-war literary formations: Charles Olson's Black Mountain, Frank O'Hara and the New York School, Robert Lowell's or Sylvia Plath's confessional writing, and the San Francisco Renaissance ushered in by Kenneth Rexroth. Nor is this to forgo asking to what degree Beat authors themselves remained Beat, or whether those like Burroughs or City Light's poet-publisher Lawrence Ferlinghetti or jazz-and-text practitioners like ruth weiss unambiguously belong in the cohort.

It is this wider graph that this book endeavours to negotiate: Beat writing down the timeline and yet as often time-specific, an interpretative map yet the particularity of given texts. The emphasis on authorship also takes into account poetics, Kerouac's 'Essentials of Spontaneous Prose', Ginsberg's open-field and breath-line theory of composition, and the anti-linear collage and cut-up devised by Burroughs and Brion Gysin and coevally deployed by Harold Norse and Kathy Acker. That, however, is not to overlook the divergent routes from Beat into beatniks and hippiedom and the myriad filters into popular culture, film, music, couture, rap, and even the American language itself. The eight successive chapters all are meant to operate within these interlocking contexts. They reflect the fact that holding out for any single Beat template, the all-purpose litmus definition, inevitably veers into difficulty. Hence the recurrence, throughout, of terms like Beat-inflected, Beat-related and Beat-connected. Even Beat Generation, or Beat Generations in one reformulation, reflects the always approximate nature of literary-cultural labels.

Chapter 1 offers a *tour d'horizon* – Beat as American counter-force and ethos. The overview of writer-players and sites calls up Manhattan's Columbia University circle and Greenwich Village and encampments in San Francisco's North Beach and Haight-Ashbury. Cold War anxiety and the atomic bomb give the one backdrop, the Eisenhower-era consumer and suburban boom the other. This disquiet at both threads through early Beat as it does the 1960s of Beat-into-beatnik. The ensuing Ginsberg and Kerouac chapters configure the two authors' careers, their achievements beyond mainstream condescension or excitable whirls of media headline. In their wake 'Insider Beats' and 'Beat Outriders' address sixteen or so names from John Clellon Holmes to Herbert Huncke, Gary Snyder to Harold Norse. This output, seamed in salute to the human spirit yet keenly investigative of its frequent dark slippages, operates in a near-opulent mix of genres. Whether alternative America or expatriate, city-modern or environmental, activist or Zen-spiritual, high serious or given to dark laughter, it is writing that so extends the literary bandwidth quite beyond Beat's usual suspects.

Time was when women's Beat participation assumedly lay outside the canon, muted, unlit. With the rise of Second Generation feminism and its footfalls in literary criticism through into the 1990s and beyond, this balance rightly has undergone shift, not just the pages of di Prima but a trove of life writing, verse and fiction. The winning of full recognition holds, too, for the authorship addressed in 'Afro-Beat'. Who more than African American Beats have claimed and displayed literary custodianship of jazz, bebop, blues, Harlem and historic black community style? The closing chapter, given over to inter-Beat and post-Beat authorship, explores legacy, associate texts from within the inaugural epoch and subsequent texts that hail, yet at the same time transpose and reinscribe, earlier tiers.

It would be disingenuous to pretend that Beat has not garnered a vast range of studies, be it critique, author profiles, biography or cultural histories. The bibliography at the end of this volume, albeit still selective, bears witness to this. *The Beats: Authorships, Legacies*, I hope, takes sufficient fresh soundings to remind why

Beat literature exerts continuing attraction, generational renewals of readership. Angelic ravings or exact pictures as may be, flare and counterpoint or black poem, Beat authorship in its time and in its legacies remains embedded not only in the dissenting America which produced it but in quite the world's wider cultural regimes.

Notes

1. Allen Ginsberg, 'Notes Written on Finally Recording "Howl"', *Evergreen Review*, 3: 10, 1959, 135.
2. Jack Kerouac, 'Belief & Technique for Modern Prose: List of Essentials', Letter to Donald Allen, 1958. Reprinted in *Evergreen Review*, 3:10 (Spring 1959) and *Good Blonde & Others*, ed. Donald Allen, San Francisco: Grey Fox, 1998, 72–3.
3. Diane di Prima, 'The Poetry Deal', *The Poetry Deal*, San Francisco: City Lights Books, 2014, 19.
4. Ted Joans, 'For you I offer . . .', *Black Pow-Wow*, New York: Hill & Wang, 1969, Preface.

CHAPTER I

Beat Origins and Circuits, 1940s–1960s

The stakes are too great – an America gone mad with materialism, a police state America, a sexless and soulless America prepared to battle the world in defense of its Authority. Not the wild and beautiful America of comrades of Whitman, not the historic America of Blake and Thoreau where the spiritual Independence of each individual was an America, a Universe, more huge and awesome than all the abstract bureaucracies and authoritative Officialdoms of the World combined.

Allen Ginsberg, *San Francisco Sunday Chronicle* (1959)[1]

There was nowhere to go but everywhere . . .

Jack Kerouac, *On the Road* (1957)[2]

Authorships, Legacies

Those drawn at the outset to the banner of Jack Kerouac and Allen Ginsberg, and to the lead accompanying figures of William Burroughs, Gregory Corso and Lawrence Ferlinghetti, had little doubt of a call to rally. To adherents, Beat seemed one of the wonders of the age: alternative, full of stir and passion, youth-oriented, spiritual while given over to sexual liberation, jazz-inclined and yielding a compendium of landmark texts none more so than *Howl and Other Poems* (1956), *On the Road* (1957) and *Naked Lunch* (1959). Here was a jolt of consciousness, a riposte, from within 1940s–50s America to the perceived dead hand of conformism and the Cold War. The follow-on 1960s, long designated a mythic change decade, re-enforces the impression, and creates footfalls that in turn have continued as far forward as the Obama–Trump century. None of which is to overlook that opinion early and late could veer quite the other way. Was this not coterie bohemianism, self-promoting, too shallow or narcissistic? Yet pathway or fad, and to adapt Ezra Pound's formula, Beat in whatever vying respects has been news that stays news.[3]

Defining Beat

First, to be sure, has to be the issue of definition, especially given that Beat has become a term of near-global vocabulary. If no single hold-all meaning presides, a number of latitudes and longitudes come into consideration. It was Herbert Huncke, Times Square hustler and addict and author of the premium-named *Guilty of Everything* (1990), who first famously passed on the word 'beat' as meaning beaten-down, life met and embodied at degree-zero. Kerouac, quite as famously, blended this notion of beat seen from the bottom tier into beatific, *beatus*, a spiritualised take on existence. His sources lie in the New Testament's beatitudes, the Catholicism of his Québecois family upbringing in Lowell, Massachusetts, and the Zen and other forms of Buddhism that manifests itself in *The Dharma Bums* (1958), the 262 choruses of *Mexico City Blues* (1959) and his Totem Press pamphlet, *The Scripture of the Golden Eternity* (1960) with its 'The awakened Buddha to show the way'.[4] Allen Ginsberg's formulation in 'Howl' (1956) of 'angelheaded hipsters' has long featured in Beat nomenclature (hard to remember that the original 1920s meaning of hipster was one who carried a hip flask of booze).[5] The titling of John Tytell's *Naked Angels: Lives and Literature of the Beat Generation* (1976), early Beat scholarship by a Greenwich Village regular, again underscores Beat's claim to spiritual as much as countercultural standing.

Jazz equally feeds into the mix, the beat of rhythm, cadence, swing.[6] Sources span the bebop and sax of Charlie Parker, the trumpet of Miles Davis, the double-bass and ensemble compositions of Charles Mingus, the clarinet of Mezz Mezzrow, the alto sax of Lee Konitz, or, from an earlier time, the throated lilt of a Bessie Smith blues. To a generation of black musicians from the Jazz Age onward to be 'hip' was to be tuned in, ear and eye, body and mind, to the lives behind each club or concert performance or the albums (vinyl and in due course CD) issued from a massively historic recording company like Blue Note Records. Beat precursor novels like

Chandler Brossard's *Who Walk in Darkness* (1952), with its Green-
wich Village down-and-out storyline and setting, or Barbara Probst
Solomon's *The Beat of Life* (1960), with its Beat-like portrait of
post-war generational malaise, both use jazz as necessary motif.
James Baldwin, himself no stranger to jazz, both in life and literary
idiom as his two-brother story 'Sonny's Blues' (1957) bears out,
insisted on the influence of a vintage black Dixie or Harlem locution
like 'beat to his socks'.[7] That is not to doubt that Beat's best-known
early voices were mainly, although not exclusively, white, mostly
male, straight or gay (often enough both), Jewish or Catholic with
admixtures of Buddhism, middle class though on occasion, as in the
case of Kerouac, up from working-class ranks, and located most
in the bohemia of New York's Greenwich Village and California's
North Beach.

Kerouac, as if to allay the claims and counterclaims, supplies
one of Beat's foundational sightlines. His 'About the Beat Genera-
tion', written the year he published *On the Road*, and opening with
an unbroken, fast-pulsed paragraph, bespeaks something akin to
devotional calling:

> The Beat Generation, that was a vision that we had, John
> Clellon Holmes and I, and Allen Ginsberg in an even wilder way,
> in the late Forties, of a generation of crazy, illuminated hipsters
> suddenly rising and roaming America, serious, bumming and
> hitchhiking everywhere, ragged, beatific, beautiful in an ugly
> graceful new way – a vision gleaned from the way we had the
> word 'beat' spoken on street corners on Times Square and in
> the Village, in other cities in the downtown city night of post-
> war America – beat, meaning down and out but full of intense
> conviction ... It never meant juvenile delinquents, it meant
> characters of a special spirituality who didn't gang up but were
> solitary Bartlebies staring out the dead wall of our civilization –
> the subterranean heroes who'd finally turned from the 'freedom'
> machine of the West and were taking drugs, digging bop, having
> flashes of insight, experiencing the 'derangement of the senses,'
> talking strange, being poor and glad, prophesying a new style
> for American culture ...[8]

The collocation of 'illuminated hipsters', 'downtown city night', and
America under the 'subterranean' purview of 'solitary Bartlebies'

sets the compass. Beat's manifesto, with lexicon to match, could not
have been more strikingly indicated.

The reference back to John Clellon Holmes, whose novel *Go*
(1952) maps the Ginsberg–Kerouac generation as a *roman à clé*,
brings into play the voice of another key participant observer.
'This is the Beat Generation', his *New York Times* column of
November 1952, offers there-at-the-time witness to a changing
American consciousness:

> Any attempt to label a whole generation is unrewarding, and yet
> the generation that went through the last war, or at least could
> get a drink easily when it was over, seems to possess a uniform,
> general quality which demands an adjective . . . The origins of
> the word 'beat' are obscure, but the meaning is only too clear to
> most Americans. More than mere weariness, it implies the feel-
> ing of having been used, of being raw. It involves a sort of naked-
> ness of mind, and ultimately, of soul; a feeling of being reduced
> to the bedrock of consciousness. In short, it means being pushed
> undramatically up against the wall of oneself. A man is beat
> whenever he goes for broke and wagers the sum of his resources
> on a single number . . .[9]

The piece, in kind with Holmes's memoirs and other novels, does
much to underline Beat as at core existential, and vexing as the term
can be, indeed spiritual. So, at least, he interprets an avant-garde
mindful of recent Atlantic and Pacific wars and a domestic economy
given over to consumer boom and acquisition. The effect, to his eye
as much as to that of Kerouac, was cultural straitjacket, an America
of dead middle-class etiquette. Melville's 'Bartleby' again does ser-
vice, Beat's sense of being pushed 'up against the wall of oneself'.[10]

LeRoi Jones/Amiri Baraka, one of the few African American
poets first implicated in Beat, succinctly looks back in his 1979
interview with Debra Edwards:

> Beat came out of the whole dead Eisenhower period, the whole
> of the McCarthy Era, the Eisenhower blandness, the whole reac-
> tionary period of the 50s. The Beat Generation was a distinct
> reaction to that, a reaction not only to reactionary politics, reac-
> tionary life style of the American ruling class and sections of the
> middle class, reaction to the conservatism and McCarthyism of

that period. Also reaction to the kind of academic poetry and academic literature that was being pushed as great works by the American establishment. So it was a complete reaction: socially, politically, and of course artistically to what the 50s represented.[11]

Albeit that his career would move on and away from Beat to Harlem and into Black Nationalist and Marxist phases, there can be no doubting its importance for him as a counter-force to the 'blandness' and 'reactionary life style' he so excoriates. But much as he proceeds to praise Ginsberg ('a good teacher', 'a great publicizer of poets') and gives a backward glance of some affection to the 'hip bohemianism' of Greenwich Village in the late 1950s, he is also not above taking a back-of-the-hand swipe. Fairly or otherwise his retrospect is summary: 'The whole Beat thing I always thought of as a publicity gimmick.'[12]

Anne Waldman, intergenerational poet heir to Beat and with it American–Buddhist literary tradition and whose pattern-poem 'Fast Speaking Woman' (1975) remains a feminist pinnacle, offers later but no less relevant bearings. In the introduction to the anthology *Beats at Naropa* (2009) she wholly recognises Beat as historic, in its way seismic. But she, too, admits hesitancy in holding so highly various a roster of writers to just the one determinative category:

> While many authors in this collection do not feel comfortable with the term 'Beat,' or feel their identity does not lie under a 'Beat' rubric, they have nevertheless been historically linked (guilt by association?) through friendships and associations with Jack Kerouac, who named it and Allen Ginsberg who ran with it. It was Ginsberg who single-handedly created the Beat literary/cultural mythology and was invested in its perpetuation for a number of reasons, not the least being the grandiose need to foist an alternative poetics onto the larger 'official verse culture' mainstream.[13]

Beat manages to overlap, but by no means fuse, all these differing tributaries.

Recognition is also due that none of the presiding first-generation names actually signed on to create a movement, political or cultural, or to become Beat legends. Allen Ginsberg, for all his role in Beat literary/cultural mythology and with 'Howl' long installed as one of

the signature texts, looked back to Beat in a 1980s interview as aris-
ing more from serendipity than any fixed ideological intent: 'Nobody
knows whether we were catalysts or invented something, or just the
froth riding on a wave of its own. We were all three, I suppose.'[14]

In his shorthand-notes introduction to *Lonesome Traveler*
(1960) Kerouac showed impatience with, as he believed it, the myo-
pia of critics who 'failed to notice beneath frenetic activity of my
true-story novels about the "beat" generation. – Am actually not
"beat" but strange solitary Catholic mystic'[15] Likewise, in 'The
Origins of the Beat Generation' (1960), and with an eye to how
On the Road had seized his era's readership, he decried the slide
of Beat into beatnik: 'It is not my fault that certain so-called bohe-
mian elements have found in my writings something to hang their
peculiar beatnik theories on.'[16] However close his friendships with
Ginsberg and Kerouac, or indissoluble from the whole phenome-
non, Burroughs even more expressly disavowed Beat as applicable
to his work. Laconic as always, he came to look back on Beat as a
hand-me-down label coarsened into sales pitch. *On the Road*, he
would observe with lowered eye, 'opened a million coffee bars and
sold a million pairs of Levis to both sexes. Woodstock rises from its
pages.'[17]

Gregory Corso: The Last Beat (2009), Gustave Reininger's doc-
umentary film has Corso saying 'You don't make a generation of
four people. Four does not a generation make.'[18] In the film docu-
mentary *Ferlinghetti: A Rebirth of Wonder* (2013) the co-founder
of City Lights Bookstore in 1953, and by his own self-designation
an old-time San Francisco North Beach radical, takes umbrage at
being designated Beat. 'Don't call me a Beat,' Ferlinghetti insists,
'I never was a Beat poet.'[19] Rather, as he still frequently emphasises,
he became the publisher of Beats and of the milestone Pocket Books
Poets Series launched with his own *Pictures of the Gone World* in
1955 and whose Number 4 issue would be Ginsberg's *Howl and
Other Poems*.[20]

Other contraflows add to the mix. Kerouac's conservatism, and
his tolerance of McCarthyism and then late-career anti-Semitism
and other ethnic slurs, ill comports with Ginsberg as Jewish liberal.
Debate continues to ask in quite what degree other than inner-circle
writing and intimacy Burroughs was Beat, and not least given that
he was older than the others by a decade, two in the case of Corso.
It is a matter of record that Ferlinghetti initially turned down *Naked*

Lunch for City Lights as 'disgusting', beyond the pale. Are there not co-Beat, or just-after Beat, or indeed post-Beat literary generations with different emphases and inclinations and which feature names, besides Waldman, as disparate as Michael McClure, Jack Micheline, Ray Bremser, Philip Whalen, Philip Lamantia, Ed Sanders (along with Tuli Kupferberg founder of satiric rock-troupe the Fugs), Lew Welch, Ted Joans, Andy Clausen, David Meltzer, Richard Brautigan, Kathy Acker, or music's Bob Dylan, Jim Morrison, Tom Waits, Patti Smith and John Lennon? Beat may have been passed down in the single label or media soundbite, but it contains any number of follow-on spirals and folds.

Beats, Beatniks, Hippies

Beat into beatnik, the transition again prompts ambiguity if not outright contradiction. 'Bloody king of the beatniks', 'I'm a Catholic not a beatnik' – Kerouac's dismay is palpable.[21] It finds an echo in the letter Ginsberg felt moved to write to the *New York Times* in May 1959: 'If beatniks and not illuminated Beat Poets overrun this country, they will have been created not by Kerouac but by industries of mass communication which continue to brainwash man . . .'[22] Whether derived from the Sputnik launched into space by Soviet Russia in October 1957 and so tinged in Cold War and Red Scare apprehension, or a Yiddish-suffixed putdown, beatnik as a term was largely aimed to disparage the Beats. Certainly, the journalist Herb Caen, who coined the term in his 2 April 1958 column for the *San Francisco Chronicle*, intended jibe rather than praise. He, like other detractors, regarded Beats as goateed men in sandals, women in black, a legion of coffeehouse poseurs in 'shades' given to the reiterative argot of 'man', 'cool' and 'square'. On the other hand, Fred W. McDarrah, *The Village Voice* photographer and creator of Rent-a-Beatnik with Ted Joans, a caper in which Joans and other poets would offer the thrill of performing their 'dissident' work in the homes of well-paying suburbanites, writes 'Anatomy of a Beatnik' for the magazine *Saga* with its fun list of requisites from beards to 'chicks dressed in black'. He also decries how the beatnik has become journalism's 'new scapegoat', 'a whipping boy'.[23] Occasionally, beatnik even served as code for criminality, dope-dealing or larceny, or, at a lesser reach, illegal squats and nuisance panhandling. Latterly, 'Beatnik Cowboy' becomes the title

of a Beat-influenced journal published since 2003 in Cambodia by
Randall K. Rogers and also the tabloid moniker for the celebrity
actor Johnny Depp, both instances of retro-naming as it were.

Definitions blur once more as beatnik elides into hippie, the
Age of Aquarius and Flower Children, and to be associated with
Haight-Ashbury communes, treks to India and Nepal in search
of transcendental enlightenment, drug regimes that turn to LSD
as much as marijuana, and a couture of flared trousers, 'granny'
dresses, feathers, shades, and Afro or ponytailed hair.[24] The best-
known apotheosis remains the Human Be-In in San Francisco's
Golden Gate Park in January 1967, a gathering of 30,000, with
many on acid and Ginsberg, Michael McClure, Gary Snyder and
Lenore Kandel among the participant names, and which leads into
the Summer of Love. Hippies saw their style musically embodied
in Jefferson Airplane (rarely more so than in Grace Slick's 'White
Rabbit'), the Glasgow-born Donovan whose 'Mellow Yellow'
released in 1966 took hold as the very expression of Flower Power,
and Scott McKenzie's 'San Francisco (Wear Flowers in Your Hair)'
written by John Philips of the Mamas and the Papas. Corso, how-
ever, in due course, would castigate Donovan, Jim Morrison and
even Bob Dylan, on grounds that they were rock or folk musicians
not poets. Use of LSD has best-known avatars in Timothy Leary,
Ivy League psychologist, author of *The Politics of Ecstasy* (1968),
and Ginsberg associate and frequent counterculture fugitive, and
Ken Kesey, whose *One Flew over the Cuckoo's Nest* (1962) would
be assumed into Beat literary ranks and whose Merry Prankster
road travels begin in 1963 with Neal Cassady at the wheel of their
rainbow-painted International Harvester school bus.

Hippiedom's dramatis personae are many, notable among them
Abbie Hoffman, activist, druggie, friend of Ginsberg, and author of
Revolution for the Hell of It (1968) and *Steal This Book* (1971), and
Jerry Rubin, Berkeley dropout, co-founder of the Yippies (Youth
International Party), the performance wit who writes *DO IT!:
Scenarios of the Revolution* (1970), and, in a keen irony, becomes
eventual Wall Street millionaire. Another name in the Beat-related
countercultural ranks is that of Peter Coyote, a founder-actor in
the Haight-Ashbury anarchist performance group San Francisco
Diggers and lifetime Zen practitioner. At an extreme reach Charles
Manson and his 'Family' transpose Beat/hippiedom into criminal
pathology, a crazed death-cult that leads to the Hollywood murder

of the actress Sharon Tate and others in August 1969. This was Beat or Beat-like 'revolution' skewed into madness, a supposed redemptive cleansing of middle-class custom and affluence. For their part hippies, and the branch into yippies (the Youth International Party founded at the close of 1967), evolve from theatrics both serious and antic into contrastingly hard-edged punk.

The music, hard but in a number of cases soft, vaults Iggy Pop and the Stooges, the Velvet Underground of Lou Reed and John Cale, the New York Dolls, the Ramones, and UK groups like the Sex Pistols (formed 1975) and the Clash (1976–86) with their aggressive shout-lyrics, piercings, tattoos, and ripped and safety-pin clothing. The last much acknowledged Burroughs and *Naked Lunch* as master script. The image, however, eases with Debbie Harry, punk madonna during the mid-1970s to early 1980s with her group Blondie. If Kerouac had no doubt that the beatnik-hippie syndrome had veered a measurable distance away from original Beat, Ginsberg serves as more of a bridge figure, especially to the hippies and a number of punk outfits. Despite media caricature Beat again resists the one all-purpose fit, the summary tag.

Yet, however Beat has morphed, or crisscrossed, the inaugural compass holds on tenaciously. It continues through a bandwidth of, say, Ginsberg's ground-breaking performance of 'Howl' at the 6 Gallery, 3119 Fillmore Street, San Francisco, on 7 October 1955 to Stephen Willis's Afro-rap adaptation on YouTube in 2014.[25] Gil Scott-Heron's spoken-sung 'The Revolution Will Not Be Televised' (1970), that of a 'bluesologist' in his own term, bridges jazz, Beat and rap. Whether the written page, campus readings, poetry slams, film or music festivals, biopics, or however baleful to certain true believers, academic and literary conferences, each has helped not only install but perpetuate Beat's evolving contour. In these respects Manhattan's Greenwich Village not only links to San Francisco's North Beach but into a huge variety of staging-posts both in-between and geographies well beyond. Outposts span Mexico and India, and cities like Paris, London, Amsterdam, Tangier and Kyoto. Beat's portability, as much as its staying power, is not to be doubted.

Two events, nonetheless, offer seminal Beat markers. The obscenity trial of *Howl and Other Poems* in 1957, following the seizure of 252 copies from the British printer by US Customs albeit that they did not press charges, led on to police raids on City Lights for sale of the book and the arrest of Ferlinghetti and his bookstore manager,

Shigeyoshi Murao, on 3 June 1957. The ensuing court case gave Beat
a spate of headlines amid which Ginsberg was to be thought either
gratuitous pornographer or free-speech hero. Jack Kerouac's appear-
ance on NBC's *Steve Allen Show* in November 1959, and his read-
ings to piano accompaniment, would be watched by over 30 million
viewers. Ginsberg, undeniably, relished the publicity, even if it took
little account of the altogether more consequential, and authentically
generous, efforts he made to edit and promote the literary work of
fellow writers. Kerouac, however, whose ebullience when drinking
masked an inherent shyness, came to regard Beat notoriety as he saw
it as cheapening the claims to serious authorship aimed for in *On
the Road* and the succeeding work. Yet allowing for this insistence
on writing unshackled from the one category, Beat remained, and
remains, nomenclature familiarly and inerasably in play.

Beat Canon

The preeminent writings, within or despite the publicity, continue
to resonate. Jack Kerouac bequeaths *On the Road*, 'spontaneous'
highway epic, which since publication has served as inspirational
American text for life taken uninhibitedly at the full. Allen Ginsberg
creates 'Howl' as the essential Beat anthem, at once portentous, a
hex, his own Talmudic incantation. In William Burroughs, Beat has
its Darth Vader whose *Naked Lunch*, with its episodic story-panels
(the cut-ups feature more in his later fiction) and often wickedly
funny-satiric thrusts, takes aim at agencies of control, media hegem-
ony and word virus. Gregory Corso, for whom Shelley was always
the inspirational spirit, lives on for a range of wryly observational
poems, one of Beat's best wits. He writes both wholly serious jest
like 'Bomb' and the more teasing 'Marriage' in *The Happy Birth-
day of Death* (1960) as well as frolicsome early poems like 'The
Mad Yak' in *Gasoline* (1958). If Beat has its inaugural gallery, these
authors and texts do duty, a literary skyline.

Each associated publication by fellow Beats adds momentum,
the resolve upon new beckonings of imagination. Lawrence Ferling-
hetti's *Pictures of the Gone World* (1955) and *A Coney Island of the
Mind* (1958) make available savvy, light-satirical talk poems, often
ekphrastic as befits a lifelong maker of canvases and line-drawings.
Neal Cassady, Denver-bred hipster of road and freight train and
Ginsberg's 'secret hero' in 'Howl' and Kerouac's Dean Moriarty
in *On the Road*, solicits his own literary nod of recognition in

the autobiography of *The First Third* (1982) and the accelerated life-register of his *Collected Letters, 1944–1967* (2004). Herbert Huncke's *Guilty of Everything* (1987), with its storying of Times Square street and drug underworld, confirms his role as one-time Beat source. Michael McClure's *Hymns to St. Geryon and Other Poems* (1959), especially a poem of Beat–Buddhist compassion like 'For the Death of 100 Whales', indicates in its verse-spacing and capitalisations the experimentalist to follow. Gary Snyder, doyen of the Pacific Northwest and lifelong student of Asian religion, writings and art, affords Beat its ranking Buddhist and eco-poet, beginning with *Riprap* from Origin Press in 1959 and nowhere more emphatic than in his summa of environmentalist imagination *Mountains and Rivers without End* (1996).[26]

Beat and Women

Axially, given that Beat notoriously has been seen as overwhelmingly an in-house male group, a boys' club of mutual promotion, not to say of bar and bed, women writers enter the frame. Starting-points summon the Glasgow-born poet and photographer Helen Adam who moves to the United States in 1939 and whose San Francisco early performance (a *Helen Adam Reader* became available in 2007) anticipates Ginsberg, with whom she was friends, and the London-born Denise Levertov who takes US citizenship in 1955 and whose imagist classic *Here and Now* (1956) was published as Pocket Poets Number Six.[27] Both, in their take on life as in their poetics, might be regarded as Beat forerunners and companions in spirit. But no name garners more deserved repute than Diane di Prima, poet, small-magazine editor, dramatist, fiction writer, autobiographer, and, in a creative lifetime from Greenwich Village to California, an encompassing Beat exemplar.

A line of feminist verse epics, besides di Prima's *Loba* sequence, evolves in Kyger's *The Tapestry and the Web* (1965) with its centre in the Penelope myth, ruth weiss's account of creative inner life, *Desert Journal* (1977), and Anne Waldman's compendious *Iovis* begun in 1993. Waldman's *Fast Speaking Woman and Other Chants* (1975), the title-poem above all, has been seminal, at once performance-piece, banner, a rally. It takes its place alongside the jazz and recitation poetry of ruth weiss, North Beach luminary. Witness narratives to Beat, autobiography and memoir, add measure, each with own inventive swerve, by Joyce Johnson, Carolyn

Cassady, Helen Weaver and Hettie Jones. Dynasty plays its role in
the writings of Edie Kerouac-Parker, Joan Haverty Kerouac and
her daughter, Jan Kerouac, and female 'road' trajectory in Bonnie
Bremser and Janine Pommy Vega. The name-list extends in differ-
ent directions, whether the posthumously published Elise Cowen,
the singer-poet Patti Smith, or key West Coast visual artists like
Jay DeFeo and Bernice Bing.[28] The impact has been considerable:
the overdue if still not wholly sufficient female repositioning of the
assumed Beat canon.[29]

Afro-Beat

Afro-Beat contributes another essential gallery of voice, jazz-seamed,
full of spoken riff, and inevitably alert to historic black culture and
America's race-lines. The upshot is a formidable roster, notably LeRoi
Jones before his Islamisation into Imamu Amiri Baraka; Ted Joans as
minstrel poet of East Village, Paris, the Maghreb and Mali; Bob Kauf-
man, whose poetry voices life at the margins with jazz and whose
Abomunist pamphlets carry his long interest in Surrealism and anar-
cho-Dada; and A. B. Spellman, jazz critic, poet, and National Endow-
ment of the Arts administrator. Each of these writers draws from the
massive archive of community history, music, sermon, speechifying
and politics. The emergence of the Black Aesthetic in the 1960s, the
view that black art and authorship should serve and be judged by its
relevance to the black community, called for 'nationalist' terms well
beyond Beat. A number of black writers, however fully alert to the
politics of race, objected, among them Ishmael Reed (who called the
leading proponents black sheriffs) and James Baldwin. Rather they
saw Black Arts as being more open to the widths of black experience
without the straitjacket of ideology or the one or another 'realist' lit-
erary form. In its wake came the postcolonial turn, African American
writing bridged to that of Africa, the Caribbean, black Latin America
or Europe. Black Beat authorship, as located in the one countercul-
tural paradigm, so has to be given yet wider anchorage.[30]

Beat Consorts

Beat was early to find consorts beyond Ginsberg and his immediates.
They yield their connecting thread. Street or spoken Beat finds voice
in Jack Micheline's *River of Red Wine* (1958), its preface penned

by Kerouac ('he has the swinging free style I like and his sweet lines revive the poetry of open hope in America') and to whom, reciprocally, homage is paid in 'Chasing Jack Kerouac's Shadow' (1982). Ray Bremser's *Poems of Madness* (1965) and *Angel* (1967) reflect a life lived under drug and prison auspices. Andy Clausen, whose performance scripts once caused Ginsberg to call him 'the future of American poetry', offers a *tour d'horizon* of life and work in his reverse-titled *Fortieth-Century Man: Selected Verse, 1996–1966* (1997). In Philip Lamantia, Beat had a San Francisco surrealist drugs and jazz co-spirit, author of collections like *Ekstasis* (1959) and *Touch of the Marvelous* (1966) and husband of Nancy Peters, City Light's executive editor. William Everson (Brother Antoninus), convert to Catholic mysticism, Beat's lay Dominican monk and long-time Berkleyite, becomes a well-known giver of spiritual counsel and public reader of his poetry from *The Crooked Lines of God* (1959) to later collections like *The Residual Years* (1997). Others, if at one remove, can include Harold Norse, variously City Lights poet, gay activist and author of *The Beat Hotel* (1983) and *Memoirs of a Bastard Angel* (1989); Hunter Thompson of New Journalist celebrity and *Fear and Loathing in America: The Brutal Odyssey of an Outlaw Journalist, 1968–1976* (2000); and Charles Bukowski, chronicler of Los Angeles low-life whose dyspepsia towards the Beats does not disguise affiliations in the compositional pitch of his fiction and poetry. It would be hard to doubt the period's Beat, or Beat-inflected, plenty.

Beat, too, has overlaps with a range of other literary consortia. Black Mountain authorship, headed by the Charles Olson of his epic *Maximus* poems and theories of projective verse and by a poet as durable and finely concentrated as Robert Creeley, supplies one connection. *Black Mountain Review 7*, co-edited with Ginsberg, would contain work by Burroughs, Kerouac and Ginsberg himself. Another is to be met in the New York School with its playful sense of city picturing and space and whose luminaries include Frank O'Hara (a particular Ginsberg friend), John Ashbery, Kenneth Koch and Barbara Guest with a second wave in Ted Berrigan, Joe Brainard and Anne Waldman. Of the confessional poets, Robert Lowell always credited Ginsberg with 'loosening' his WASP New England classicism. The San Francisco Renaissance poets, for whom the writer-polymath Kenneth Rexroth served as titular presence, have their own discrete standing. But the West Coast literary work of Robert

Duncan, Jack Spicer, Madeline Gleason, Lew Welsh, Philip Whalen, William Everson, Philip Lamantia and the painter-poet Kenneth Patchen, frequently connects to Beat poetics, and not least in the writings of Lawrence Ferlinghetti who tactically and by location straddles both domains.

Beat Ethos

Beat's ethos at the outset was to be one of unfettering, a rebuke to Middle America's staid paradigm of career and suburb, office and corporation, and for which Whitman's 'Song of the Open Road' (1856) was not infrequently invoked as the relevant anthem. Even the Good Gray Poet, however, could not quite have anticipated Beat's morph into voluminous regimes of art, adventuring, dissent, sexual plurality, pot, amphetamine and the heavier drugs, jazz, and Buddhist spiritual and meditative regimens. The ever greater un-closeting of gay, lesbian and sexually pluralistic behaviours would find notable figuration in Ginsberg's lifetime partnering with Peter Orlovsky and his campaigns for recognition of same-sex rights and equality. The goal was to urge reconnection to an altogether more vital 'open' America, whether bequeathed by Whitman, Blake and Thoreau or energised by the immediacies of popular culture and a plurality of music from jazz, bebop, blues and scat to rock and roll. But as Beat and the larger activism of which it was a part took aim at the politics of the Pentagon and the CIA, the nuclear industry, censorship, and the running sore of the Vietnam War, it did not lessen frequent denunciation as gesture, play-acting.

The currents once again eddy a number of ways at once. In the one respect Beat signified social and cultural breakout, a boldest strike for liberation, youth energy and exuberance. There were, and still are, those who think Beat authorship taken in the round amounts to little short of a post-war literary succession to the 1840s–50s American Renaissance or to the modernist efflorescence of the Fitzgerald–Hemingway 1920s. On the other hand, in life and in art, Beat drew critique as a butt for jibes and lofty editorials. Norman Podhoretz, Ginsberg's classmate at Columbia, in *Partisan Review* in 1958 indicts 'a movement of brute stupidity and anarchy know-nothingness'.[31] Robert Brustein, Yale and then Harvard drama professor, likewise speaks in *Horizon* for 1958 of 'the cult of unthink'.[32] The most waspish comment likely belongs to Truman

Capote, speaking on the David Susskind show *Open End* in 1959: 'None of them can write. Not even Mr. Kerouac . . . [It] isn't writing at all – it's typing.'[33] Either way, amid the acclaims and denunciations since publication of 'Howl' and *On the Road*, Beat has carried its own frisson, the paradox of clandestine text and yet bestseller.

Further contradictions include Ginsberg on a number of occasions self-vauntingly nude yet also applauded winner of the National Book Award for Poetry in 1974. Kerouac increasingly lets drink get the better of him, but he remains the novelist of *On the Road* given rapturous acclaim by Gilbert Millstein in his *New York Times* review for September 1957 ('There are sections . . . in which the writing is of a beauty almost breathtaking').[34] The shock-horror stirred in Main Street citadels of respectability like high schools, churches, masonic lodges or municipal libraries managed the unmeant but predictably ironic effect of helping make Beat a recurrent source of controversy. Moreover, the lives involved, and their successes and losses, cannot but grow sharper in memory than with the death of Cassady on a rail track close to Guanajuato, Mexico in 1968, the drink-induced final haemorrhage of Kerouac in St. Petersburg, Florida in 1969, and subsequently, the demise of Ginsberg in Manhattan and Burroughs in Lawrence, Kansas in 1997 and of Corso in Minnesota in 2001.

The Rise of Beat

However customarily thought a generation, Beat, in fact, has been continuously in view across successive time periods since its stirrings in the 1940s. The signature writings that appear in the 1950s and 1960s, and Beat as an ethos, an aesthetic, indeed have their footfalls long into the next century. In this respect, the actual historic and literary origins of Beat, and the timelines involved, of necessity require note. If immediate enough at the time, they have increasingly come to be seen in the larger frame of reference. In the wake of scholarship, documentary film, different conference and journal retrospectives, the once startling outburst of energies transposes into remembered annals, a Beat chronicle.

Ginsberg's invitation to Kerouac to share his dorm room at Columbia University in 1944 inaugurates their lifetime association, the one a pre-Law student, the other on a football scholarship. Both serve briefly and at different times in the Merchant Marines.

Lucien Carr, turbulent and beauteous leader in Ginsberg's student circle and who introduces him to Burroughs (Carr and Burroughs had known each other in the St. Louis of their boyhood), is arrested in 1944 for the knife-murder and Hudson River disposal of the body of his athletic sexual harasser, David Kammerer. Both Burroughs and Kerouac, whom Carr sought out after disposing of the body in the Hudson, will be called as material witnesses and be ordered to deposit bail money. Based on these events they co-author *And the Hippos Were Boiled in Their Tanks* in 1945, conceivably the first-ever Beat novel, unpublished until 2008. It can be read for the relationships involved, and the speculations arising, as against John Krokidas's version of events in his biopic *Kill Your Darlings* (2013).

Carr's circle, not only Ginsberg and Kerouac but Hal Chase (the Chad King of *On the Road*) whose Columbia teachers include leading literary-academic names like Harrison Ross Steeves, Lionel Trilling and Mark Van Doren, proposes that their times, too, require A New Vision or Season. They invoke the Rimbaud of 'Le Bateau ivre' (1871) and *Une saison en enfer* (1873), the latter with its bitter iterations of ennui and call for a derangement of the senses, and W. B. Yeats's *A Vision* (1925), with its emphasis on the occult and automatic writing, as sponsoring texts. The first edition of *Howl and Other Poems*, as subsequently Ginsberg's *Plutonian Ode and Other Poems, 1977–1980* (1982), will contain warm prefatory dedications to Carr.

Ginsberg in 1948 undergoes the vision of believing he hears the Romantic visionary William Blake reading 'Ah! Sunflower', 'The Sick Rose' and 'Little Girl Lost', which will inspire his entire writing life and help shape 'Howl'.[35] Echoing Blake's emphasis on ingenuous response to the world and in anticipation of the Buddhist teaching of Trungpa, he deploys the mantra of 'first thought, best thought', a gloss much to accompany Kerouac's 'spontaneous prose' narratives. His arrest in 1949 for a stolen goods episode in which Huncke had stashed loot at his apartment leads, by way of creating a defence, to his being sent for 'rehabilitation' at the Columbia Presbyterian Psychiatric Institute. There he shares wards with Carl Solomon, a fellow-patient full of literature even as he receives electroconvulsive therapy, the dedicatee of 'Howl', and who himself will become a Beat freelancer in his City Lights Dada pamphlets *Mishaps Perhaps* (1966) and *More Mishaps* (1968).

In 1950 in the Village Ginsberg encounters Corso, damaged Reform School street survivor sent to Bellevue Hospital for psychological treatment, a teenage veteran of The Tombs and Clinton State Prison having in 1947 been sentenced to three years for robbery. His attention, aroused at one and the same time by Corso's poetry and looks, will become a lifelong support. In 1953 Ginsberg becomes romantically involved with Elise Nada Cowen, friend of Joyce Johnson and Joan Vollmer, heterosexuality for all that Ginsberg and Cowen looked uncannily similar in face and stature which will give way when he meets Peter Orlovsky in California in 1954. It also places him yet further inside the orbit of William Burroughs.

Kerouac marries Edie Parker in 1944 in the wake of the Carr affair for which her family had provided his bail money. However mythologised as Beat America's Ulysses, Kerouac also married two more times: Joan Haverty follows in 1950, with whom he will father Jan Kerouac (a novelist in her own right) in 1952, and Stella Sampas, with whom he and his mother live first in Lowell, then Florida, in 1966. In 1946 he meets Neal Cassady through Hal Chase. Their encounter begets a profound homocentric alliance, the alter-ego mirror of the author and Western roughrider whose best-known fictional incarnations will be Sal Paradise and Dean Moriarty. The legendary coast-to-coast road trips Kerouac and Cassady undertake in 1947 and 1949 constitute the basis for *On the Road*. Kerouac's 120-foot scroll version of *On the Road*, typed up from previous part-drafts in three coffee-fuelled weeks and at times more sexually explicit than the Viking first edition, gets completed in 1951. In due course, and after sale at Christie's Manhattan to Jim Irsay, owner of Indianapolis Colts for $1.9 million, it becomes an art object, a feature of travelling library and museum exhibits. In 1952 he completes *Doctor Sax* while visiting Burroughs in Mexico, a fertile period for him which leads on subsequent publication of *The Subterraneans*, *Maggie Cassidy* and *Mexico City Blues*.

Burroughs, who moves to New York in 1943, gets his heroin supply from Huncke, the beginning of a long association albeit that Huncke finds himself intimidated by Burroughs's intellect and voluminous reading. In 1951 Burroughs's William Tell shooting of Joan Vollmer, his intelligent, Barnard-educated common-law wife and former roommate of Edie Parker, in Mexico City causes him to flee back to the United States. Drunken accident or bravura, it will do nothing to lessen his fascination with firearms. Ace Books, established by Carl Solomon's uncle A. A. Wynn as a mass-market paperback business, publishes *Junky* in 1953 under Burroughs's pseudonym of William Lee. In 1954, a year after the brief affair with Ginsberg that then eased into enduring friendship, Burroughs moves to Tangier, the Maghreb writer-colony home of Paul and Jane Bowles and hashish centre, where his creative collaborations with the painter-experimentalist Brion Gysin, co-creator of the techniques of cut-up and fold-in, will begin before continuing in Paris. He will also welcome Kerouac, Ginsberg and Corso to Tangier in 1955 and receive their editorial help in fashioning, and on Kerouac's part the very naming, of *Naked Lunch*.

The October 1955 6 Gallery reading (Ginsberg, Lamantia, McClure, Whalen and Snyder), under the baton of Kenneth Rexroth and with Kerouac bellicosely distributing wine from his jug and shouting 'Yeah! Go! Go!', and to which he gives fictional expression in *The Dharma Bums* (1958), is followed with the publication of *Howl and Other Poems* by City Lights. United States Customs, however, in 1957 confiscates imported copies from its British printers. Shigeyoshi Murao, the bookstore clerk (and eventual manager) responsible for selling the book and himself a collagist writer and editor whose *Shig's Review* was launched in 1960, is put under arrest. The ensuing court case becomes national news even though Judge Clayton W. Horn of the San Francisco Municipal Court rules that the poem is not obscene. At the time of the 6 reading, only Philip Lamantia, mentored by André Breton in Paris, married to Nancy Peters of City Lights, and a poet given over to alterity and the play of dissonant voices, has a full-length book in print, *Erotic Poems* (1946). In 1956, after years of breakdown and institutionalisation, Ginsberg's mother Naomi dies and he writes his bold, self-liberating *Kaddish and Other Poems, 1958–1960* (1961) in her memory.

In 1958 Ginsberg and Orlovsky are living in Paris at the bottom-of-the-market Beat Hotel, 9 rue Gît-le-Coeur, run by the garrulous but sympathetic Mme Rachou. Their co-residents include Burroughs, the British electronics experimentalist Ian Sommerville (Burroughs's lover and who contributes to the cut-up technique), Corso, whose first collection *The Vestal Lady on Brattle and Other Poems* appears in 1955, Gysin, Norse and an international roster of painters, photographers and fashion models. By the end of the decade not only the canonical trilogy of 'Howl', *On the Road* and *Naked*

Lunch will be in available, but an expanding galaxy of Beat work.
That numbers the short comic-surreal film *Pull My Daisy* (1959),
co-directed by the Swiss émigré photographer Robert Frank and the
New York painter Alfred Leslie with narration by Jack Kerouac and
music by the long-time Beat-connected composer David Amram. It
offers a classic piece of improvisational Beat whimsy with bit-parts
by Ginsberg, Orlovsky and Corso. Serendipitously or not, stops and
starts, Beat inexorably has become a loop, a circle of publication and
creative interconnection.

The publication of Norman Mailer's *The White Negro* in *Dis-
sent* (Summer 1957), and then as a City Lights pamphlet (1967),
heralds hipsterism, and, by implication, Beat, as a form of existen-
tial authenticity. Black Americans, forced by the historic racism of
Dixie and city street and tenement to negotiate life at the edge, now
have, if not their equivalent, then something supposedly in kind. 'In
such places as Greenwich Village,' Mailer opines, 'a ménage-à-trois
was completed – the bohemian and the juvenile delinquent came
face-to face with the Negro, and the hipster was a fact in Ameri-
can life.'[36] The hipster (male whereas women have become 'chicks')
assumes renegade status, running to black survival rules and style
('So there was new breed of adventurers, urban adventurers who
drifted out at night looking for action with a black man's code to fit
the facts' , 3). The essay, not without charges of reductive profiling
('Any Negro who wishes to live must live with danger' , 3), took on
a life of its own, a banner for dissident (and so Beat) white hipster-
ism from one of New York's own bad-boy literati.

The American 1960s hold special luminosity in the Beat calen-
dar as they do across the overall board, political and cultural. One
span runs from Ginsberg's *Kaddish* to Kerouac's *Vanity of Duluoz:
An Adventurous Education, 1935–1946* (1968), the last written
but dealing with earlier life history in the fictional-autobiograph-
ical Duluoz saga. Another runs from Burroughs *The Soft Machine*
(1961), the surreal cut-up narrative of searching for the Mayan hal-
lucinogenic drug yagé across various Latin American countries, to
Ted Joans's 'The Wild Spirit of Kicks: In Memory of Jack Kerouac'
(1969) with its uppercase celebration of 'THE FUEL OF A GEN-
ERATION/AT REST/AT LAST'.[37] Di Prima's *Dinners and Night-
mares* (1961), her multiform collage of Beat life and voices, likewise
opens the decade, and it can be said to close with Joans's *Afrodisia:
New Poems* (1970) in which jazz, blackness and sex are bound into

spoken verse. Taken in all, the period positively abounds in shared creative vitality – not the least the Rent-a-Beatnik featuring readings and performance for a white suburban clientele. 'ADD ZEST TO YOUR TUXEDO PARK PARTY . . . RENT A BEATNIK' ran the *Village Voice* advertisement.

Little Magazines

It is also an era, the 1950s again overlapping into the 1960s, in which, like other traditions of the avant-garde, Beat arises through totemic small magazine publications. Among the foremost has to be *Evergreen Review*, founded in 1957 by 'Barney' (Barnet) Rosset, and early and throughout the 1960s to publish extracts of work by Ginsberg, Kerouac, Burroughs and McClure. It comes to be thought virtually the Beat house journal.[38] Others add to the ranks, often mimeographed broadsheets or pamphlets both hand-stapled and hand-distributed. LeRoi Jones's *Yugen* (1958–62), eight issues with layout and editorial work by Hettie Jones and billed as 'a new consciousness in arts and letters', puts almost every Beat name into its pages. In this it overlaps with *Floating Bear* (1961–71), the monthly mimeograph newsletter co-edited by Jones and di Prima through 37 issues and which led to Jones's arrest for the supposed dangerous erotica of a portion of his play *Dante's System of Hell* in issue number 9.

On the West Coast Bob Kaufman, with John Kelly and William Margolis as co-editors, creates *Beatitude Magazine* in 1959, Issues 1–7 weekly, 8–35 monthly, then published at irregular intervals through to 1996. Simply mimeographed and bound, 20 or 30 cents a copy, it proved a sterling outlet for Beat voice. *City Lights Journal*, begun under Ferlinghetti's editorship in 1963 and with Ginsberg on the cover of Issue 1, gives space not only to Beats but a wide range of innovative American and international writing. These, and companion journals like Lita Hornik's *Kulchur*, Michael McClure's *Arc II/ Moby I* and *Journal for the Protection of All Beings*, and Paul Carroll's *Big Table*, with mention of the *Chicago Review* controversy in 1959 after publication by the editor Irving Rosenthal of excerpts from *Naked Lunch* and Edward Dalhberg's 'Further Adventures of Priapus' (1959), provide other outlets. Ira Cohen, Bronx-born poet, eventual filmmaker and a leading name in the international underground based in Morocco in the early 1960s, publishes GNAOUA (a Berber naming) given over to swathes of countercultural writing. Cid

Corman's *Origin* (1951–84), begun in Boston and continued from his base in Kyoto, opens its pages to include Beat-linked poets from Snyder to Waldman. Wallace Berman, pioneer of assemblage art, publishes folio mail-packages under the name of *Semina* (1957–64) and reprints work by Ginsberg, Burroughs and McClure along with names from Bukowski to Jean Cocteau. These often daring forums and networks give validity, and needed vital circulation, to Beat literary activity.

Cassady's release from San Quentin in 1960 after serving two years on a marijuana charge by chance also sees the publication of Donald M. Allen's *The New American Poetry 1945–1960*, the decade's most influential anthology. A seasoned Grove Press editor, Allen's foresight as to the changing American poetic order merits considerable salute. His celebration of the impact of modernism in William Carlos Williams, Ezra Pound and Charles Olson, and their role in opening new American avenues of imagination, remains well placed. Amid the groupings of Black Mountain, San Francisco and New York School poets, forty-four voices in all, albeit only four of them belonging to women, Allen's assignment of Beats to a section of their own (to include twelve choruses from *Mexico City Blues*, 'Howl', and Corso's 'Marriage') especially does service as a benchmark.

To this end, too, the contributions to 'Statements on Poetics' by Kerouac, Ginsberg, Snyder and LeRoi Jones, underpin Beat as aiming for not only New Vision but advances in literary voice and form. Notably the formulations include Kerouac on prose rhythm ('an endless one line poem called prose') – his 'Essentials of Spontaneous Prose' is couched earlier but sees print in 1953 – and Ginsberg from his 'Notes on Howl' on 'breath-units'. Beat, almost for the first time, is to be thought radical but actually un-aberrant, a body of work possessed of its own coherence. A number of admirers, against the cavils and even dismissals, saw an imaginative furthering of the genealogy adumbrated in William Carlos Williams's *In the American Grain* (1925).[39]

Literary, Arts and Music Contexts

If Beat authorship runs through the decade, however, that should not underplay coexistent, and sometimes rival, other literary streams. James Baldwin's *Another Country* (1962) tackles the culture's colour-line and sexual knots even though critics thought it a drop from the Dixie to Harlem memory narrative of *Go Tell It on the Mountain* (1953) and the articulate command of the essays gathered in *Notes of a Native Son* (1955), *Nobody Knows My Name: More Notes of a Native Son* (1961) and *The Fire Next Time* (1963). Saul Bellow's *Herzog* (1964) draws upon a Jewish America of both learning and desire. Flannery O'Connor's posthumous story collection *Everything That Rises Must Converge* (1965) takes the back country and Bible fundamentalism of the Deep South into unprecedented Gothic fashioning. Truman Capote's *In Cold Blood* (1966), farm murder and capital punishment, becomes the classic forebear of the non-fiction novel. Robert Lowell's *For the Union Dead* (1964) triumphs as confessional verse and genealogy. Edward Albee's play *Who's Afraid of Virginia Woolf?* (1962) disembowels middle-class marriage as an image of the state-of-the-nation. War as nightmare comedy has its incarnations in Joseph Heller's absurdist novel *Catch-22* (1961) and Kurt Vonnegut's time-travel *Slaughterhouse-Five* (1969). These all contribute to a crowded terrain, the sense of an era unremittingly about writer business and in which Beat, no less than other authorship, contends for right of place.[40]

To focus on Beat is also not to disregard art activity similar in countercultural resolve. Andy Warhol's Manhattan 'Factory' studios (1962–4), with their demimonde art-party happenings, drag culture, film and silk screens, attracts Ginsberg as a visitor. The era is one of late modernism trending towards the postmodern, as is evinced by Robert Rauschenberg's 'combine' graphics, the comic-strip parodies of Roy Lichtenstein, the atonal 'chance' counterpoint of John Cage's music, or the avant-garde dance choreography of Merce Cunningham. Indie film like Jack Smith's *Flaming Creatures* (1963), with its gender-bends fantasia, suitably appeals and shocks. Lenny Bruce delivers brilliantly sardonic improvisational stand-up. Off Broadway and Off-Off Broadway has the Living Theater, Julian Beck and Judith Malina productions like Jack Gelber's *The Connection* (1960) with its drug panorama and jazz interludes, or Kenneth Brown's *The Brig* (1963) set in a marine world of drills and punishment.

These respectively coexist with the one or another aspect of the Beat aesthetic, and in a number of cases to be made subject to bouts of censorship and prosecution.[41] Indubitably, a sense of the 1960s invokes popular culture, in no respect more emphatically than in the music to be heard on vinyl, cassette or TV. Beat linkages are many.

The balladry of Bob Dylan, a classic 1963 composition like 'Blowin' in the Wind' or his 1964 album *The Times They Are a-Changin'*, and of Joan Baez, not least a poetry and song compilation like *Baptism: A Journey through Our Time* (1968), give their respective measure of the times. Folkniks was one usage given them. The Ginsberg–Dylan friendship begins in 1963, partly a generational passing of the baton according to Ginsberg.[42] He frequently would avow Dylan to be the greatest poet of modern America, prophetic in the light of the 2016 Nobel Prize for Literature. One notable indication occurs in the card-flip screening of the proto-music video for 'Subterranean Homesick Blues' with a full-bearded Ginsberg standing to one side of the frame and whose sweater round his shoulders looks on first sight like a prayer shawl. Ginsberg, too, would both applaud recordings like *Highway 61 Revisited* (1965) with its hugely successful if acerbic 'Like a Rolling Stone' and 'Desolation Row', and encourage Dylan's own prose writing, none more so than *Tarantula*, drafted in 1964–5 and published in 1971, with its Burroughsian cut-up surrealism and filtered-in allusions to Corso and fellow Beats.

Dark-matter Beat lyrics, drugs to transgender, are to be heard from Lou Reed, Tom Waits, and Burroughs-titled groups like Soft Machine founded in 1966 and Steely Dan in 1971. The 'English Invasion' also means the Beatles, themselves named in part for the Beats, and the Rolling Stones. For West Coast hippie-beat good cheer there are the Mamas and the Papas and the Beach Boys as against the sombre lyrics of the Doors; both carry drug experience into their music. Janis Joplin's raw blues vocals in albums like *Big Brother and the Holding Company* (1967), and her hippie dress and hair styles, could not but imply Beat as affiliation. 'All Along the Watch Tower', initially written and recorded by Bob Dylan for his *John Wesley Harding* (1967), and then covered by Jimi Hendrix with his electric guitar virtuosity in 1968, takes Beat into electric rock.

All of these registers emerge as Frank Sinatra and Bing Crosby keep the mainstream crooner legacy in play while Elvis Presley, first with Sun Records and then on through the 1960s with RCA, parlays a fusion of Dixie rockabilly and Afro-blues rhythms into monumental hit parade success and Las Vegas concert spectaculars. Jazz, even so, as played in Manhattan and Chicago clubs or on record or tape, remains the preferred sound-wrap for Beat illuminati like Kerouac and Corso as for Jones/Baraka, Joans, Kaufman and Spellman. Kerouac's *Mexico City Blues* speaks of Charlie Parker as 'the perfect musician' in Chorus 239. Corso's 'For Miles' says of the trumpeter 'Your sound is fault-less/pure & round/holy/almost profound'.[43] Ted Joans titles one of his best-known poems 'Jazz Is My Religion'.[44]

The 1963 Vancouver Poetry Conference, featuring Ginsberg alongside Olson, Robert Creeley, Denise Levertov and Robert Duncan, underscores Beat's further expanding reach. In February 1965 Ginsberg is in Prague, after deportation from Cuba for his 'decadent' support of gay poets, where he is crowned Kral Majales (King of the May), arrested for drunkenness, and where he will write the poem 'Kral Majales' naming himself the 'Buddhist Jew / who worships the Sacred Heart of Christ (and) the blue body of Krishna'.[45] The Berkeley Poetry Conference of July 1965, with Donald Allen among its organisers, has him reading along with Joanne Kyger, Robert Duncan and John Wieners. In 1966 Burroughs moves to London, in part to begin his apomorphine treatment, in part to complete *The Ticket That Exploded*. The momentous Woodstock Festival of August 1969, with Hendrix offering his guitar version of 'The Star-Spangled Banner' in the early hours of the festival's final morning, can be said to draw hip, Beat and rock into the moment's end-of-decade single coalescence.

Historical Contexts

The yet larger historical context in which Beat arises, and then takes hold, may well risk well-known pitfalls when given in decades or synopsis. But it, too, requires being taken into account. The America that emerged from World War II stood tall as victor, the first modern superpower of both the Atlantic and Pacific. Increasingly through the 1950s and 1960s manufacture shifts to white-collar office employment (the majority of the workforce by 1956), the writ one of Main Street and suburban nuclear family, wife-homemakers, baby boom, commutes along routes brought into being by the Highways Act of 1956, and replete in consumer durables whether TV (owned by more than 70 per cent of Americans by 1960), phone, television, fridge, or the two-car garage. Whatever the areas of poverty, rural or urban, the majority landscape bespoke material well-being, genuine shelves of abundance. Beat's critique was that this came at a cost of fatal un-creativity, the self reduced to dollar-chasing and commodity. 'Howl' takes its aim, plangent, accusatory. But no writing displays greater animus than that of Burroughs, a detestation angled above all at white suburbia and for him its dire co-optive monotony.

If, too, the 1950s, running into the early 1960s, indeed yielded an America at once comfortably affluent, a family-centred white mainstream, there could be no doubting this was also an Age of Anxiety. For behind the World War II 'greatest generation' returnees from the European and Japanese theatres lay the age presaged by the bombings of Hiroshima and Nagasaki in 1945 during the Truman administration. The sight of the atomic cloud became iconic as Corso's poem 'Bomb' attests, the more so as Cold War politics set in with Soviet Russia the adjudged threat and America supposedly vulnerable to fifth-column communist conspiracy. The House Un-American Activities Committee (HUAC), with its roots in the Red Scare of the 1920s, arises, and the McCarthy hearings of the early 1950s follow. Edgar Hoover's FBI begins its COIN-TELPRO wiretap and domestic espionage operations in 1956, and is subsequently revealed to have bugged Martin Luther King Jr. and other Civil Rights activists. Ginsberg and Kerouac both come under surveillance as subversive of consensual America, to be thought variously both political and sexual threats to the realm.

Subversion allegedly lay everywhere, whether borne out by the initial Hollywood blacklist of 1947, the Julius and Ethel Rosenberg spy trial of 1951, accusations of collusion even in the senior ranks of the Pentagon, or subliminally in a film like Don Siegel's *Invasion of the Body Snatchers* (1956) with its pods and zombie-like human replicas. John Frankenheimer's *The Manchurian Candidate* (1962) gives the paranoia a slightly later airing in its Korean War–era plotline of Soviet–Chinese brainwashing and assassination. A particular animus was reserved for the arts, screen and literary names to include Orson Welles, Dashiell Hammett, Lillian Hellman, Lena Horne, Lauren Bacall, Charlie Chaplin, Arthur Miller or Pete Seeger, not to mention Dalton Trumbo, driven by blacklist exclusion to become the clandestine scriptwriter of Stanley Kubrick's *Spartacus* (1960). The Beats could hardly escape being caught up in the hysteria, the narrow phobias and anti-intellectualism. As late as 1965 Corso would be fired from a teaching post at the State University at Buffalo for refusing to sign a document denying he was a communist. *Naked Lunch*, banned in Boston in 1962, goes all the

way to the Massachusetts Supreme Court in 1966, with testimony
from Mailer and Ginsberg, before being absolved of the charge of
obscenity.

America's political bow into the 1960s can be said to begin with
Eisenhower's Farewell Address of January 1961 with its warning
about the rise of a military–industrial complex and its ever-burgeon-
ing budget. The Cuban Missile Crisis of October 1962, Kennedy's
blockade and Khrushchev's stand-down, adds to the sense of nerves
being frayed. The war in Vietnam (1961–75), more televised than
any previous war, disrupts the decade like a running sore. The litany
involves saturation bombing, use of the nerve gas Agent Orange, a
massacre like that of Mai Lai in 1968, and the estimated more than
a million deaths overall albeit far fewer for American troops. US
military body bags and casualties give accusing evidence of a failing
conflict, as does the rising number of draft refusers or refuseniks
and peace activists, Ginsberg and Ferlinghetti unremittingly among
them. Anti-war politics are to be met with in different protest groups
of which Students for a Democratic Society (SDS), the Weathermen
and the Berkeley-generated Free Speech Movement were radical
manifestations and which erupt into police and crowd violence at
the Democratic Convention held in Chicago in 1968. Among those
monitoring the politics and Mayor Daley's police regime are Tom
Hayden, the major force behind SDS's *The Port Huron Statement*
(1962) with its New Left manifesto call for a socialist order, the
black performer-activist Dick Gregory, Jean Genet, the satirist Terry
Southern, and Ed Sanders, Ginsberg and Burroughs.

The 1960s was also a time of tense race relations, Dixie colour-
line and city ghetto. Black America, with figureheads in Martin
Luther King and Malcolm X, takes on segregated Mississippi or Ala-
bama and tenant poverty in Harlem or Chicago's South Side. King's
'I Have a Dream' at the March in Washington on 28 August 1963
still echoes (preceded, it is easily overlooked, by Bob Dylan singing
'When the Ship Comes In'). These politics lead to Lyndon John-
son's presidential signing of the Civil Rights Act of 1964 and Voting
Rights Act of 1965, even as black inner cities explode against racist
police and housing practices in this and the ensuing years. 'Burn
Baby Burn' becomes the mantra – Watts in 1965, Detroit in 1967,
with outbreaks in Harlem, Bedford Stuyvesant and Washington,
DC. Black Panthers find voice in Eldridge Cleaver, the SNCC (Stu-
dent Non-Violent Coordinating Committee) in Stokely Carmichael,

and Malcolm X emerges as chief lieutenant to Elijah Muhammad, Chicago-based leader of the separatist Nation of Islam. The assassinations of Malcolm in February 1965 in the Audubon Ballroom, and of King in the Lorraine Motel, Memphis, in April 1968, creates lasting trauma. Jones/Baraka pre-eminently, as he moves on from Beat, will refract these histories.

Black Power was not alone in making race, ethnicity or gender a focus in the national consciousness. Chicano/a and Filipino/a farm-labour activism is to be met in the AFW (American Farm Workers) under the leadership of César Chávez and Dolores Huerta, not least the Delano Grape Strike of 1965. AIM (American Indian Movement) is founded in Minneapolis in 1968 by Dennis Banks, Clyde Bellecourt and their compeers. The Asian American Movement rises in Berkeley and San Francisco State University in the later 1960s, a Pacific American political alliance given literary re-remembrance in Karen Tei Yamashita's epic ten-story-panel I-Hotel (2010).[46] The accounts of student and worker activism also accord Beat abetting countercultural reference. The gay movement emerges from the Stonewall riot-protests of 1969, the Manhattan club venue a memorial against homophobic police harassment. Beat, out front or implicitly, again contributes to the wider context of renegade time and place.

At the same time, Beat often enough faced the accusation of being absent without leave from politics. That does considerable injustice. There is every reason to think Ginsberg and Ferlinghetti politically aware poets, committed to First Amendment rights, anti-militarism, and, in Ginsberg's case, to gay equality. Both, throughout, display a keen eye and activism as to CIA, FBI and other machinations and to neocolonial forays into Latin America. In Nicaragua they meet with the poet and priest Ernesto Cardenal and other Sandinista-supporting writers. Marches, anti-war demonstrations from Vietnam and Cambodia onwards, give further credence, whether protests at the Pentagon (Ginsberg's 'Pentagon Exorcism' in Planet News applies), or at the nuclear installation in Colorado's Rocky Flats (Ginsberg, again, comes into play with 'Plutonian Ode' and its indictment of 'Satanic industries').[47]

Ginsberg often and in plenty returns to the political fray. His wry poetic diatribe 'America', published in Howl, leaves little doubt of his historical familiarity with radicalism, be it the Irish American labour organiser Tom Mooney, his mother Naomi's Communist

Party affiliation, or his colloquial mockery of Cold War paranoia ('them Russians and them Chinamen'). *Planet News, 1961–1967* (1968) includes 'Wichita Vortex Sutra', one of his fiercest anti-war compositions, and 'Television Was a Baby Crawling toward That Deathchamber', with its swathe of indictments of media-biased political news to capital punishment. In *Plutonian Ode and Other Poems, 1977–1980* (1982) his 'Verses Written for Student Antidraft Registration Rally 1980' indicts missile systems and their shadow-bearing power of nuclear destruction.

Kerouac would advert often to his nostalgia for the working-class diligence of his parents in Massachusetts beginnings, and the Republican Party values that underpinned it. His drink-fuelled rants against the counterculture, and shies at Ginsberg for his protest marching, both honour and yet complicate that heritage. Few Ferlinghetti poems have stayed more keenly in mind than 'Tentative Description of a Dinner Given to Promote the Impeachment of President Eisenhower'(1958), again a poem with its focus on nuclear threat, and 'One Thousand Fearful Words for Fidel Castro' (1961), with its take on US ideological and military reaction to the Cuban Revolution.

In Burroughs's case the issue falls more towards his own species of anti-politics, those of the libertarian-anarchist in no doubt of the worthlessness of everyman politics. They include his distaste for all organised religion. A radio interview of 1982 has him averring, 'If I'm anything I'm an elitist.' He also argues for firearms ('I'm interested in weaponry', 'The answer to violent crime is an organized and armed citizenry)'.[48] In the same sweep he confirms commitment to raising his pen in imagery drawn from supply-and-fix drug addiction against, as he sees it, global power-systems, the controlling matrix of authority, state and law.[49] His longstanding misogyny no doubt makes for an extreme. But it is a homocentrism he conspicuously shares with Ginsberg, whose 'This Form of Life Needs Sex' in *Planet News* reads: 'I will have to accept women / if I want to continue the race'.[50]

These attitudes lie oddly, not to say chauvinistically, out of step in the light of the feminist debate stirred by Second Wave voices like Betty Friedan's *The Feminine Mystique* (1963), the founding of the National Organization of Women (NOW) in 1966, and the Afro-womanist and Latina movements to be associated with writer-activists like Alice Walker and Gloria Anzaldúa.[51] If it can be said that 'politics' have a place in the universe of Ginsberg, Kerouac and Burroughs it lies well outside Democratic or Republican party affiliation (albeit that Kerouac liked to say he came of a Republican-voting family). The same, if not more so, holds for Jones/Baraka in racial politics, Ferlinghetti in his anti-war writing, and Snyder and Waldman in ecopolitics. Their dissent, however maverick, takes its grounding from commitment to self-freedom and art in the face of institutional authority.

End of the 1960s

If, for the 1960s, the flag was sex, drugs and rock and roll, the signs towards decade's end begin to indicate slow-down, the need for res-pite. There had been the exhaustion brought on by Vietnam, the marches and boycotts in the name of more equitable civil rights, the city race-fires, student protest, and the assassinations of John Ken-nedy (1963), Malcolm X (1965), Martin Luther King (1968) and Robert Kennedy (1968). America may have retained its position as the world's leading economy, but post-industrialism increasingly threatened in the rise of rustbelt unemployment and family-farm dispossession. The cities, despite the corporate wealth and the condo high-rises, get yet further mythologised into sites of after-dark criminality, ethnic otherness, and enclaves of risqué bohemi-anism like the Beats. The Kennedy–Johnson years of progressive optimism soon give way to Watergate and the Nixon impeachment hearings (1973–4). The early Internet use by the US Department of Defense in 1969 presages a future of cyber-technology. That same year Neil Armstrong and Buzz Aldrin walk the moon, a marker not only of space exploration but space militarisation. Beyond chronol-ogy, the nation, Beats included, begins to feel more or less done with the 1960s.

Easy Rider (1969), hipster road movie with a drugs-and-guns apocalyptic ending, suggests one kind of coda. A wider transatlantic effect had been anticipated in an anthology like *The Beat Genera-tion and the Angry Young Men* (1958). Scholarship has increasingly given attention to Beat achievement, a sure sign not just of arrival but moving-on. Allen's *The New American Poetry, 1945–1960* (1960), in company with City Lights's *Beatitude Anthology* (1960) and Thomas Parkinson's *A Casebook on the Beat* (1961), helped point Beat towards canonisation and classroom. Bruce Cook's *The Beat Generation: The Tumultuous '50s Moment and Impact on Today* (1971), one of several early route maps, now looks more a work of advocacy than analysis. Jayne Kramer's transcriptions of talk and opinion in *Allen Ginsberg in America* (1969) and Ann Charters's pioneer *Kerouac: A Biography* (1973) pave the way for Beat biographies ahead. Given these and similar perspectives, the original Beat movement perceptibly edges towards legacy, granted that Beat literary output at the same time continues, whether Ginsberg's *Angkor Wat* in 1968 or di Prima's *Memoirs of a Beatnik* in 1969.

Beat recordings and recovered literary drafts suggest that Beat and its writings have become archives, resources for research. Ginsberg's reading of 'Howl' for KPFA Pacifica in October 1956, like that at the 6 Gallery, assumes historical status. William Burroughs, in his characteristic flat St. Louis drawl, tapes an interview with Ginsberg and Corso in 1961 to be put into print in the *Journal for the Protection of All People*. Jack Kerouac, drink-addled, makes his memorable last-ever TV appearance to discuss Beat and hippies on William Buckley's *Firing Line* for PBS in 1968. These readings and screenings, the interviews and collections, head towards storage, many later accessible on-line and by web page.

The Boulder founding of the Naropa Institute by the exiled Tibetan monk Chögyam Trungpa Rinpoche in 1974 centred in Buddhist studies, and its incorporation of the Jack Kerouac School of Disembodied Poetics with its emphasis on literary-creative writing, takes on particular status as custodial Beat centre. The principal inaugural faculty of Ginsberg, Waldman, di Prima and John Cage, having extended invitations to a host of poets, establish a tradition that has long continued. Under the baton of Waldman and colleagues, and over time, a huge assemblage of Beat memorabilia, whether manuscript, readings, lectures or artwork, and sound or video, has become a working archive. Each and all add to the implication of Beat's original pennant shading into remembrance even as Naropa itself endeavours to move forward into ever newer 'investigative' poetics.[52]

Ginsberg, Kerouac and Burroughs, famed but still far from cultural mainstream, so consolidate status. Celebrity has beckoned, posthumously as in life. Ginsberg and Burroughs, especially, are remembered for work and conference and festival appearances but also their TV and billboard commercials. The signs came early. In 1956 Ginsberg's poem 'America', duly ironic, could ask 'Are you going to let your emotional life be run by Time Magazine?'[53] By 1969 *Time* magazine's review of *Allen Ginsberg in America* is headed 'Odd Man In'.[54] *Kerouac, the Movie* (1985), with speaking contributions from Ginsberg, Burroughs, Carolyn Cassady and

Ann Charters, situates Kerouac as belonging both to Beat's trajectory from the 1940s to the 1960s and to the American history that followed in its wake. Burroughs appears in Peter Blake's 1965 assemblage-cover for the Beatles' paradigm-shifting 1967 album *Sgt. Pepper's Lonely Hearts Club Band* but also 1990s Nike shoes and clothing publicity. Commemoration gathers and extends. The evolution of Beat beyond the 1960s, however, and the fuller legacy and perspectives, will invite its own mapping.[55]

Notes

1. Allen Ginsberg, *San Francisco Sunday Chronicle*, 26 July 1959.
2. Jack Kerouac, *On the Road*. This sentence is taken from the original Teleprinter Scroll.
3. Ezra Pound, *ABC of Reading*, London: G. Routledge and Sons, 1934; New Haven: Yale University Press, 1934.
4. Jack Kerouac, *The Scripture of the Golden Eternity*, New York: Totem Press/Corinth Books, 1.
5. 'Angelheaded hipsters' appears in the third stanza of 'Howl'. Allen Ginsberg, *Howl and Other Poems*, San Francisco: City Lights Books, 1956, 9.
6. For a conscientious and greatly energetic account, see Preston Whaley Jr., *Blows Like a Horn: Beat Writing, Jazz, Style, and Markets in the Transformation of U.S. Culture*, Cambridge, MA: Harvard University Press, 2014.
7. James Baldwin, 'If Black English Isn't a Language, Then Tell Me, What Is?' *New York Times*, 29 July 1979. Reprinted in James Baldwin, *The Price of the Ticket: Collected Non-Fiction, 1948–1985*, New York: St. Martin's Press, 1985, 649–52. 'Sonny's Blues', first published in *Partisan Review* in 1957, is included in Baldwin's story collection *Going to Meet the Man*, New York: Dial Press, 1965.
8. Jack Kerouac, 'Aftermath: The Philosophy of the Beat Generation', *Esquire*, March 1958, 24.
9. John Clellon Holmes, 'This Is the Beat Generation', *New York Times Magazine*, 16 November 1952.
10. For a thorough account of the etymology of Beat, and the respective roles in its creation by John Clellon Holmes and Jack Kerouac, see Steven Watson, *The Birth of the Beat Generation: Visionaries, Rebels and Hipsters, 1944–1960*, New York: Pantheon, 1995.
11. 'LeRoi Jones in the East Village', in Arthur and Kit Knight (eds), *The Beat Vision*, New York: Paragon House, 1987, 131.
12. *The Beat Vision*, 131.
13. Anne Waldman and Laura Wright (eds), *Beats at Naropa*, Minnesota: Coffee House Press, 2009, 13.

14. Glen Burns, *Great Poets Howl: A Study of Allen Ginsberg's Poetry, 1943–1955,* Frankfurt: Peter Lang, 1983.
15. Jack Kerouac, *Lonesome Traveler,* New York: McGraw, 1960, Introduction.
16. *The New York Journal-American,* 8 December 1960. Kerouac's 'The Origins of the Beat Generation', published a year earlier in *Playboy,* June 1959, gives another version: 'People began to call themselves beatniks, beats, jazzniks, bopniks, bugniks, and finally I was called the "avatar" of all this . . . I went one afternoon to the church of my childhood . . . and had a vision of what I must have really meant with Beat . . . the vision of the word Beat as being to mean beatific.'
17. William Burroughs, *The Adding Machine,* New York: Seaver Books; London: John Calder, 1986, 180.
18. *Gregory Corso: The Last Beat* (2009), dir. Gustave Reininger.
19. *Ferlinghetti: The Rebirth of Wonder* (2013), dir. Christopher Felver.
20. For a range of perspectives, see Maria Anita Stefannelli (ed.), *City Lights: Pocket Poets and Pocket Books,* Rome: Ila Palma, Mazzone Editori, 2004.
21. Jack Kerouac, 'bloody King of the beatniks'. The phrase appears in *Big Sur* (1962) with Kerouac under the guise of Jack Duluoz. 'I'm a Catholic not a beatnik' is to be found in a 1969 interview with the *Tampa Bay Times.*
22. Allen Ginsberg, Letter to the *New York Times,* 11 May 1959. Reprinted in *The Letters of Allen Ginsberg,* ed. Bill Morgan, Boston, MA: Da Capo Press, 2008, 223.
23. 'Anatomy of a Beatnik'. Reprinted in Ann Charters (ed.), *Beat Down to Your Soul,* New York: Penguin Books, 2001, 377–87.
24. For an informed account of the Beat–punk nexus, albeit as manifested in New York, see Victor Bockris, *Beat Punks: New York's Underground Culture from the Beat Generation to the Punk Explosion,* New York: Open Road Media, 2016.
25. Stephen Willis, http://youtube/ULhNDeAy13A
26. Snyder's role in fashioning a West Coast and Pacific Northwest 'Beat' domain is illuminatingly studied in Timothy Gray, *Gary Snyder and the Pacific Rim: Creating Countercultural Community,* Iowa City: University Press of Iowa, 2006.
27. *A Helen Adam Reader,* ed. Kate Prevallet, Orono, ME: National Poetry Foundation, 2007. Denise Levertov, *Here and Now,* San Francisco: City Lights Bookshop, 1957.
28. Cowen's writing has long needed collecting and editing. Fortunately, there is now *Elise Cowen: Poems and Fragments,* ed. Tony Trigilio, Boise, ID: Ahsahta Press, 2014.
29. I offer a selective map of this writing in 'Un-shadowed Women: A Beat Contour', in Frida Forsgren and Michael J. Prince (eds), *Out of the*

Shadows: Beat Women Are Not Beaten Women, Kristiansand, Norway: Portal Books, 2015, 25–36.

30. Key texts for the Black Aesthetic include *Black Expression: Essays by and about Black Americans and Their Creative Arts*, New York: Weybright & Talley, 1969, and *The Black Aesthetic*, New York: Doubleday Anchor, 1971, both edited by Addison Gayle Jr. Major analysis of the postcolonial turn is to be found in Henry Louis Gates Jr. and Anthony Appiah (eds), *Race, Writing and Difference*, Chicago: University of Chicago Press, 1986; Henry Louis Gates Jr., *Figures in Black: Words, Signs and the 'Racial' Self*, New York: Oxford University Press, 1987; and the same author's *The Signifying Monkey: A Theory of Afro-American Criticism*, New York: Oxford University Press, 1987.

31. Norman Podhoretz, 'The Know-Nothing Bohemians', *Partisan Review*, xxv (Spring 1959), 305–18. Republished in Norman Podhoretz, *Doings and Undoings: The Fifties and After in American Writing*, New York: Farrar, Straus and Company, 1964.

32. Robert Brustein, 'The Cult of Unthink', *Horizon*, 1:1 (1958), 38–45, 134–5.

33. For a fuller account, see Barry Miles, *Jack Kerouac, King of the Beats: A Portrait*, New York: Henry Holt, 1998, 223.

34. Gilbert Millstein, 'Books of the Times', *New York Times*, 7 September 1957.

35. For an appropriate account, see Luke Walker, 'Allen Ginsberg's Blakean Albion', *Comparative American Studies*, Special Beat Issue, 11:3 (September 2013), 227–42.

36. Norman Mailer, *The White Negro*, San Francisco: City Lights Books, 1967, 3.

37. Ted Joans, 'The Wild Spirit of Kicks: In Memory of Jack Kerouac', 1969. Reprinted in *Teduction: Selected Poems, 1949–1999*, Minneapolis: Coffee House Press, 1999, 97.

38. Rosset's contribution to Beat and countercultural America at large (he died in 2012) is recalled in his posthumous work *My Life in Publishing and How I Fought Censorship*, New York: OR Books, 2017.

39. William Carlos Williams, *In the American Grain*, New York: A & C Boni, 1925.

40. References are as follows: James Baldwin, *Another Country*, New York: Dial, 1962; *Go Tell It on the Mountain*, New York: Knopf, 1953; *Notes of a Native Son*, New York: Dial, 1955; *Nobody Knows My Name: More Notes of a Native Son*, New York: Dial, 1961; *The Fire Next Time*, New York: Dial, 1963; Saul Bellow, *Herzog*, New York: Viking, 1964; Flannery O'Connor, *Everything That Rises Must Converge*, New York: Farrar, Straus and Giroux, 1965; Truman Capote, *In Cold Blood*, New York: Random House, 1966; Robert Lowell, *For the Union Dead*, New York: Farrar, Straus and Giroux,

1964; Edward Albee, *Who's Afraid of Virginia Woolf?*, New York: Atheneum, 1962; Joseph Heller, *Catch-22*, New York: Simon & Schuster, 1961; and Kurt Vonnegut, *Slaughterhouse-Five; or the Children's Crusade*, New York: Delacorte Press, 1969.

41. Jack Gelber, *The Connection*, New York: Grove Press, 1960; Kenneth Brown, *The Brig*, New York: Hill & Wang, 1963, 1965.

42. This comment, and others, is made by Ginsberg in *No Direction Home: Bob Dylan* (2005), the biopic directed by Martin Scorsese.

43. Gregory Corso, 'For Miles', *Gasoline*, San Francisco: City Lights Books, 1958, 44.

44. Ted Joans, *Teducation: Selected Poems, 1949–1999*, Minneapolis: Coffee House Press, 1999, 9.

45. 'Kral Majales', Allen Ginsberg, *Planets News, 1961–1967*, San Francisco: City Lights Books, 1968, 90.

46. Karen Tei Yamashita, *I-Hotel*, Minneapolis: Coffee House Press, 2010.

47. Allen Ginsberg, 'Pentagon Exorcism', *Planet News, 1961–1967*, San Francisco: City Lights Books, 1968, 143; 'Plutonian Ode', *Plutonian Ode and Other Poems, 1977–1980*, 15. For a full account of 'political' Ginsberg, see Eliot Katz, *The Poetry and Politics of Allen Ginsberg*, Beatdom Books, 2015.

48. BBC Radio 1, 11 November 1982.

49. See, in this respect, Eric Mottram, *William Burroughs: The Algebra of Need*, Buffalo: Intrepid Press, 1971, 108.

50. 'This Form of Life Needs Sex', *Planet News, 1961–1967*, San Francisco: City Lights Books, 1968, 33–5. In *The Job: Interviews with William Burroughs*, New York: Grove Press, 1970, Burroughs makes the following observation: 'In the words of one of a great misogynist's plain Mr Jones, in Conrad's *Victory*: "Woman are a perfect curse." I think they were a basic mistake, and the whole dualistic universe evolved from that error', 116. He goes on to say: 'In *The Soft Machine* I propose that the sexes be separated, that all children be raised by males and all female children by women. The less the two sexes have to do with each other, the better I think', 125.

51. Betty Friedan, *The Feminine Mystique*, New York: W. W. Norton, 1963.

52. Something of this Naropa tradition is annotated in Sam Kashner, *When I Was Cool: My Life at the Naropa School*, New York: Perennial, 2005. Kashner was Naropa's first-ever student.

53. 'America', *Howl and Other Poems*, San Francisco: City Lights Books, 1956, 31–4.

54. *Time*, 8 August 1969.

55. The issue of legacy, and Beat culture and history after the 1960s, is addressed in Chapter 8.

CHAPTER 2

Allen Ginsberg: Public Privacy

I GREET YOU AT THE BEGINNING OF A GREAT CAREER,
WHEN DO I GET THE MANUSCRIPT OF 'HOWL'?

Lawrence Ferlinghetti (1955)[1]

> I liked it that you sort of bubbled out of the '50s
> Complete and Bardic
> Full voiced and Howling
> I didn't have to know
> really whence he came
>
> but only that he was There
> Fully there
> Completely there
> with a voice I trusted
>
> to lead me to the Best Minds

Ed Sanders, 'Ginsberg Reading at the
Living Theater Early '59' (2009)[2]

Ginsberg and the Beats

Lawrence Ferlinghetti, having been present at the 6 Gallery reading of 9 October 1955, resuscitates Ralph Waldo Emerson's historic letter of 21 July 1855 to Walt Whitman, and almost exactly a century later sends his telegram to Allen Ginsberg.[3] It is the start of proceedings that will lead to publication of *Howl and Other Poems* in 1956 as a City Lights classic in the Pocket Poets Series. Ed Sanders, Greenwich Village habitué, writer-musician, founder of the Peace Eye Bookstore in the Lower East Side of New York City and Fugs performer, reprints his fond retrospective homage to Ginsberg in the collection *Let's Not Keep Fighting the Trojan War* (2009). Echoing the opening line of 'Howl', 'Best Minds' adds a canny intertextual flourish. Both these declarations, distinctive as they are one from another, re-emphasise Ginsberg's poem as breakout, inerasable Beat touchstone.

By the time of Ginsberg's death in 1997 it was clear how formidable, and across the decades how popular, had become his 'great career' with 'Howl' as the major pivot. More than anyone, and not only on account of 'Howl' and his other verse but his always considerable public and private presence, it fell to him to keep Beat alive as a continuum of voice, repertoire, cultural politics. Poet first and above all, Ginsberg always exhibited the still further repertoire of campaigner, teacher, traveller, practitioner of meditation, media and festival presence, and self-revelling celebrity. These different incarnations, on any number of occasions, readily overlap and fuse.

Life, as literature, has him the Kerouac and Burroughs ally onward from his Columbia University and Lucien Carr years. Legend follows, perhaps even more so since his death, and to embrace in its orbit Huncke, di Prima, Solomon, Orlovsky and, in due course, Snyder. The literary confluence reaches from Frank O'Hara in New York to Lawrence Ferlinghetti in San Francisco, with Whitman as the great progenitor of private life as public life. There is the Buddhist Ginsberg, a syncretic Buddhism at once Tibetan and otherwise with admixtures of Theravada, and the life-long student of the dharma, Buddha's teachings. He was also long drawn to Hindu practice, student of the Vedas and Upanishads and typically given to citing a scripture like the Prajnaparamita Sutra for its precepts on human suffering.[4] His Hare Krishna/Hare Rama chants, using squeeze box and finger cymbals, and his insistence upon the principle of love as highest spiritual aim in universal consciousness, become a hallmark. Who, too, doubts 'sexual' Ginsberg, the lifelong love with Peter Orlovsky, and his unabashed statements of same-sex preference and practice? He early assumes gay activist status not only in the United States but controversially in visits to Soviet-era Cuba, Czechoslovakia and Russia.

Both in his secular and spiritual history, and though his work shocked much Jewish respectability, he also never ceased to see himself the cultural heir to the Torah and Kabbalah. His role as politically aware activist rarely abated, the multiple Vietnam and anti-nuclear protests, the Pentagon demonstrations and censorship court trials, the Free Speech movement, or the visits to the Sandinistas with Ferlinghetti in 1982 and 1986. The speaking out for legalisation of marijuana and other drugs yields frequent headlines. The Naropa presence – classes, readings and in-house relationships – augments his example of creative exemplar, even guru. A huge international reputation accrues, his works are widely translated, and even as he at the same time acts as herdsman of companion literary talent. Ginsberg may well have seemed to be always on stage, which stirred predictable snipes of over-eagerness for the limelight, the fame hound. In fact, there was ever the private, kindly Ginsberg, the wholly committed figure behind the writings and his causes and stances.

In taking on a selection of compositions from across his writing, the point is to show Ginsberg at imaginative work, the width and yet particularity of his powers of word. These, to one degree or another, all come under Beat colours, a flag of general identity within which he stakes every claim to his own originality. It also takes cognisance of his poetry as spoken idiom, much of it engagingly reinforced in his immediately recognisable New York/New Jersey vocal delivery and patterns of emphasis and intonation. The evidence from the live readings, through the decades from the 6 Gallery reading in 1955 to his last-ever author event at the Booksmith store in Haight-Ashbury in 1997, and often delivered with musical accompaniment, continues in the abundance of available records, tapes, CDs, broadcasts and videos. Few poets can more have given better auditory embodiment to the printed page than in his recordings of *Howl and Other Poems* (Fantasy, 1959), *Holy Soul Jelly Roll: Poems and Songs, 1949–1993* (Rhino/Word Beat 1995), *The Ballad of the Skeletons* (Mouth Almighty/Mercury Records 1996) with Paul McCartney and Philip Glass, and his superb three-hour cassette reading of Kerouac's *Mexico City Blues*.[5]

Howl and Other Poems inaugurates the trajectory, to be followed by each collection from *Empty Mirror: Early Poems by Allen Ginsberg* (1961) through the dozen or so successors like *Kaddish* (1961), *Reality Sandwiches* (1963), *Planet News* (1968), *The Fall of America* (1973), *Mind Breaths* (1978), *Plutonian Ode* (1982), *White Shroud* (1986), *Cosmopolitan Greetings* (1994) and the valedictory *Death and Fame* (1996).[6] This output takes its place alongside the lifetime flow of correspondence, whether with Kerouac, Cassady or Snyder, or with the Burroughs of *The Yage Letters* (1963) and the unbroken back-and-forth exchanges between the two of them.[7] It also embraces the work notebooks, the India travel journals,[8] the frequent interviews, the film appearances and photography of the kind posthumously displayed as 'Beat Memories' at Greenwich Village's Grey Art Gallery in 2013.[9] Nor, it bears repeating, does it minimise the unselfishness of his role as editor of the work of others. His career, incontestably, yields nothing short of a genuine compendium, the writings through to each multifaceted show of cultural-political activity. Of necessity, however, 'Howl' compels first point of call.

'Howl'

Estimation of 'Howl' has circled almost every which way, from near-euphoric welcome, a defining bardic poem for the age, to accusations of shrillness, an obscene torrent. But one historic early response takes on quite special resonance, that of Ginsberg's own poet-father, Louis Ginsberg, Newark High School teacher and the author of collections like *Morning in Spring and Other Poems* (1970).[10] His letter of 29 February 1956, on receiving a draft of 'Howl', offers soundings, a gauge that still captures the immediate impact: 'It's a wild, rhapsodic, explosive outpouring with good figures of speech flashing by in its volcanic rushing. It's a hot geyser of emotion suddenly released in wild abandon from the subterranean depths of your being.'[11]

To engage with 'Howl' is indeed to entertain terms like rhapsody, geyser, depths of being. These terms of reference can also be read alongside those of the introduction from William Carlos Williams, established light of American poetry's imagist tradition and Ginsberg's older fellow poet from Paterson, New Jersey. Williams, too, seizes upon 'courage' and 'faith' saved out of 'defeat' and, in phrasing that has long attached itself to the poem, takes it upon himself to warn: 'Hold back the edges of your gowns, Ladies, we are going through hell'.[12] Quite another take, however, came from Robert Frost: 'It's not very good – just a pouring out . . . "Howl" is not real; one can't howl on for so many pages.'[13] A vote in favour or not, the poem remains fully if controversially installed as landmark, a contender as centrepiece of modern American verse.

Pitched for the ear as much as for the eye, Parts I, II and III of 'Howl', together with the Footnote, put on offer Ginsberg's personal witness statement as to a time out of joint.[14] It does so with fierce energy, his performative scroll-down or intersequence of dynamic verse paragraphs.[15] For throughout these strophes, as he often called them, Ginsberg is about the sighting and contestation of regimes of predatory materialism ('the narcotic tobacco haze of Capitalism', 11), disquietude at the atomic bomb ('a cloud of sexless hydrogen', 17), individual breakdown ('invincible madhouses', 18), and whose overall figuration lies in the destructive Canaanite fire-god Moloch ('Moloch in whom I sit lonely! Moloch in whom I dream Angels', 17). 'Unobtainable dollars' and 'running money' prevail (17). The 'sphinx of cement and aluminum' (17) ravages the creative impulse. 'Robot apartments' (18) and 'invisible suburbs' (18) incarcerate the citizenry. The implication is of America turned unholy, a regime of soul-less (and sexless) acquisition under whose appetite nothing other than 'the poem of life' has become 'butchered' (16).

It is against this darkening light, much though the poem can be flamboyantly playful, that Ginsberg's 'best minds' are to be imagined having reacted even to the point of fantasticality. Madness haunts the soul. Cold War ideological phobias about Russia and China rule. From the acclaimed opening line ('I saw the best minds of my generation destroyed by madness, starving hysterical naked', 9) through to the last iteration of 'Holy' ('Holy the supernatural extra brilliant intelligent kindness of the soul!', 22) the poem tracks deficits but also redemption, lives pushed to the parapet yet saved in the discovery of the sanctity of all existence.[16] 'Howl', thereby, seeks to perform both hex and healing.

'Best minds', Ginsberg once suggested, was ironic. If so, it nevertheless meant 'best' to him in terms of companionship of spirit, co-resistance at whatever price against the loss of humanity he sees within an America increasingly having sold short (or just sold) the original dream. Each, as Part I of the poem enumerates, raises the cry of opposition, whether 'a lost battalion of platonic conversationalists' (10), jazz players and followers, highway and boxcar cross-America hitchers, Zen-practitioners, druggies on smack or Benzedrine, asylum patients like Carl Solomon and Ginsberg's mother Naomi, followers of Kabbalah, sexual adventurers of every gender, or, in a deft reflexive touch, the 'stanza-writers' who 'scribbled all night' and engage in 'the noun and dash of consciousness' (16).

His own Beat confraternity stand foremost among those acknowledged in the revolt. To this end the dedication to the collection overall apostrophises Kerouac as the 'new Buddha of American prose', his 'bop prosody' the pathway into an 'original classical literature'.

Burroughs's *Naked Lunch* wins sportive plaudits too as 'an endless novel that will drive everybody mad'. Cassady's *The First Third*, in like manner, allegedly can enlighten even Buddha. All these writings, 'published in Heaven' to go along with the rest of the encomia, confirm the cadre. These, in 'Howl' itself, move on to Neal Cassady as indeed 'the secret hero of these poems' (12), Tuli Kupferberg, poet-songster of the Fugs 'who jumped off Brooklyn Bridge' (14), actually the Manhattan Bridge, after a nervous breakdown, and Carl Solomon as fellow writer-patient (16). They, and the legions 'who' did this or the other, are to be denominated 'the crazy shepherds of rebellion' (21) or, in one of Beat's best-known rubrics, 'angelheaded hipsters' (9). In them, and theirs, lies if not full counterforce then custodians of alarm at the Moloch of 'pure machinery' (17), 'running money' (17) and a whole cityscape of desexualised 'granite cocks' (18).

Moloch, as projected in Part II of the poem, is envisaged as having taken sway. In units again linked by opening word, Ginsberg constructs a whole ledger of damage. Moloch variously manifests itself as 'jailhouse', 'cannibal dynamo', 'endless oil and stone' and 'sexless hydrogen' (17). Its regime mutilates, often enough kills, illumination. Beat's enlistees, or given the poem's Buddhist undertow *bodhisattvas* from Manhattan and beyond, make for the resistance. Their 'highs', 'epiphanies', 'holy yells' and 'farewells' might be near-absurdist badges of warriordom. In a nice touch of comic deflation they might each take to street or river 'carrying flowers' (18). But the effect, especially for partisans of the poem, is one of impassioned indictment, an exhilarating flyting or exorcism. The unpersuaded, however, again see, and hear, hysteria. Whichever holds, and across the 'Moloch' verses, there can be little denying language as unremitting as exclamatory.

In alighting upon Carl Solomon in Part III, patient in the Rockland State Psychiatric Hospital with its ECT and lobotomy practices and to whom *Howl and Other Poems* is dedicated, Ginsberg invokes Solomon the Dadaist who once anarcho-comically threw potato salad at his college lecturers. The repetition of 'I'm with you in Rockland' (19–20) underwrites not only personal psychosis ('we are great writers on the same dreadful typewriter', 19) but national psychosis ('the United States that coughs all night and won't let us sleep', 20). Solomon's delusions may well rule ('you've murdered your twelve secretaries', 19, or 'you accuse your doctors of insanity', 20).

Old-time politics may almost comically flatter to deceive with the dream of utopia ('the Hebrew socialist revolution against the fascist national Golgotha', 20). 'The Internationale', again in absurdist spirit, can be sung by 'twentyfive-thousand mad comrades', 20). But Solomon is to be conjured into mind as 'dripping from a sea-journey across America in tears to the door of my cottage in the Western night' (20). Although this might be read as the West to East Coast compassion of the one poet for the other, yet more is involved: the poem's Ginsberg and Solomon share a psychic register, America and its 'best minds ' torqued and psychologically self-injuring.

'Footnote to Howl' promises balm, a better order of the human spirit. World and soul, tongue and genitalia, sax-playing and marijuana, crucially and self-referentially, poem and reader-hearer, are to be hallowed. The same holds in the listing of 'holy' Orlovsky, Ginsberg himself, Carr, Kerouac, Huncke, Burroughs and Cassady (21). These 'marijuana hipsters' (21), each a Beat 'madman' amid the 'solitudes' of skyscraper and pavement (21), invite having bestowed upon them 'Holy forgiveness! mercy! charity! faith!' (22). That holds from New York to Istanbul, and across time, whether clock-specific or eternity. Herein, nothing less, lies the 'bop apocalypse' (21) and 'kindness of the soul'(22) to counter Moloch's predations. The Footnote, in rhythms that re-enact Judaeo-Christian liturgy and anticipate Ginsberg's interest in Buddhist chant, bids to bring hope out of lamentation.

The contour of sight and sound in 'Howl' presses hard throughout. However vexatious an opening phase like 'negro streets at dawn'(9), with its implicit stereotype, the poem moves quickly to embrace visionary 'Mohammedan angels' (9), a land-and-sea corridor of 'Canada & Paterson' (9), and New York's own city ambit of Brooklyn Bridge, Madison Square, Union Square, Wall Street, Harlem, Chinatown, the Empire State, the Bowery, Bellevue, Rockland, the Hudson River and Bickford's Restaurant, with a nod both to 'Zen New Jersey' (10) and 'the filthy Passaic' (14). These geographies further extend to Burroughs's drug domain of 'Eastern sweats and Tangerian bone-grindings and migraines of China' (10). The 'streets of Idaho' (11) with their 'visionary Indians' (11) or a 'Chicago' of burned manuscripts (11) add locale. The homocentric ocean, with its 'caresses of Atlantic and Caribbean love' (12) beckons. Cassady's Denver (14) points to road America and North Carolina's Rocky Mount where Kerouac decamps to 'cultivate . . . tender Buddha' (15), give their coordinates. The Los Alamos

Atomic Test Site and the wail of its 'sirens' (11) serve warning of
the end of days, even if Alcatraz, California's legendary island peni-
tentiary, can inspire 'sweet blues' (15). The poem's topographies
steer revealingly between the actual and hallucinatory.

Given the raft of accompanying cultural references, whether to
Plotinus, Edgar Allan Poe, St John of the Cross, Paul Cézanne and
Christopher Columbus ('the brilliant Spaniard', 11), one also has
the obligation to recognise serious learning amid the often startling
symptoms of personal and generational disorder. Deistic formulae
like the Hebrew 'eli eli lama sabachthani?' ('My God why has thou
forsaken me?', 16), in emulation of Jesus's cry of abandonment, or
the euphoria of becoming 'Pater Omnipotens Aeterna Deus' (16),
which he took from Cézanne, add allusive weight. The networks
within, and behind, Ginsberg's epic do not come cheap.

In addressing these different reaches, replete with 'holy' epilogue,
'Howl' also invites acknowledgement of compositional strategy. This
is to go beyond each often scintillating fertility of image which has
the best minds 'listening to the crack of doom on the hydrogen juke-
box' (10), or being 'dragged off the roof waving genitals and manu-
scripts' (12), or finding themselves embroiled in 'the lamb stew of
the imagination' (3). Ginsberg himself supplies helpful guidelines in
the letter he wrote in response to the poet Richard Eberhart's 'West
Coast Rhythms', published in *The New York Review of Books* in
1956, which while praising the poem complained of 'negativity', the
denial of slightest American benevolence. The letter speaks explicitly
of 'poetry techniques', 'Howl' as 'an experiment 'with uses of cata-
logue, the ellipse, the long line, the litany, repetition etc.'[17]

To hand, also, is his answer to John Hollander's hostile review
of *Howl* in *Partisan Review* for spring 1957 ('a dreadful little vol-
ume').[18] This account is likewise full of prosodic detail, Ginsberg's
great concern to have the poem's measure, its organising poetics,
fully grasped. Part I, he begins,

> uses repeated base *who*, as a sort of kithara BLANG, Homeric
> (in my imagination) to mark off each statement, each rhythmic
> unit. So that's experiment with longer & shorter variations on
> a fixed base – the principle being, that each line has to be con-
> tained within the elastic of one breath.

For Part II 'the basic repeated word is Moloch. The long line is now
broken up into component with "rhythmical punctuation"'. Part III

'perhaps an original invention [is] a sort of free verse prose poem STANZA form invented or used here'. The 'Footnote to Howl', Ginsberg insists, 'is too lovely & serious a joke to try to explain. The built-in rhythmic exercise should be clear, it is basically a repeat of the Moloch section. Its dedicated to my mother who died in the madhouse and it says I loved her anyway.' On this section-by-section account the proliferations of vision, intent and execution, fold into carefully thought-through architecture.[19]

The longer line, or 'mind breath' in the title of his later collection, acts as organising principle. It is to be met as though delivered to the rhythmic pluck of the kithara or ancient Greek lyre. The first-word repeats of 'who' and 'Moloch', and also by implication of 'I'm with you' and 'Holy', act as single-word hinge. The Carl Solomon sequence, evidentiary, a whole paradigm of symptoms and sympathies takes form in stanzas of prose verse ('I'm with you in Rockland / where you scream in a straightjacket that you're losing the game of the actual pingpong of the abyss', 19). The 'Footnote' again turns to reiteration for incantatory impact. As poetics these all are brought into play to support and serve, fully calculated fashioning. Ginsberg, from the outset, saw himself pledged to the Whitman tradition, the seer but like his mentor also the artificer, possessed by vision but equally resolved upon requisite craftsmanship.

Controversy has continued to hover. Does 'Howl' seize and persuade or, to the contrary, risk treading close to rant? Are admirers right to proclaim the poem monumental and under full prosodic control, or do doubters hit the mark in speaking of pathology, unanchored fervour? Issues of obscenity continue to arise, whether gay couplings with 'saintly motorcyclists' (12) or the heterosexual 'innumerable lays of girls' (12). The allusions to illicit drugs still arouse murmurs, marijuana (9) as everyday choice, but also peyote (10) and heroin (15). Yet allowing for these, and other critique along the spectrum, it would be fair to say that modern American poetry whether Beat or beyond has become unimaginable without according 'Howl' due place.

Howl and Other Poems

Howl and Other Poems, assuredly, offers more than the title-poem. Other inclusions, for which three might do duty, long have won status as markers in the early Ginsberg canon. 'A Supermarket in California', albeit that it works at altogether more subdued pitch than 'Howl', gives grounds to be thought another primary Beat anthem. The Whitman of 'Song of Myself', cited on the collection's title-page, again comes into play as presiding tutelary spirit. It falls to Ginsberg's speaker to exercise the privilege of voice, but Whitman serves as silent colloquist, the one poet paired in loneliness and male-on-male desire across time and amid America's plenty. From the first stanza's 'What thoughts I have of you tonight Walt Whitman' (23) the poem opens at exact right pace into sustained reflection, privacy of feeling made public.

Ginsberg has his speaker match his 'hungry fatigue' (23) and his 'shopping for images' (23) with Whitman as both 'lonely old grubber' (23) and yet always 'lonely old courage-teacher' (24). Kindred isolates, they are also kindred *flâneurs*, night-walkers silhouetted against neon-lit supermarket abundance with its aisled overflows of fruit. Emphasis thereby falls upon 'our solitary fancy' (23), 'our odyssey' (23), the colloquy of the two-for-one. In invoking Spain's great modernist poet ('and you, Garcia Lorca, what were you doing down by the watermelons?', 23), the poem adds a further affiliate both in writing and gender. Among other facets, Ginsberg is writing tribute, fellowship whether literary or sexual, with chosen and wholly honoured forebears.

Tone in 'A Supermarket in California' counts for much, if not almost all. The invitation to intimacy runs warm, never without irony, a gesture of beckoning. Whitman's poetry has its 'enumerations', but how not to savour the speaker's own equivalent – the fantasy foodways of 'peaches' and 'penumbras', 'aisles of husbands', 'wives in the avocados', and 'babies in the tomatoes' (23), along with queries as to pork chop butchering, the price of bananas and the taste of artichokes (23)? A touch of tease is to be heard in Whitman's 'eying the grocery boys' and Ginsberg's being 'followed in my imagination by the store detective' (23). Their 'never passing the cashier' (23) neatly encapsulates the larger journey beyond the store visit, one of life cycle and repetition.

As the poem progresses, the sense of 'our odyssey' (23) takes on transcendence: Whitman and Ginsberg, metaphorically at least, to traverse time as much as space ('Where are we going, Walt Whitman?', 23). Their 'stroll', their 'dreaming of the lost America of love' (24), their 'silent cottage' (24), and even arrival after death across the River Lethe, position them as joined across time at the poetic hip. The intimacy of affiliation, 'dear father, graybeard' with poet-son (24), is unmistakable and considerably moving. 'Sunflower Sutra', true to its Vedic/Buddhist title, offers epiphany, the inspirational yellow-gold durability of the flower even in death as reproach to an America of waste. It makes perfect sense in this regard that Ginsberg summons his other great visionary mentor, William Blake, although it would be far from inappropriate to link the image to the sumptuous still-life sunflower series of the great Dutch painter Vincent van Gogh. The mood, for 'companion' Ginsberg and Kerouac (28), again is contemplative, their 'thoughts of the soul' (28) during a San Francisco railroad sunset inflected as 'bleak', 'blue', 'sad-eyed', 'rheumy-eyed', 'hung over', 'tired' and yet 'wily' (28). Kerouac's call to 'Look at the Sunflower' (28) releases a flood of further images, Blakean euphoria on the one hand, 'Hells' of 'dank muck' on the other (28).

The dead sunflower before them, corolla, spikes, seeds, and 'sunny hair', remains like a valiant sentinel ('Unholy battered old thing', 29) against 'worse-the-dirt' industrialism and cultures of consumption and throwaway paraphernalia (29). The risk might have been of sentimentality, too easy a contrast. But Ginsberg keeps his imagery precise, even aggressively anatomical ('the cunts of wheelbarrows', 'the milky breast of cigars', 'wornout asses of chairs', 'sphincters of dynamos', 29), as though only this blunt usage can convey the force of the scene before him. The ensuing outburst ('A perfect beauty of a sunflower!', 29) virtually enacts relief, the sudden elevation of spirit caught in the poem's own measure. Credit rightly accrues to the performative verve of the writing.

The flower itself, despite being 'broken like a battered crown' (28), inspires –'You were never no locomotive, Sunflower, you were a sunflower!' (30). The slightly askew grammar gives colloquial edge to the declaration. Sceptered with the flower the poet can now deliver 'my sermon to my soul, and Jack's soul too, and anyone who'll listen' (30). The closing verse paragraph lattices sermon and image: the rejection of 'our skin of grime' (30) and the relish of 'beautiful golden sunflowers inside' (30). The prospect is of regeneration from shadow, the sunflower-self redeemed from some 'dread bleak dusty imageless locomotive' (30). In a closing line run-on, vintage Beat in styling, the poem's 'mad locomotive riverbank sunset Frisco hilly tincan evening sitdown vision' (30) calls for nothing less.

'America' displays the Ginsberg of wit as much as seriousness, a plaint layered in tongue-in-cheek riff. It assumes the voice of put-upon parent speaking to the nation as if to an errant child. Ironic

finger-wagging descends upon a catalogue of political and cultural
waywardness, chastisements clearly meant to carry import but leav-
ened by wit. The aim can be 1950s war mentality ('Go fuck yourself
with your atom bomb', 31), sexual repression ('When will you take
off your clothes?', 31), censorship ('America why are your libraries
full of tears?', 31) or self-preening affluence ('America when will
you send your eggs to India?', 31). The poet within the poem speaks
from margins, his own financial penury but also end-of-tether
expenditure of spirit ('I've given you all and now I'm nothing', 31,
and 'I can't stand my own mind', 31). A kind of under-the-weather
grumpiness prevails ('I don't feel good don't bother me', 31). No
poem can be written until the poet finds 'my right mind' (31), a
pathway out of being put upon by 'insane demands' (31). This
opening volley works to engage, critique made over into a game-
some bridge to the reader.

The tactics involve mock alarm ('Burroughs is in Tangiers I don't
think he'll come back it's sinister', 31). Pseudo-apologies give their
nudge ('I'm trying to come to the point', 31). A confessional CV, as
it were, layers yet further tease into the serious issues at hand. The
speaker acknowledges his heretic sentimentality about the Wobblies
and unrepentant youth-time communism. Smoking joints, refusal of
the Lord's Prayer of Christianity, the implied anti-Semitism visited
on Uncle Max from Russia, and perhaps above all, 'mystical visions
and cosmic vibrations' (32), play into the roster's disjunctions. *Time*
magazine, best-selling of all national weeklies, is invoked to indict
a Henry Luce businessman standard of Americanness ('Are you
going to let your emotional life be run by Time Magazine?', 32).
Yet antithetically the speaker bids to be also America's voice, albeit
the upshot, 'I am talking to myself again' (32). The poem offers
ingenious vent to these alternating currents, raillery with purpose.

Throughout the final sequences Ginsberg turns cliché yet further
back on itself. 'I haven't got a chinaman's chance' (32), with its built-
in Cold War Asia reference, gives the one instance. 'My ambition is
to be President despite the fact that I'm a Catholic' (33), with its ref-
erence back to John F. Kennedy, gives another. To counter America's
'silly mood' (33), as though the nation were throwing a hissy fit,
Ginsberg engages in an anachronistic campaign to recognise past
radicalism and injustice. The names drawn from history all bespeak
dissidence, from the labour activist Tom Mooney, wrongly sentenced
in 1916 for the bomb explosion in San Francisco's Preparedness Day

Parade, to the executed Massachusetts anarchists Sacco and Vanzetti in 1927. The list extends to the Scottsboro Boys, falsely accused and imprisoned in white supremacist Alabama in the 1930s, and to Scott Nearing, Pennsylvania's veteran Marxist-pacifist from World War I. The labour organiser Mother Bloor (Ella Reeve Bloor) and the co-founder of the American Communist Party Israel Amter further underscore the poem's line of dissent. 'Everybody must have been a spy' (33) reads the gloss, apt for versions of American as ever at risk of left-wing conspiracy.

It remains for the speaker himself to assume child or pidgin register, language pared down into parodic mumble, and thereby synchronised with the lowest terms possible of Cold War phobia. Phrases, each building on the other, mockingly coalesce ('it's them bad Russians. / Them Russians them Russians and them Chinamen, And them Russians', 33). Russia becomes 'The Russia', some ghoulish bear pledged to 'eat us alive . . . take our cars from out our garages . . . grab Chicago' (33). In making parody of stereotype, discomforting bigotry ('Him make Indians learn read', 'Him need big black niggers', 34), Ginsberg makes no compromise. The infantile language guys infantile bias. Reverting, finally, to the persona of reporter poet ('this is the impression I get from looking at the television set', 34), and to seemingly bemused scrutineer ('America is this correct?', 34), he can then offer his real credential in the playful sincerity of 'America I'm putting my queer shoulder to the wheel' (34). 'America' reflects 'Beat' Ginsberg in indicative agility, the readiness of esprit, the command of overall measure.

Kaddish

Ginsberg has always made psychological and sexual self-exposure a large part of his theatre, an 'open' life, an 'open' aesthetic. Poetry like 'Siesta in Xbalba' in *Reality Sandwiches*, with its sexual dream soliloquy set in Chiapas, Mexico, or the 'Black Magicians' sequence in 'THE CHANGE: Kyoto-Tokyo Express' in *Planet News*, with its genital explicitness, give instances. Ginsberg, or his persona, assumes centre-place in most of his poetry, the self as register even when the issue is the subjugation of self or ego to the greater spiritual cause.

The title-poem of *Kaddish*, however, ranks among the most unsparing in its remembrance of Naomi Ginsberg's breakdown and death. The Kaddish prayer itself, fairly short, several verses, and a Hebrew paean to God and the writ of peace, contrasts with the poem's chronicle of copiously particular fissure. For Ginsberg is no mere dutiful member of the *kaddishim*. Rather he writes trauma, the jagged and at times savage family saga of filial love veering into disaffection and to include his own first sexual coming-out. The plainness of the dedication to his mother, 'For Naomi Ginsberg, 1894–1956' (7), belies not only the poem's plenitude but its emotional pitch ('Blessed daughter come to America, I long to hear your voice again', 29). 'Kaddish' deserves to stand with 'Howl' among quite the most affecting of all Ginsberg's verse.

Departure points start with appropriate discord, the poet's walking in Greenwich Village under winter sun after a sleepless night thinking of his mother and perusing the Kaddish, and yet at the same time having given ear to Ray Charles 'shouting blind' the blues (7). Shelley's *Adonaïs* (1821), written on the death of Keats ('the soul of Adonaïs, like a star, / Beacons from the abodes where the Eternals are'), has been Ginsberg's reading but also 'the Hebrew Anthem' (7) and 'the Buddhist Book of Answers' (7). Panels of memory augment. They call up Naomi's childhood arrival from *shtetl* Russia and marriage to Louis, career as New Jersey classroom teacher, fervid radical politics, early hospitalisations, and the final decay whereby 'once long-tressed Naomi of Bible' (31) becomes the 'old woman of skulls' (31). Death itself ('God's perfect darkness', 12) is made to stalk the poem for which the allusion to 'Emily Dickinson's horses – headed to the end' (11) makes the perfect analogy.[20] Ginsberg might also well be echoing the grief bound into Whitman's eulogy to Lincoln in 'When Lilacs in the Dooryard Bloom'd' (1865). But these correspondences go only so far as the poem becomes almost a fever chart.

Naomi's dying, and the harrowing downward pathway that leads into it, is dubbed 'a few images' (31). In fact, 'Kaddish' more resembles a brilliantly exhaustive profile, a map of pathology. The language takes on emblematic force, a code or hieroglyphics of 'electric shocks' (13), the young child who screams 'Lady of Death' at Naomi (13), her fantasy of 'Hitlerian invisible gas' (15), the 'three big sticks left in her back by gangsters' (21), and 'the wires in her head' (33). Each features within the dense family net, whether Ginsberg as her nurse offspring, his lawyer brother Eugene, Louis as despairing and unfaithful husband, Naomi's siblings, Elanor and

Max, and the uncles and aunts of lives variously lived as far apart as Newark and The Hague. Each also comes shadowed in Naomi's reeling sense of history, Trotsky's Russia to the Lower East Side, worker unions to US branch of the Communist Party (CPUSA). Detail brims, whether Naomi dishevelled and delusional (she offers to cook for God), or Allen raw in horror (he imagines her offering herself to him sexually), close to her then repelled, and provisionally at last reconciled. The poem's verse form, the one paragraph literally and as it were urgently hyphenated into the next, gives measure to the abrupt life-swings for both mother and son.

Amid his mother's psychological unthreading Ginsberg himself unthreads, his own sexuality, call to poetry, the redemptive journey to California, and the need to reach equilibrium as expressed in the poem's devotional closing 'HYMMNN' that recapitulates Naomi's broken mental state ('with your eyes of shock . . . with your eyes alone', 35) and offers the dissonant sound of birds cawing over her buried ashes in Long Island (36). For Naomi's body acts throughout as the poem's focal battle site, the obstetric scars, the eventual lobotomy, the fallen breasts, the extra weight brought on by medication, the shrieks but also silences, and her very genitals. She is likened to the biblical Ruth with Ginsberg himself the Svrul Avrum (Israel Abraham).

The disastrous early-boyhood bus journey with her to a rest home in Ocean County's Lakewood localises the still larger journey out of his mother's balance into un-balance. Yet though edging beyond sanity, and being subjected to the fierce electro-convulsive therapy, surgery and tranquilliser regimes, Naomi is to be remembered saying to her son 'Get married Allen, don't take drugs – the key is . . . in the sunlight at the window' (31). The marriage and drug advice for all its unintended irony, and likewise the fortuitous Blake-like vision of sunlight as key, make for rare poignancy.

'Wichita Vortex Sutra'

Buddhism, like Hinduism, was early to attract, and then give sustenance to, Ginsberg's concern with how best to face both the fractures within himself and a warring world-order. He persists as advocate of self-awakening, consciousness and illumination. His India travels with Orlovsky during 1962–3 (and for part of the time with Snyder and Kyger) took him to Calcutta, Benares and

Patna as well as to the Ganges as sacred river to witness rites of purification. He admired the sadhus and other holy men, practised yoga, learned the cosmic pluralism embodied in deities like Vishnu, Brahma, Shiva and Kali, and studied the Vedas and sutras. In his various Japan stays he relished first-hand Kyoto's temple culture and the Buddhism that sieves into considerable swathes of his writing. Much of the Asia reading he took from Snyder and Kerouac, especially Buddhism's Noble Truths, and the meanings of karma and bodhisattva, he would see also reflected in the Kerouac of *The Dharma Bums*, *Mexico City Blues* and *Desolation Angels*.[21]

These underpin his tenaciously held anti-war beliefs and rarely to more manifest effect than in 'Wichita Vortex Sutra', one of the presiding poems of *Planet News*. The itinerary format, accretive, spontaneous, also has its resemblances to Kerouac's itinerary in *On the Road*.[22] News snippets heard on the radio of his VW camper enter as though a cycle. Storefront names, highway route numbers, local allusion ranging from the Wabash rail track to a *Wichita Eagle-Beacon* headline like '*Kennedy Urges Cong Get Chair in Negotiations*' (128), feed the diary. The main focus, however, lies in war, and the way language has wilfully been suborned to normalise both the Vietnam War and all other military-colonial conflicts from Algeria to Indo-China (123). To this end the poem draws upon both Buddhist precepts of compassion and the Prajnaparamita Sutra vision of giving easement to suffering. Ginsberg looks also to the example of Hindu ascetics (Shambu Bharti Baba heads the list), withdrawal from human proneness to conflict. The outcome resembles a reel, linear and collagist and delivered in small-block line measure.

His self-appointed role, as he tours Kansas in 1966 for readings ('I come / lone man from the void, riding a bus ... on the straight space road ahead', 111), is to un-vortex war, and with it the corrosive double-talk of the kind which uses 'pacification' for carpet bombing:

> I lift my voice aloud,
>   Make Mantra of American language now
>   pronounce the words beginning my own
>   millennium
>   I here declare the end of War! (127)

Language so traduced ('conflicting language, language proliferating in airways', 121) and 'all this black language writ by machine' (124) takes on a life of its own, the power to ensnare and misdirect. The

ALLEN GINSBERG 55

evidence is to be met in Lyndon Johnson's presidential edicts, Robert McNamara's managerial techno-speak at the Defense Department, impersonal draft forms, and the military's dubious recruitment sign ('Careers with a Future', 118). Ginsberg leaves no doubt of the need for counter-language against these 'formulas for reality' (119). 'I search for the language / that is also yours –' (126), asserts the poem, adding the perfect laconic rider 'almost all our language has been taxed by war' (126). That Kansas lies at the continental centre of the United States adds important figural meaning. Wichita, set upon the Plains, and the very siglum of everyday 1960s Middle America, is to be understood for its connections, tacit or not, to the war ferocity of Vietnam. Wichita's workplaces, high schools, streets, eateries, churches and newspapers, their quotidian normality or insouciance (the 'Pepsi Generation' is invoked at one point, 115), may well exist at every seeming remove from 'the defoliated Mekong Delta' (132). But Ginsberg insists upon the link, the fault-line in consciousness. How, the poet asks as he road-drives his way through Kansas, to transform this most symptomatic of American cities, and its state, and indeed the nation-at-large, into a centrifuge for peace over war? 'Wichita Vortex Sutra', Beat–Buddhist mantra, endeavours to arrive at an appropriate answer.

Selected Verse

Ginsberg's role in carrying Beat beyond the United States cannot be understated. Latin America, Europe and Asia each provide spans of geography but rarely without taking the poet's eye well beyond mere site. The two-part short poem 'Havana 1953', in *Reality Sandwiches*, works symptomatically.[23] First on offer is Cuban night-heat, the café vista of partying 'midnight drinkers', Latin guitar and mariachi music, fleshly women in silk and pimp-gambler machos, and from the bar cheap shots of Cuba Libre. Second, another café, acts to locate the poet's isolation 'observing the square, alone' 20). These contrasts pair into the larger perceptual terrain of sound and silence, local *alegría* and foreigner's paranoia, in sum two ways of being within conjoined but distinct Americas.

'Kral Majales' (King of the May), in *Planet News*, brings Europe into view, more exactly the 1960s Eastern Europe of then Czechoslovakia.[24] The poem so conjures a sense of place, Prague, but also a sense of time, the ongoing Cold War. Crowned as festive monarch

by university students, Ginsberg's deportation in accordance with
the iron-bound strictures of the party regime likely has as much to
do with the image of his kind of Americanness as anything else. One
of his notebooks with sexual and other annotations reaches police
hands. Charges go up of drunkenness. Gay liaisons are mooted
(he is called 'BOUZERANT', or 'fairy', by an agent, 89). To the
authorities who keep him overnight in prison he is a stir to subver-
sion, America's best-known public poet but also a decadent. Yet
as May King, folk mythology's bringer of fertility ('the power of
sexual youth', 90), both in his own right and as the persona given
in the poem, he positions himself as would-be liberator.

The charge of aberrance against him from the authorities reflects
not least his venturing to speak as unflatteringly of Marxism as of
capitalism. The one is 'eyeglasses and lying policemen' (89), the
other 'Napalm and money in green suitcases' (89). He allies his own
travails with those of Kafka and sees himself perceived by Prague's
bureaucratic apparatchiks as less the King of the May than alien
virus. He posits his true King of the May credentials as those of
imagination, a necessary creative and sexual *disponibilité*. 'Human
poesy' (90) stands as his calling card. He signs himself 'of Slavic
parentage and a Buddhist Jew' (90). He testifies that he has heard
'the voice of Blake in a vision' (90). As he flies to London under
orders, to Islington's Bunhill Fields and to the greenery of Hamp-
stead Heath, he looks back (and down) at the Czechoslovakia that
juridically has expelled him from 'our kingdom' (91). The impli-
cation of a royal 'we' adds its tweak. As his poem makes clear,
the protocols of his kingdom, as against those of 'Police Station'
Prague, derive from the politics of imagination over the grip of any
one ideological orthodoxy.

Among Ginsberg's abundance of geographic poems, *Angkor
Wat* (1968), issued initially in pamphlet size, again stands out, his
Hindu-Buddhist and all-one-night Beat reflections on war and peace
as inspired by Cambodia's formidable temple complex.[25] Written in
the nearby township of Siemréap, in June 1963, it situates within the
single mid-length poem a dialectic of beatitude and the world's poli-
tics of conflict, of the time-present of the Vietnam War and time-past
as inscribed in the Khmer architecture and friezes, and, far from least,
of self and desire. Ginsberg exhibits a fine eye for the topography,
whether temple halls and tree roots ('long snaky toes spread / down

the lintel's red / cradle-root / elephantine bigness', 314) or engravings of Buddha and supplicant dancers ('reassurance from Buddha's / two arms / palms out', 327). That, too, involves him is the contradictory call to become a true *bodhisattva* yet possessed of his call to sexual flesh (his dream of coitus with 'a Cambodian sweet policeman', 324). The poem's centre so lies in his exploration of who he is, the poet-self of spirit and body, East and West, and between Buddhist quietude and the world's political and military noise.

Late Ginsberg

The publication of *Death & Fame: Last Poems, 1993–1997* has not always been thought to represent Ginsberg at strength. But the collection gives illumination to a preceding literary output both full of self-mirror ('My Sad Self' in *Reality Sandwiches* or 'Ego Confession' in *Mind Breaths*) and physical sexuality ('Please Master' in *The Fall of America*, 'Hardon Blues' in *Mind Breaths* or 'Love Comes' in *White Shroud*) and yet generosity towards others ('Who Be Kind To' in *Planet News* or 'Elegy for Neal Cassady' in *The Fall of America*). It also conjures up a poetry focused in America ('Who Runs America?' or 'Stay Away from The White House' in *Mind Breaths*) yet always navigatory of the wider world ('Patna-Benares Express' in *Planet News* or 'Ayers Rock/Uluru Song' in *Mind Breaths*).[26] In this respect *Cosmopolitan Greetings: Poems, 1986–1992* (1994) re-emphasises Ginsberg seeking to speak to worlds beyond America, truly the transnational bard. The last poems, if not exactly a recapitulation of these directions, carry any number of shared threads.

The self-absorption takes on quite a medical emphasis given Ginsberg's physical setbacks in the decade, the minor strokes and Bell's palsy and the eventual final tumours brought on by hepatitis C. His plaints make their way uninhibitedly into the poems. 'How will you feel when you can't breathe?' he asks in 'Bowel Song' (35). 'Hepatitis Body Itch' hints of likely physiological lead-on to what he terms 'corpse cancer' (77). Haemorrhoids become an accompanying affliction in the untitled 'This kind of Hepatitis can cause ya / Nosebleed skin itch bowel nausea' (94). Buttocks and evacuation are made over into reminders of the terminal fade of body function in 'Excrement' (16–17). These anatomies, never least his sphincter, have about them a certain ruthlessness as if Ginsberg will have no

truck with evasion of the body's pathway towards death. That does
not erase, even in decline, the element of playfulness that never left
him, as attested in a poem like 'Richard III':

> Toenail-thickening age on me,
> Sugar coating my nerves, leg
> muscles lacking blood, weak kneed
> Heart insufficient, a thick'd valve-wall
> Short of breath, six pounds
>   overweight with water –
> logged liver, gut & lung – up at 4.a.m.
>   reading Shakespeare. (67)

Nor does he flinch from recognition of his life's narcissism as he
makes clear when, in the contrarily titled 'Objective Subject', he
avers 'It's true I write about myself / Who else do I know so well?'
(75). In 'Multiple Identity Question' he takes up a note of self-
mockery. If he has had laurels, fame, professorships, he is also now
the senior citizen with discounts at Alfalfa's Healthfoods, in all a
'relative phantom nonentity' (41).

Yet there is also the ongoing politically aware Ginsberg, responsive
as ever to arbitrary power and war. Against a backdrop spanning the
1990–1 Gulf invasion, the 1993 Bosnia-Herzegovina conflict and the
Oklahoma City Bombing in 1995, he continues the assignment he gave
himself at the outset to achieve peace-ability amid embattled times.
'New Democracy Wish List', addressed to the Clinton White House,
might almost be a manifesto, his indictments of nuclear technology,
fossil fuels, lack of accessible AIDS medicine, continued criminalisa-
tion of marijuana, and CIA, NSA and FBI interventions and surveil-
lance. He calls for eco-foods, conservation, ecological health. But to
relieve any suggestion of liberal platitude he also seams this advocacy
in typical aphoristic wit, whether 'Sexuality's loose not fixed. Legalize
it' (2) or 'Reward educators as handsomely as plumbers' (3).

Other like-oriented verse takes on the ruinous Balkan wars ('Peace
in Bosnia-Herzegovina', 4–5), the Right's contempt for alternative
America ('Newt Gingrich Declares War on "McGovernik Counter-
culture"', 20), and market globalisation as 'money tree' ('World Bank
Blues', 64–6). The title-poem, 'Death & Fame', written a month or
so before his death, sutures this personal and public Ginsberg. The
closing lines imply a Buddhist awareness of a life lived in the face of

pending demise. But they also, in a typical layer of Ginsberg drollery, ease any undue solemnity with a nod to the force of the absurd in his own history: 'Everyone knew they were part of "History" except the deceased who never knew exactly what was happening even when I was alive' (70). The note of coming retrospect was anticipated in the one-stanza poem 'What Relief' (*Plutonian Ode and Other Poems, 1977–1980*), an almost rueful wariness that he might pass insufficiently noticed into history:

> If my pen hand were snapped by a Broadway truck
> – What relief from writing letters to the *Nation*
> disputing tyrants, war gossip, FBI –
> My poems'll gather dust in Kansas libraries,
> adolescent farmboys opening book covers with ruddy
>   hands. (82)

The notion of his work gathering dust verges on the unlikely. Pen and protest, poetry even in the America of mid-point Kansas, and a coy nod to young manhood: the ingredients point to both long-aborning and continuing Ginsberg.

Notes

1. Bill Morgan (ed.), *I Greet You at the Beginning of a Great Career: The Selected Correspondence of Lawrence Ferlinghetti and Allen Ginsberg, 1955–1987*, San Francisco: City Lights, 2015, 1.
2. Ed Sanders, *Let's Not Keep Fighting the Trojan War: New and Selected Poems, 1986–2009*, Minneapolis: Coffee House Press, 2009, 45.
3. Letter from Emerson to Whitman, 21 July 1855. Whitman reprinted the letter in the appendix to his 1856 edition of *Leaves of Grass*.
4. This favourite Ginsberg sutra with its emphasis on 'No suffering, no cause of suffering' is also quoted on the title-page of *Selected Poems, 1947–1995*, London: Penguin Books, 1996.
5. *Mexico City Blues Read by Allen Ginsberg*, Boulder: Shambhala Lion Editions, 1996, 2 cassettes. Ginsberg himself gives a bibliography of his recordings up to 1982 (as well as written work) in *Plutonian Ode and Other Poems, 1977–1980*, San Francisco: City Lights Books, 1982, 108–10.
6. Full annotation is given in the bibliography at the end of this volume.
7. See Bill Morgan (ed.), *The Letters of Allen Ginsberg*, Philadelphia: Da Capo Press, 2008 and *The Yage Letters*, with William Burroughs, San Francisco: City Lights Books, 1963.

8. Allen Ginsberg, *Journals: Early Fifties Early Sixties*, New York: Grove Press, 1977; *Journals Mid-Fifties, 1954–1958*. New York: HarperCollins, 1994, and *Indian Journals, March 1962–May 1963*, San Francisco: Dave Haselwood Books, 1970; republished San Francisco: City Lights Books, 1974.

9. In this regard, see Allen Ginsberg, *Snapshot Poetics*, San Francisco: Chronicle Books,1993, and *Photographs*, Altadena, CA: Twelvetrees Press, 1991.

10. Louis Ginsberg, *Morning in the Spring: And Other Poems*, New York: Morrow, 1970. In his Introduction Allen Ginsberg writes, 'Confronting my father's poems at the end of his life, I weep at his meekness and his silent recognition of that pitiful Immensity he records of his own life's Time, his father's life time, & the same Mercy his art accords to my own person his son', 14–15.

11. Louis Ginsberg to his son, 29 February 1956. For the full correspondence between the two, see Allen Ginsberg and Louis Ginsberg, *Family Business: Two Lives in Letters and Poetry*, New York: Bloomsbury, 2001.

12. William Carlos Williams, 'Howl for Carl Solomon', *Howl and Other Poems*, San Francisco: City Lights Books, 1956, 8.

13. Cited as personal reminiscence in Jeffery Meyers, *Privileged Moments: Encounters with Writers*, Madison: University of Wisconsin Press, 2001, 8.

14. For the text as first written, see *Howl, Original Draft Facsimile, Transcript and Variant Versions*, ed. Barry Miles, New York: Harper & Row, 1986.

15. I have given full analysis of this dimension of the poem in *Modern American Counter Writing: Beats, Outriders, Ethnics*, New York: Routledge, 2010, 13–16. It is, however, worth requoting Ginsberg's own summary of how the poem is ordered: 'Howl is an "affirmation" of individual experience of God, sex, drugs, absurdity etc. Part I deals sympathetically with individual cases. Part II describes and rejects the Moloch of society which confounds and suppresses individual experiences and forces the individual to consider himself mad if he does not his own deepest senses. Part III is an expression of sympathy and identification with C.S. (Carl Solomon) who is in the madhouse, saying that his madness is basically his rebellion against Moloch and I am with him, and extending my hand in union.' *To Eberhart from Ginsberg: A Letter about HOWL*, Lincoln, MA: Pennean Press, 1976.

16. All page references are to *Howl and Other Poems*, San Francisco: City Lights Books, 1956.

17. *To Eberhart from Ginsberg*.

18. Richard Eberhart, 'West Coast Rhythms', *New York Times Book Review*, 6 September 1956. Reprinted in *To Eberhardt from Ginsberg*,

19. Reply to Hollander's review. Ginsberg's letter of 7 September 1958 recapitulates much of what he wrote to Eberhart but with even greater local prosodic detail.
20. Emily Dickinson, 'Because I could not stop for death'.
21. The definitive study in these respects is Tony Trigilio, *Allen Ginsberg's Buddhist Poetics*, Carbondale: Southern Illinois University Press, 2007.
22. Allen Ginsberg, 'Wichita Vortex Sutra', *Planet News, 1961–1967*, San Francisco: City Lights Books, 1968, 111.
23. Allen Ginsberg, *Reality Sandwiches, 1953–60*, San Francisco: City Lights Books, 1963, 17–20.
24. 'Kral Majales', *Planet News, 1961–1967*, San Francisco: City Lights Books, 89–91.
25. Page reference is to Allen Ginsberg, *Collected Poems, 1947–1980*, New York: Harper & Row, 1984, 314.
26. Each of these poems is also to be found in Allen Ginsberg, *Selected Poems, 1947–1995*, New York: HarperCollins, 1996; Penguin Books, 1997, 2001.

CHAPTER 3

Jack Kerouac: Road, Jazz, Zen

Oh, and Kerouac? Jack still jumps
with the same beat genius as before,
notebooks filled with Buddha.

Allen Ginsberg, 'Dream Record: June 8, 1953'[1]

How inseparable you and the America you saw yet was
never there
to see: you and America, like the tree and the
ground, are one and the same . . .
a Beat Christ-boy

Gregory Corso, 'Elegiac Feelings American (for the dear
Memory of John Kerouac)' (1970)[2]

Contours

To open an account of Jack Kerouac with Allen Ginsberg's early
acclaim as to the novelist's 'same beat genius' and taste for Bud-
dhism can hardly be less than fitting. Theirs, for a time, seemed the
classic duopoly, Beat's respective voices of 'spontaneous' prose in
which *On the Road* took all before it and of the 'mind breath' verse
so operatically enacted in 'Howl'. In 'Elegiac Feelings American',
written shortly after Kerouac's death in October 1969 and a req-
uiem to their lifetime's friendship despite the occasional sparring,
Gregory Corso gives recognition to the writer who for him had been
an inspirational counter-force in biography and word ('And what
has happened to our dream of beauteous America, Jack?'). Both
Ginsberg and Corso, from the early to the later years, bespeak utter
fondness, the sense of having been implicated in the unremittingly
creative if often erratic presence of Kerouac's life.

Other tributes, likewise first-hand, add a further cross-ply of
bearings. John Clellon Holmes in his celebrated 'The Philosophy

of the Beat Generation', written for *Esquire* in February 1958, her-
alded the dynamic pulse of Kerouac's writing but also his envisaging
of Beat as a 'spiritual quest' beyond hedonism or celebrity.³ William
Burroughs, one of a host of interviewees in the greatly engaging
film documentary *What Happened to Jack Kerouac?* (1986), insists
on Kerouac's literary workmanship before his part in politics or
media: 'I don't think he ever took part in a demonstration or signed
a petition.'⁴ Lawrence Ferlinghetti in 'The Canticle of Jack Kerouac'
(1987) summons popular-myth 'road' Kerouac but also his French
Canadian name tag ('Ti-Jean' for 'Petit-Jean') and family French
patois or *joual*:

> And then Ti-Jean Jack with Joual tongue
>   disguised as an American fullback in plaid shirt
>   crossing and recrossing America
>   in speedy cars . . .⁵

Michael McClure, co-Beat poet and author of the play *The Beard*
(1965) with its juxtaposition of Billy the Kid and Jean Harlow as
American archetypes, in 2013 recalls the 1955 6 Gallery reading
where he, too, read with Ginsberg and others and gives a coun-
ter to the image of Kerouac as the rowdie full of wine and shout:
'I thought I was the shyest person around until Allen Ginsberg
brought Jack Kerouac round to my house in San Francisco. Jack
had a deep-down shyness – way more than me.'⁶

Bearings, too, are to be found from music. David Amram, Beat-
connected composer and virtuoso of the jazz French horn who
co-inaugurated jazz and poetry with Kerouac at New York's Brata
Gallery in 1957, remembers that 'He had a phenomenal ear. It was
like playing duets with a great musician.'⁷ Bob Dylan's 'On the Road
Again', from his album *Bringing It All Back Home* (1965), echoes
Kerouac's title to take surreally worded aim at suburban norms
('You ask why I don't live here anymore, Why? How come you have
to ask me that?'). In the 1980s Dylan would also be heard to say
'*On the Road* changed my life as it changed everyone else's'. Patti
Smith, songster of the watershed album *Horses* (1975) and author of
Just Kids (2010) with its memoir of 1970s Beat-punk times in Hotel
Chelsea and her relationship with Robert Mapplethorpe, doyen of
homocentric photography, recognises the Kerouac possessed of an
abiding sense of vocation. Interviewed for the screen documentary

One Fast Move or I'm Gone: Kerouac's Big Sur in 2008, and with
an eye to his overdrinking and bouts of depression, she observes, 'He
wasn't a perfect man but he had moments of perfect clarity.'[8]

The plethora of different life studies, more than a dozen since Ann
Charters's pioneering *Kerouac: A Biography* (1973), underlines his
continuing draw, whether pre-eminent portraits like Gerald Nicosia's
Memory Babe: A Critical Biography of Jack Kerouac (1994), Barry
Miles's *Jack Kerouac: King of the Beats* (1998) or, latterly, Joyce
Johnson's full-throttle account of the best writing years in *The Voice
Is All: The Lonely Victory of Jack Kerouac* (2012) with its salutary
observation 'his works live on, while the Beat Generation has not
existed for a very long time'.[9] But they also encompass competitive
writer-closeness as in Holmes's *Gone in October: Last Reflections
on Jack Kerouac* (1985) or the coming-of-age Beat-era memoir of
his sister Elizabeth Von Vogt in *681 Lexington Avenue: A Beat Edu-
cation in New York City, 1947–1954* (2008). These can be read
alongside the remembrance of tangled, challenging love affairs with
Kerouac in Johnson's *Minor Characters: A Young Woman's Coming-
of-Age in the Beat Orbit of Jack Kerouac* (1983) and Helen Weaver's
The Awakener: A Memoir of Jack Kerouac and the Fifties (2009).
Kerouac, as though himself the embodiment of existential theatre,
long came to create a focus almost on a par with his writing.

The upshot, across the board, is the sense of Kerouac's self-
enclosure yet also needfulness, his writer's quiet and concentration
yet alcoholic noise and itinerary impulses. That takes on especially
greater weight given the gathering public fanfare in the wake of
On the Road whose publication Gilbert Millstein in his celebrated
1957 review for the *New York Times* announced as 'an authentic
work of art' and 'the most important utterance yet made by the
generation Kerouac himself named years ago as "beat" and whose
principal avatar he is'.[10] As Johnson recalls in *Minor Characters*,
Kerouac at the time could not resist being taken aback at his fame,
much as he was understandably delighted to read Millstein's words
in early-morning Manhattan. It bears noting that the *New York
Times* regular review editor, the austere Orville Prescott who also
in his time panned Nabokov and Gore Vidal, was reported to have
detested *On the Road*.

The way-stations in Kerouac's history have long become famil-
iar. They extend from birth as Jean-Louis Kérouac within a migrant
blue-collar Catholic and Québecois family and his Lowell, Mas-
sachusetts boyhood through to the final years in Florida and death

of cirrhosis of the liver.[11] The publication in 1950 of *The Town and the City* (1950), his debut novel given over to the extensive French Canadian and Irish American dynasty takes its setting in Massachusetts and Manhattan. Both *Maggie Cassidy* (1959), the blighted teenage romance between the 'Canuck half-Indian' Jack Duluoz and his first-love Irish American girl, and *Doctor Sax* (1959), childhood gothic and Freud-inflected fantasy, likewise draw from intimate but little veiled early autobiographical sources. That involves his being tied into the Oedipal knot with his tough but also needful mother, Gabrielle, Mémère as she was known, and the haunt that followed on the death of his brother Gerard of rheumatic fever aged nine in 1926 and to which his 'book of sorrows', *Visions of Gerard* (1963), gives Buddhist-Catholic and guilt-laden remembrance. 'My holy brother', he calls Gerard in *Desolation Angels* (1965).[12]

Vanity of Duluoz: An Adventurous Education, 1935–46, written in 1966 but published after his death, maps the early years as though a narrative diary. The course of events takes in his classes and sports at Lowell high school, then Horace Mann preparatory school and follow-on football scholarship to Columbia; the early US navy camp and Merchant Marine seagoing 1940s in the wartime Atlantic when he drafted the still unpublished *The Sea Is My Brother*; the inaugurating Manhattan encounters and intimacies with Ginsberg, Burroughs and Cassady; and the Lucien Carr/David Kammerer murder and arrest of Kerouac and Burroughs as material witnesses in 1944. There would ensue his 1940s and 1950s trans-America highway adventuring and cross-border drive into Mexico with Cassady, his firewatcher and Zen lone sojourn in the Pacific Northwest's Cascade Mountains, later recounted in *Desolation Angels*, and the several trans-Atlantic forays. Peripatetic, a kind of willed homelessness even as he kept his vocation strong, whether in the United States, Mexico, France and other Europe, or North Africa, becomes a hallmark. Each increment contributes to a sense of momentum edging as much towards the virtual as actual.

The writer's boltholes and residences add circumstantial time and place to his story, whether West 188 Street, Manhattan, where he roomed with Edie Parker and Joan Vollmer in 1943–4, or Hartley Hall at Columbia University, where Ginsberg first invited him as roommate in 1944, or the Rocky Mount and Big Easonburg Woods in North Carolina where he stayed with his sister and family a number of times throughout the 1940s and 1950s. The San Francisco apartment of Neal and Carolyn Cassady also plays its part, not least as the stage for their sexual imbroglio and where he wrote most of *The Subterraneans* (1958) with its extemporaneous 'bop prosidy' and anatomy of citied interracial love. Other locales include Orizaba Street, Mexico City, out of which arises both *Mexico City Blues* and *Tristessa* (1960), the latter with its portrait of a beauteous title-heroine Mexican hooker fatally caught up in morphine addiction; Ginsberg's rented Berkeley cottage in 1955; the 'funny little peaked almost Chinese cabin' on Desolation Peak where he served as a firewatcher meticulously recalled in *The Dharma Bums* (1958: 231); and Ferlinghetti's cabin in Bixby Creek Canyon in July 1960, where he wrote *Big Sur* (1962) with its chronicle of his downward-spiralling writer's breakdown and failure to handle celebrity.

Hyannis, Massachusetts, marks his return to home turf where Ann Charters would visit and create the first bibliography of his work in 1966, and where in Lowell he completed *Vanity of Duluoz*, which on a notably boozy occasion he took round to Charles Olson in coastal Gloucester. Olson, guru of Black Mountain and the *Maximus* poems, gave it no plaudits.[13] Finally, in 1968, the year of his infamous drink-filled televised interview with William F. Buckley on *Firing Line*, he takes up residence in St. Petersburg, Florida, with Stella Sampas whom he had married in November 1966 as an act of convenience to help care for his mother (she had suffered a major stroke in 1966). At the time of his death he was seeking a divorce. The final abode, after collapsing of a haemorrhage, would be his room in St Anthony's Hospital.

Life and legend evidently fold one into the other, but all too often at the cost of recognition of his literary smarts. Once *On the Road* had launched there would be the public fame and each press conference and public reading whereby, to his dismay and even anger, his name became code for beatnik-ism or hippiedom. For within the trajectory stand the fourteen or so novels whose core he nominated the Duluoz epic, his intended *roman fleuve*. Inspired in part by John Galsworthy's *Forsyte Saga*, in part by his Breton and French Canadian family legacy, he always hoped this body of work would bestow the honorific of latter-day Proust upon him (he was also early to read Balzac and Céline in French). Writing to Malcolm Cowley at Viking Press in 1955 he insisted that 'when I'm done, in about 10, 15, years, it will cover all the years of my life, like Proust, but done on the run, a running Proust'.[14] It was in this vein that he also worked at different times on *Visions of Cody* (post. 1972), his

story-epic centred upon Cody/Cassady and overlapped with other
material that had fed into *On the Road* and his other texts, and in
which he employs a kaleidoscope of narrator voices.

The output hardly stops there. *Sartori in Paris* (1966), the novella
first serialised in *Evergreen Review* and given over to his ten-day stay
in France in 1965 ostensibly researching Breton ancestry, opens into
forays into the contrast of capital city and region, *joual* and standard
French. It extends to both *Mexico City Blues* and his shorter poetry,
notably *Scattered Poems* (1971), *Heaven and Other Poems* (1971)
and *Pomes All Sizes* (post. 1992), together with the compositions
gathered in *Book of Haikus* (post. 2003), his play *Beat Generation*
written in 1957 but unperformed until 2012, the prefaces, studio and
television recordings, and, of major consequence, his lifelong trove
of pencil-scribbled notebooks.[15] The voluminous letter-writing might
constitute an epistolary novel in its own right, urgent, exhilarated,
and a major resource for his operative poetics, especially the long lost
'Joan Anderson' letter: 'I got the idea for the spontaneous idea of *On
the Road* from seeing how good old Neal Cassady wrote his letters
to me, all first person, fast, mad, confessional, completely serious, all
detailed . . .'[16] Kerouac as Beat's would-be Marcel Proust, diligently
in search of his own time past and writing with rare energy on the
run or not, might still have to contend against the ambiguous hagiog-
raphy of ever the 'gone' hipster. But he was, as he remains, foremost
the author.

On the Road

As in the case of Ginsberg, selective texts do duty for the larger
round, the *carpe diem* ethos, the vital readiness of the Kerouac
voice. *On the Road*, almost of obligation, invites first billing. Its
celebrity, without doubt, has become a filter to negotiate, variously
massive Beat bestseller and *ur*-text, existential life-road manual in
five acts, and the renowned compositional model of 'first thought,
best thought'. In Sal Paradise as narrator, and Dean Moriarty as
fabled companion and second self, the novel sets forth America as
literal but also figurative topography, to be met in liberating (and
let it be said abidingly masculine) itineraries of highway, landscape,
city and coast. Enthusiasts are quick to assert how the novel's rush
of aliveness stirs admiration, the adventuresome panorama of close
encounters with the Beat fraternity, the road trips and hitching, the

freight-hops, talk, jazz, sex, kicks and partying, the city buzz of New Orleans or San Francisco, and, not least, the symptomatic relish of burgers in Manhattan, cold beer in Denver, or apple pie and ice cream in the Plains. Even those who think *On the Road* a false deck of cards, over-euphoric, plotless, or increasingly dated 'Boy's Own' fare, concede that it possesses powers to attract ear and eye.

To this end, the novel's voice and its workings invites continued attention. For in the chronicling of his 'road' apprenticeship across the one and several time-bands, Sal speaks in a manner at once full of evidentiary speed yet often lyric, at its best as wholly prepossessing as that to be heard in, say, Twain's *Huckleberry Finn* or Fitzgerald's *The Great Gatsby*. The signature so offered at the outset marks ground-zero ('everything was dead', 3). Detail is filled in: the split-up with his wife, the unspecified illness, the dependence on his aunt, the 'hanging around the campus' (3), and the rain-strewn mistaken attempt to head west by Bear Mountain before embarking on Route 6 and then the mythic Route 66. 'My whole life', he says, 'was a haunted life, the life of a ghost' (15). The adventuring to follow leads into a kind of magnification, a narrative of arousal and spectacle.

Dean is its embodiment, to be remembered as 'a young Gene Autry' (4), 'a western kinsman of the sun' (19), the athletic and always highly sexual Denver jailbird and car-thief full of volubility, witness, idiom, and yet who comes into Sal's life 'to learn to write' (5). He features as beatified petty-criminal, the westerner, the street-savvy Denverite, 'son of a wino' (35) and the car-driver supreme, with Sal as his East Coast Boswell.[17] Dean's 'excited way of talking' (9) gives off its own infection. He will bond with Carlo Marx as frenetic colloquist. As centrifugal figure Dean possesses, like one of the consecrated outcasts in a Jean Genet text, 'the tremendous energy of a new kind of American saint' (35). Sal sees himself and Dean 'embarked on a tremendous season together' (38). In this regard, Sal's existential hunger, and Dean's answering call, yields the novel's best-known passage, the need to join the ranks of 'the ones who are mad to live, mad to talk, mad to be saved, desirous of everything at the same time, the ones who never yawn or say a commonplace thing, but burn, burn, burn, like fabulous roman candles' (7). The effect, for better or otherwise, is rhapsodic, one of paean, even if Dean is also acknowledged to be clearly blemished, feckless, the joy rider as second-by-second opportunist.

Given these interacting points of departure, *On the Road*, autobiographical fiction as it has been called with a regard especially to the influence of Melville's evidentiary first-person fictions, moves inexorably into narration of each working high and yet often surprisingly of each sour low and breakup. 'I was ready for anything' (79) Sal offers as credo. In Central City, the site of drink and partying revels after he has made it to Denver with the Colorado Rockies as backdrop, he speaks of 'a new beat generation that I was slowly joining' (48). In Mill City, near San Francisco, with Remi Boncoeur, he designates the black and white mixed community 'so wild and joyous a place I've never seen since' (53). Los Angeles yields 'the beatest characters in the country' (77). In his encounter with Terry, the diminutive *campesina* with whom he is smitten and with whom he picks cotton in the San Joaquin Valley before moving to her farmworker hometown of Sabinal, he thinks himself among 'the great fellahin people of the world' (89). However, that will not prevent his abrupt abandonment of her and her child when he returns to New York ('Well, lackadaddy, I was on the road again', 92). It is a road both external and interior, an America of thrill, highway sight and sound, but always, and reflexively, of Sal himself as the writer with 'my notebook' (88).

Each sequence acts on these cues with always as presiding motif 'the purity of the road' (121), 'the holy road' (125). Dean even pronounces that 'the road is life' (192). He makes it into a declension of 'holyboy road, madman road, rainbow road, guppy road, any road' (229). The continent's space, as it were, reverberates within him, and in Sal to a lesser extent, its stage-coaching aboard each Greyhound and Trailways bus, factory and farm produce truck, bureau car and freight locomotive, and the succession of iconic Hudsons, Plymouths, Buicks, Cadillacs, Coupés and Ford Sedans. The geographies involved again take on luminosity, a westering lustre as against the ground zero of the New York's Times Square and the drug sub-world of Elmer Hassel.

The Mississippi River becomes 'the great brown father of rivers' (127), New Orleans 'mad jazz' (127), San Francisco 'the fabled city' (165), Chicago a heady sax and blues-bebop metropolis that 'glowed red before our eyes' (216), with Los Angeles a 'wild humming night' (79) and Mexico City 'a long, spectral Arabian dream' (264). Wider Mexico belongs to 'these vast and Biblical areas of the world' (274). Which is not to deny Sal's disenchantment in Cheyenne, Wyoming with its faux 'Wild West Week', kitsch cowboys and contrived storefront décor. Kerouac writes as though steering between literal and impressionist canvas, a mediation of the factuality of Manhattan

and San Francisco, the vast prairie Midwest, the highways of motel
and road-sign, or the vernacular speech and music, and an American
dreamscape that can be visionary, even numinous ('As we crossed
the Colorado/Utah border I saw God in the sky in the form of huge
sunburning clouds', 165).

The peopling of Sal's world likewise transposes Beat's actual his-
torical players into emblematic *dramatis personae*. Dean, as always,
assumes central focus. With a nod to Dostoevsky, he becomes 'the
Idiot, the Imbecile, the Saint of the lot . . . the HOLY GOOF' (176),
or as Sal calls him in a vision before they head to Mexico 'a 'burning
shuddering frightful angel' (236). Under a counter-perspective his
mistreatment of Camille and the children and inveterate philander-
ing makes him the butt of Galatea Dunkel's reprimand: 'You have
absolutely no regard for anybody but yourself and your damned
kicks' (176). Sal himself, when ill with fever and abandoned by
Dean in Mexico, will deliver the judgement: 'When I got better
I realized what a rat he was' (276). Dean may well incarnate
euphoric Beat as 'the root, the soul of Beatific' (176), but, under his
biographer's alternatingly compelled and disenchanted gaze, he is
also by journey's end the broken-thumbed figure last seen in street-
corner Manhattan 'ragged in a motheaten raincoat' (280).

Other portraiture, drawn from recognizable originals (Ginsberg,
Huncke, Burroughs, Carolyn Cassady), finds matching voice. They
take person in Carlo Marx and his 'nutty surrealist low-voiced staring
talk' (9), the elusive supplier-user Elmer Hassel with his 'hip sneer' (9),
Old Bull Lee as laconic sage, gun fetishist and marijuana grower on his
Louisiana holding who 'dragged his long, thin body around the entire
United States and most of Europe and North Africa in his time only
to see what was going on' (129–30), and Camille, 'well-bred, polite
young woman' (158) but also talented line-drawing artist and Dean's
infinitely put-upon spouse and mother to his children. Encounters,
varied, long or short term, each give off their own storyline within
Sal's own orbit. They number Dean's hot-rodding and Sal's temporary
security-guard work at the naval yard, the memory-filled truckers and
hobos, the exuberant Minnesota brothers delivering farm machinery
with their motley hitchhikers aboard the speeding deck truck, and the
different love partners (Dean's Marylou, Camille and Inez, the 'thin
fag' pickup driver, and Sal's Rita, Terry and Laura).

On the Road has long stirred controversy, at the sillier end an
affront to respectability, a danger to youth. More serious discussion

sees it as either breakthrough narrative or a tilt towards the facile open to Truman Capote's deflationary charge of mere typing. Other disquiet has also surfaced over time. Is the misogyny somehow understandable, historic, and, however evident, not actually endorsed by the text? Should there be offence or not offence to be taken at Sal's self-disenchantment with his own jaded cultural whiteness and in compensation 'wishing I were a Negro . . . a Mexican, or even a poor overworked Jap' (164) or believing Mexicans Indians like other indigenes 'basic, primitive, wailing humanity' (255) – his novella *Pic*, published posthumously in 1971 and written in the colloquial voice of a black boy making his way from North Carolina to Harlem in post-war America, has raised similar concerns. How persuasive is a Mexico of exotic Latin sexuality, brothels, weed, drink and all other anything-goes pleasures to be reached across a 'magic border' (249) and where life is 'dense, dark, ancient' (273)?

None of which is to deny how the novel makes for ardent human parade, the turnings both of event and personality caught stirringly in the narrator's road-diary Beat eye. Kerouac's style, the first-person passion of voice, is not to be denied – heedful, engaged, appetitive. It little surprises that, whatever the misgivings, *On the Road* has far from lost either critical or popular standing. To the contrary: Kerouac's American 'life' chronicle, Beat but also beyond-Beat, clearly gives grounds for believing it will continue to endure in all its singular inscriptive fluency.

True Story Novels

A quartet of further 'true story novels' in his own often repeated phrase, albeit none as canonical as *On the Road*, confirms the stride always to be associated with Kerouac. Each, again, deploys a working persona, the author by design both teller and to a large degree his own tale. In the case of *The Dharma Bums*, often thought his best workmanship for how it somewhat de-accelerates the usual spontaneity, the narrative falls to Ray Smith, Easterner, Buddhist-in-the-making, and companion spirit to his fellow writer-poet in the Gary Snyder figure of Japhy Ryder. Their Zen camaraderie (each a 'fellow Bodhisattva', 61), the literary networks that include the Ginsberg-like Alvah Goldbook ('wailing his poem . . . with arms outspread', 13), and the thinly veiled figures of Rexroth, McClure, Whalen, Lamantia, Neal Cassady and the ill-fated suicide Natalie Jackson,

with the 6 Gallery reading as reference point, along with the exuber-
ant Berkeley and hillside Marin County picnics (especially that for
Japhy's impending departure to Japan) and Japhy's Zen-mandated
sex practices with his various women followers, all flow into the
unfolding single narrative.

But the keystone lies in the eventual 'big mountain climb' (35)
up the Matterhorn in California's eastern sierras, ecology as near
formidable as its Swiss namesake and undertaken with their oddball
librarian companion Henry Morley (John Montgomery). The nar-
rative pitches Ray, and his eco-seasoned mentor Japhy, as indeed
bodhisattvas or *bhikkhu* in spirit and pledged to find *dharma*, the
search for 'the wheel of true meaning' (5). 'We were two strange dis-
similar monks' (176) runs Ray's description. Yet for all the invocation
of the Buddha, or the compassionate god-figures of Avalokiteshvara
and Kwannon, or the Diamond Sutra with its doctrine of empti-
ness, or the ninth-century 'Cold Mountain' Taoist poet Han Shan, or
Japhy's vision of 'the great rucksack revolution' (97) as a fist against
suburban and TV America ('I'm scared of all this American wealth,'
he says, 93) , or even Ray's 'Path of Buddhism' and Taoist/Wu Wei
'non-doing' or 'active inactivity' creative meditations at his sister's
woodland homestead in North Carolina (41), they both remain ine-
luctably American in word as much as world.[18]

Their Salvation Army and Goodwill clothes, boots and sleeping
bags, the provisions and wine, the sport and film cultural allusions,
update ancient Asia into the modernity of the American West with
the mountains as transnational time-and-place linkage. The trek also
has its pratfalls and jokes, whether Morley's failure to drain his car's
crankcase against the cold and his yodelling or Ray's sight of Japhy,
goat-like and without his pants, leaping boulder to boulder each
almost mock-comically signposted with imitation ducks. Kerouac's
considerable achievement is to keep the different ligatures of his sto-
rying not only accessible but tightly voiced.

In part this derives from the text's discernible but un-intrusive
reflexivity. 'By God it's a haiku in itself' (55) Ray says of the Sierra
range. Japhy, in turn, pays Ray the tribute of 'learning to write spon-
taneously and all that' (55). An early trail is said to have 'a kind of
immortal look to it' (61). Japhy, on top of the Matterhorn, gives out
his 'mountain-conquering Buddha Mountain Smashing song of joy'
(84). Having subsequently moved on to Desolation Peak, Ray lauds
the vista for the 'tremendous sensation of its dreamlikeness' (235).

Each precept likewise plays into the trek, typically the remembrance of the Zen sayings 'When you come to the top of the mountain, keep climbing' (83–4) and 'I had really learned that you can't fall off a mountain' (85). Kerouac leaves little doubt that he can write beautifully of the natural landscape, but if true to fact his language is also cannily figurative, a poetry.

It is within this kind of perceptual frame that Kerouac situates both Buddhism ('You know to me a mountain is a Buddha' testifies Japhy, 62) and ecology ('Buddha fields', 148, 'my alpine yard', 234, reads Ray's take on the landscape). Kerouac manages these dimensions with genuine prowess in *The Dharma Bums*, a work he himself said came out of his own best California years and clearly written from his centre. He is known to have wanted the word 'Beat' to be kept off the cover description, yet that does not in fact close the case. For all that Kerouac's novel might call to mind kindred 'spiritual' texts like Thoreau's *Walden* (1954), with its Massachusetts pond setting, or latterly Garrett Hongo's *Volcano* as a Zen and natural history autobiography centred in Hawai'i (1995), all manner of Beat trace makes its impact. The case is well founded to think *The Dharma Bums* classic Beat writing shorn of the label.

'Meantime I wrote and got an assignment for the coming summer as a fire look-out for the U.S. Forest Service on Desolation Peak in the High Cascades in Washington state' (142). *The Dharma Bums* so carries into *Desolation Angels*, the one work threaded sequentially into the other despite the change of narrator in Jack Duluoz for Ray Smith. Each major phase of *Desolation Angels* as usual comes busy in event ('I wake up and I'm on Desolation Peak, 25, 'I'm on the road', 95, 'Everything's happening', 136, 'Now we're famous writers more or less', 275), along with a slew of gnomic reflections ('to be *and* not to be', 5) and pressures of memory ('overflowing', 62). Kerouac, moreover, again monitors his own voicing of the text, not least on account of the later parts having been written after a several years gap. In his mountain hut he speaks of seeing 'a reflection of myself in the black window' (37) and of 'My desk . . . littered with papers, beautiful to look at thru half-closed eyes' (37). He rues 'the horror of my literary notoriety' (227) and counsels his reader to 'take another look at me to get the story better' (234). Life narrative, discursive opinion, remembrance, authorial self-circling: the upshot is busiest weave.

Duluoz's sixty-three-day sojourn as hermit firewatcher, as pre-figured in *The Dharma Bums*, lacks nothing in the way of Snyder-inspired ecological plenty, be it 'firs motionless in the blue morning' (25), 'the dense electrical air' (40) of a Cascades storm, or 'the eternity and solitude of mountain snowy rocks' (69). He also gives himself to full discursions into 'Zen Mystery' (57), a succession of haiku moments, and various expressions of self-obeisant homage to Saint Francis. But for all 'my mountainside contentment' (28) he also confesses to boredom, surges of memory involving his Low-ell family childhood, past loves, time and bets at the horse-track, and above all the un-Thoreauvian need for human interaction with his fellow literary roustabouts. Coming down the mountain he also leaves no doubt of his relish that 'ahead of me are adventures with even madder angels' (93), not least visits to burlesque in Seattle and to 'the whole fabulous movie of San Francisco' (121), be it sex, wine or the fabled poetry renaissance. Pastoral shades into urban, mountain into city.

The California sequence has him relishing jazz at The Cellar, sharing group talk and pace with Ginsberg, Cassady, Bob Kaufman, McClure, Robert Duncan, and Peter Orlovsky and his brother as 'Bohemians and Subterraneans' (148). He especially eulogises the wit and inventive dissonances in the poetry of Corso as Raphael ('Raphael is Socrates', 208). These exhilarations Duluoz gives their own gloss –'it's the beat generation . . . the beat of the heart' (127). The Mexico that follows, written as retrospect, is delineated as un-puritan, a whole body-and-mind cultural alternative to the United States and typified in the freewheeling Club Bombay. Duluoz writes in pencil and candlelight in his rooftop space, listens to the ground-floor junk-fuelled discourses of Bull Gaines (Bill Garver), and shares Aztec-pyramid and street wanderings under the guid-ance of Irving Garden (Ginsberg).

The New York of return, and where Duluoz fears that the noto-riety of *On the Road* will forever unbalance him ('a big book that will change America' Garden calls it, 260), bespeaks love affairs with Joyce Johnson and Helen Weaver, albeit tainted by a betray-ing vein of misogyny, and the rum episode in DC where Corso has been generously invited to stay in the residence of Varnum Random (based on the poet Randall Jarrell). Duluoz admits to guilt at writ-ing a spontaneous-styled Beat poem inside Jarrell's home to spite the more orthodox Library of Congress laureate whose work he has earlier dismissed. The Africa, Europe and, once again, return-to-America epilogues carry their own key vignettes, whether Hubbard (Burroughs) in Tangier looking 'like an insane German Philologist in Exile' (314) and composing *Nude Supper* (*Naked Lunch*), a London in Teddy Boy and Soho mode, or California as now supposed police state emblematically struck by an earthquake. 'Passing through' serves as sectional heading for all these sequences. It speaks exactly to *Desolation Angels*, Kerouac's narrative of a world perceived to be transient, material, yet also Zen-spiritual and populated by fellow 'dharma bums', and which he opts to voice at all habitual velocity.

The Subterraneans (1958), set in early 1950s North Beach and with its account of the interracial love affair between Leo Percepied ('I'm not a hoodlum but some kind of crazy saint', 7), and Mardoo Fox ('tattered holy Negro Joan of Arc', 31), arouses an ongoing deep well of contention. Does it or not veer into cartoon stereotype of white master/black handmaiden? How persuasive are the Wilhelm Reich ponderings, genuine insight into gender behaviour or cod psychology of sexual 'unbecloudedness'?[19] When Percepied, his name French for pierced foot in an echo also of Oedipus, speaks of 'my old dream of wanting to be vital, alive like a Negro or an Indian or a Denver Jap or a New York Puerto Rican' (70), is he pandering to cheap atavism or paying good-faith homage? Henry Miller and William Burroughs were early to lavish praise, their shared regard for Kerouac's truth to feeling. But equally there has been harsh rebuke – 'a nasty bit of business, indeed' and especially its 'woman-degrading, racist and homophobic attitudes' writes Warren French.[20] These splits continue to grate uneasily.

But a point of convergence lies in Kerouac's manner of fictionalising this intense lover relationship.[21] No text of his quite more fulfils his 'spontaneous' poetics than *The Subterraneans*, so much so that both Ginsberg and Burroughs prompted him to encode his compositional approach. The upshot, 'Essentials of Spontaneous Prose' (1958), to be read in company with his other short manuals like 'Belief & Technique for Modern Prose' (1959) and 'The First Word' (1959), insists upon the exigency of 'undisturbed flow from the mind of personal secret idea-words'. Throughout the novella 'spontaneity' wholly applies, the Joycean runs of consciousness, barely punctuated monologue and dialogue, the cross-folds of thought process and spoken disclosure, and typically Mardou's letter about the psychology of their relationship and the implacable parsing of it given by Leo.

To be sure Kerouac is infinitely about the 'subterranean hip generation' (23), a full citied diary of the usual suspects, be it Ginsberg as Adam Moorad, Corso as Yuri Gligoric, and Sam Vedder as Lucien Carr, with spot appearances like that of Arial Lavalina for Gore Vidal. The currency, as ever, lies in kicks, night partying, drink and unabated writer talk in clubs like The Mask. Sexual permutations hardly go missing, those of Leo, Mardou and Yuri, with a gay dimension in the Leo–Arial flirtation and their male court. Jazz serves as almost a religion, with Charlie Parker, 'king and founder of the bop generation' (12), the high priest, and with savvy allusions to a range of other jazz stylists like Gerry Mulligan, Art Blakey and Thelonious Monk. But the main drama lies in the relentless, embattled Leo–Mardou equation. 'No girl ever moved me with a story of spiritual suffering and so beautifully' (36) attests Leo. Mardou, often impatient with fellahin male talk, emerges from their fervour and all of its racial as much as emotional baggage, to give her closing 'I want to be independent' (111). Love or not, they are frequently 'spent with sex' (76).

Written high on Benzedrine in a three-day bout at his mother's dining table, *The Subterraneans* avails a range of interpretation. Race, and its pre-emptive shadow, hovers throughout. Black skin plays against white skin, Mardou as 'black Cherokee' (45) against Leo as Canuck with a trace of Mohawk who designates himself 'a bum, a drunkard' (104). Sexuality overlaps, whether Mardou's understanding of women as trophy, conquest, the more so if under white male gaze further exoticised by colour, or Leo's self-uncertainty as to his tending androgyny. The both of them are to be heard as voices of probe, accusation, discontent with psychoanalysis (Mardoo's therapy both helps and vexes her) and guilt as in Leo's recognition that he cannot take Mardou south to the colour-line Carolinas of his white family. The speed, the synaptic leaps of idiom, keep all these elements in play, a triumph of instinctive stagecraft to admirers, a confusion of racial and sexual signals to the un-persuaded.

Vanity of Duluoz: An Adventurous Education, 1935–1946, with its recapitulation of Kerouac's Massachusetts/Connecticut boyhood through marine service in the North Atlantic to Greenwich Village writerhood, acts as both bridge and epilogue to the Duluoz cycle. If the last written, it goes back to beginnings, ostensibly the thirteen-book narrative meant for Stella Sampas (addressed as 'wifey' throughout) a would-be explanation of the life that gave rise to his creative identity. Fond as to 'Autumn nights in Massachusetts' in the 1930s (9) in contrast with the 'Mandala Mosaic Meshed-up world' of 1967 (10), and sour at the cost of his own eventual fame in a TV age and in the wake of *On the Road*, this is assiduous memory-fiction once more and again under the alias of Jack Duluoz albeit with Kerouac's own lightly veiled parenthetical reflections and meta-commentary. Aptly the narrator chooses to call his work one of 'football and war' (193), a series of 'cameos' (53) and 'this mosaic' (56), and as if mock bravura, 'this whole insane tirade of prose called a book' (201).

Detail, as always, comes in busiest currents and eddies. The credo, his self-reflection in the wake of being denied a sports vocation, is explicit:

> Go into the American night, the Thomas Wolfe darkness, the hell with these bigshot gangster football coaches, go after being an American writer, tell the truth, don't be pushed around by them or anyone else or any of their goons. (92)

Duluoz as alter ego bows in with a full sports cv, the football and track star who progresses on an athletics scholarship to Columbia University yet who is also the bookish young reader of H. G. Wells's *Outline of History* and the *Encyclopedia Britannica*, Homer's *Iliad* and *Odyssey*. Declaring himself the aspirant journalist and writer, almost reflexively, he gives a novelist's attentive eye to time and context underscored not a little by his repertoire of literary allusion. Wolfe repeatedly features for his endeavours in first-person fiction like *Look Homeward, Angel* (1929) to capture America's plenitude, as among others do Joyce, Melville, Rimbaud, Tolstoy and T. S. Eliot. Kerouac from the start may well have been the jock, the seaman, the traveller. But *Vanity of Duluoz* holds little back in also brandishing his writer affinities.

Each 'cameo' does service in this regard. The sports sequences brim with team particulars, scores, pranks, locker-room jock behaviour, and the broken leg that signals the end of his athletics career. The Duluoz/Kerouac dynasty, with its Celtic roots in Brittany and Cornwall, and the portraiture of his blue-collar father and tough, fervently Catholic mother, are given near-poetic attention. Whether 'deckrat' (120) in the marine service and off coastal Greenland,

or patient at Bethesda having been certified psychiatric for train-
ing indiscipline, or the voyager to London and Liverpool during a
pause from the blitz, or his life under sexual threat from the bosun
of the *S.S. Robert Treat Pain* with its echo of Herman Melville's
Billy Budd and the love–hate of Claggart for the winsome Billy, the
effect is one of hecticity, an unyielding imaginative appetite for new
sight and sound. His meeting with Big Slim, storyteller, would-be
hobo, and temporary fellow-escapee from their military hospital,
might almost be a mirror reflection of himself. These, each, he puts
under history's shadow of World War II and its bitterly personalis-
ing impact in the death on the beaches of Anzio, Italy, of his best
friend, 'Sabby' Savakis (Stella's brother Sammy Sampas). He dis-
closes the broader aesthetic pattern in his shipboard return from
London: 'And it was that last morning before we got ready to sail
to Brooklyn that I devised the idea of "The Duluoz Legend"' (190).

No one 'cameo', however, more has drawn attention than the
murder story as he tells it of Claude de Maubris (Lucien Carr) and
Franz Mueller (David Kammerer), the latter's impossible passion and
stalking of his Dionysian blond love-object and its calamitous out-
come in the knife-death and river disposal of the body at Maubris's
hand. The affair has long become Beat tableau, Duluoz (Kerouac)
and Hubbard (Burroughs) as material witnesses with interventions
from Irwin Garden (Ginsberg), the payment of Duluoz's court bond
by his lover Johnnie (Edie Parker) and their subsequent marriage
and breakup, and the return to seafaring by Duluoz. As though epi-
logue, all passion spent ('I had goofed throughout wartime and this
is my confession', 261), he re-summons the Village and its writer-
bohemian places (42nd Street, Times Square, Harlem) and, poign-
antly, his father dying of cancer. The final word of counselling his
wife to sleep implies the life led as one of dream reality yet also his
own wakeful writer's truth.

Blues and Poetry

Kerouac's poetry has a major centrepiece in *Mexico City Blues*,
the chorus-sequence written in 1955 and aimed to emulate 'a long
blues in an afternoon jam session on Sunday' as he calls it in his
brief but hospitable frontispiece. Variously it has been designated
Whitmanesque Long Poem, a sutra replete with copious Buddhist
references, and his Catholic-inflected spiritual meditation on life's
entrances and exits. Given, too, that Kerouac and Ginsberg were

much in correspondence during its writing, about both conscious-
ness and poetics, it adds weight to regarding *Mexico City Blues* and
'Howl' (the title was actually suggested by Kerouac) a like-minded
match. But never least as the poem ranges through self, identity, the
harmonies and disharmonies of the world, he is writing word-jazz
in an attempt to forge a scriptural equivalent of Charlie Parker or
John Coltrane in improvisational style and riff.

This jazz-blues accent holds throughout the choruses as they
alight on each unfolding major theme. The 34th Chorus, as a voice
within a voice, suggests freeform composition, a roaming sax or
horn:

> I have no plans
> > No dates
> > > No appointments with anybody
>
> > So I leisurely explore
> > > Souls and cities . . .

To ask, as the last line of the Chorus does, 'That's enough, isn't it?',
gives something of the tease that frequently surfaces in the poem.
It takes little time to discern that Kerouac indeed is emulating the
improvisation of a jazz set. Scat, wordplay, counterpoints of high
idea with folksy colloquialism all enter the one overall field of the
poetry's 'musical' reckoning and whether the compass is Beat as
movement, family, spirituality or the great jazz illuminati.

The 5th Chorus has him turn to Beat's fraternity, Ginsberg
('KIND KING MIND / Allen Ginsberg called me'), the Burroughs of
his pen-name in *Junkie* ('William Burroughs / Is William Lee), and
Corso whom he associates with German medieval lyric poets ('The
Italian Minnesinger'; 'the Haunted Versemaker / King / of Brattle
Street'). Neal Cassady is given his nod several times over, likewise
'nuts like Carl Solomon' (27th Chorus). His biological family calls
up similar proximity. In the 148th Chorus he calls to mind himself
as 'Ti-Jean' (or Petit Jean). The 19th Chorus gives homage to his
sacral lost brother Gerard ('Christ had a dove on his shoulder / –My
brother Gerard / Had 2 Doves / and 2 Lambs / Pulling his Milky
Chariot'). His blue-collar father has his place in the 103rd Chorus
('straw hat, newspaper in pocket / Liquor of the breath' yet also to
be recalled 'like a shadow') as, in the 237th Chorus, does his always
and determinative mother ('Ma mere [*sic*], tu es la terre').

Religious myth holds attention from start to finish. Buddhahood, as it is called in the 182nd Chorus ('The Essence of Existence / is Buddhahood'), gives one focus. The 65th Chorus even provides a vernacular route-map:

> To understand what I'm sayin
> You gotta read the Sutras.
> The Sutras of the Ancients, India
> Long ago . . .

Catholic mysticism comes into play, often inter-plied with Buddhism. In this respect, Buddha's mother Damema elides with the Virgin Mary, not to say his mother Gabrielle. Mexico, or 'Azteca' with its figurative 'Aztec radio' (Chorus 116th), yields indigenous mythologies of Quetzalcoatl, serpent gods, floods and blood. The span is one of a generic mythical family with a shared transcendent dynasty despite all the evident fissures. On this basis, Michael McClure perceptively terms *Mexico City Blues* a 'religious visionary poetic statement', a register of humanity's fault-lines but also of its reach for redemption.[22]

Inevitably, however, jazz both in motif and as reflexively embodied in the poem's fashioning, holds centre-place. Mexico itself, its *latinidad*, becomes 'Mexico City bop' (43rd Chorus). The presiding avatar lies in Charlie Parker, Kansas's bebop sax maestro who in the 239th Chorus is said to have 'looked like Buddha' and whose playing is that of 'the Perfect Musician' with its ethos of 'All is Well'. In calling him a 'Great musician and a great / creator of forms', Kerouac tacitly refracts his own ambition in *Mexico City Blues*, that of the poet who in the closing 242nd Chorus positions himself as about nothing if not keeping vigil on the world ('I am the Guard').

The poems that were first gathered in *San Francisco Blues*, composed in 1954 but published posthumously, give forward pointers not only to *Mexico City Blues* but to the wider body of his verse. The Introduction that speaks of composing each as a 'jazz blues chorus' underwritten by 'the musician's spontaneous phrasing & harmonizing with the best of time' could not be more apt. That holds for the extended *flâneur*-style title-sequence 'San Francisco Blues' or poems like 'Daydreams for Ginsberg' ('all world / roaring–vibrating—I put it down') and 'Rimbaud' ('Rimbaud, hit me over the / head with a rock'). Haiku reflects his other direction. His admiration for Bashō and other classic practitioners led to a proliferation on his own part as born out in his *Book of Haikus* (2003). He showed anything but hesitation in incorporating a number into texts like *Desolation Angels*, typically:

> While meditating.
> I am Buddha –
> Who else? (75)

Road, jazz, Zen and always spontaneity, act as Kerouac's loadstones, the figurings within but also far beyond *On the Road*.

Notes

1. Allen Ginsberg, 'Dream Record: June 8, 1955', *Reality Sandwiches, 1953–60*, San Francisco: City Lights Books, 1963, 48.
2. Gregory Corso, 'Elegaic Feelings American', *Elegaic Feelings American*, New York: New Directions, 1970. John (for Jack) Kerouac is in the original.
3. John Clellon Holmes, 'The Philosophy of the Beat Generation'. Reprinted in Ann Charters (ed.), *Beat Down to Your Soul: What Was the Beat Generation?*, New York: Penguin, 2001, 228–38.
4. *What Happened to Jack Kerouac?*, dir. Richard Lerner and Lewis MacAdams, 1986.
5. Lawrence Ferlinghetti 'The Canticle of Jack Kerouac', *These are My Rivers: New and Selected Poems*, New York: New Directions, 1993.
6. Jonah Raskin, Interview with Michael McClure, *SFGate*, 15 November 2013. This point is again reinforced by David Amran in his obituary for Kerouac written in October 1969 and published in *Evergreen Review*, 1970: 'Jack was a private person, extremely shy. When he drank, he became much more expansive, and this was the only part of his personality that became publicized.'
7. David Amran, Obituary, *Evergreen Review*, 14:74, January 1970.
8. Patti Smith, *Just Kids*, New York: HarperCollins, 2010. Hotel Chelsea was also where Kerouac wrote *On the Road*. *One Fast Move or I'm Gone: Kerouac's Big Sur*, dir. Curt Worden, 2008. The title is shared with the blues/rock documentary by Ben Gibbard and Jay Farrar.
9. Joyce Johnson, *The Voice is All: The Lonely Victory of Jack Kerouac*, New York: Viking, 2012, xx.
10. Gilbert Millstein, 'Books of the Times', *The New York Times*, 5 September 1957.
11. For the French Canadian lineage and influence, see Victor-Lévy Beaulieu's pioneer study, *Jack Kerouac: essai-poulet*, Éditions du Jour, 1972, trans. *Jack Kerouac: A Chicken Essay*, Toronto: Coach House, 1975, and Maurice Poteet (ed.), *Textes de l'exode: recueil de textes*

sur l'émigration des Québécois aux État-Unis (XIXe et XXe siècles,
Montreal: Guérin Littérature, 1987. These need to be read against
Hassan Melehy's recent and definitive *Kerouac: Language, Poetics,
and Territory*, London: Bloomsbury, 2016.

12. *Desolation Angel*, New York: Penguin, 1966, 2012, 293.
13. The *Journal of Beat Studies*, 5 (2017), issued in honour of Ann Charters,
     reprints the long-out-of-print bibliography and Charters's own remem-
     brance of working with Kerouac. See also A. Robert Lee, 'Correspond-
     ences: Melville, Olson, Charters', 45–51.
14. Cited in David Barnett, 'Visions of Jack Kerouac', *The Guardian*, 24
     July 2016.
15. These notebooks, together with Kerouac letters and artworks, were
     acquired in 2001 by the New York Public Library for their Henry W.
     and Albert A. Berg Collection.
16. The 'Joan Anderson letter', unfound until 2010 in Oakland, is Kerouac's
     own term – based on the name of a one-time girlfriend of Neal Cassady.
17. In *Desolation Angels*, in which Sal has morphed into Jack Duluoz
     and Dean into Cody, the Dr Johnson–Boswell trope is made explicit:
     'Cody . . . as in Dr. Johnson whom I also Boswelled in another life-
     time', *Desolation Angels*, 163.
18. For a helpful annotation of the Buddhist and connected allusion in the
     novel, see Gregory Stevenson, 'Explanatory Notes to Jack Kerouac's
     The Dharma Bums', *Pilgrims to Elsewhere: Reflections on Writings
     by Jack Kerouac, Allen Ginsberg, Gregory Corso, Bob Kaufman, and
     Others*, Roskilde: EyeCorner Press, 2013, 65–80.
19. Wilhelm Reich's *The Function of the Orgasm*, originally published in
     Vienna in 1927, had become required counterculture reading by the
     1950s, a riposte to Freud and an influence on Burroughs (with his
     orgone box) as much as Kerouac.
20. Warren French, *Jack Kerouac*, New York: Twayne, 1986, 46.
21. Fortunately, we now have a version of the relationship by Alene Lee
     (1931–91), on whom Mardou Fox is based (Irene May in *Big Sur*).
     Her daughter Christina Diamente, on the *Beatdom* website, looks back
     to the relationships with Carr and Ginsberg as well as Kerouac and
     explains how Alene, a first-class mind and recognised as such within
     Greenwich Village and New York circles, albeit much overlooked even
     in the accounts of Beat women, denied having held many of the views
     attributed to her by Kerouac. Their relationship, moreover, took place
     in New York, not San Francisco. No doubt to help disguise the actual
     affair, Kerouac shifted locales.
22. Michael McClure, *Scratching the Beat Surface: Essays on New Vision
     from Blake to Kerouac*, San Francisco: North Point Press, 1982, 75.

CHAPTER 4

Front Row: Insider Beats

None of us wanted to go back to the gray, militaristic silence, to the intellectual void – to the land without poetry – to the spiritual drabness. We wanted to make it new and we wanted to invent it and the process of it as we went into it. We wanted voice and we wanted vision.

> Michael McClure, *Scratching the Beat Surface: Essays on New Vision from Blake to Kerouac* (1982)[1]

Dissent is not un-American.

> City Lights Bookstore Celebration Banner (2001)[2]

Make It New

Michael McClure's remembrance of the 6 Gallery reading in 1955, and his determination shared with his platform co-readers upon a *new* iteration of 'making new', captures much of Beat's early literary spirit. Here, in San Francisco but with New York in the mix, were to be departures and arrivals, an adieu to 1950s 'drabness', the call to emergent inventions of 'voice' and 'vision'. McClure himself would play his own part, as, beyond Kerouac and Ginsberg, would others who belong in Beat's front row. Each of these bequeaths their own Beat dissent, a forum of markedly individual, even idiosyncratic contributing signatures.

The City Lights banner, in keeping with Ferlinghetti's North Beach poet-bookseller radicalism, underlines the right of Beat as indeed all related other counterculture to hold out for free speech. As a slogan 'un-American' summons McCarthyism, blacklists, surveillance and the compendious private files of the Director of the FBI J. Edgar Hoover, tactics and resources often malignly unconstitutional whereby speaking truth to power is curtailed and even demonised.

Beat would have its several close encounters in this respect, not least
City Lights Bookstore itself for harbouring books (largely meaning
pornography) supposedly insulting or at least upsetting to the pub-
lic round. The banner astutely memorialises American dissent as
having given grounds for persecution throughout American history
from 1600s New England witch-trials to HUAC investigations of
the early 1950s.

John Clellon Holmes: Jazz in the Night

John Clellon Holmes long has been a necessary person of interest in
the Beat consortium. In *Go* (1952), especially, a map-chronicle of
Beat formation, he had written the classic *roman à clé*. 'My vision
of the time' he calls it in the foreword to a 1976 reissue.[3] It stands
alongside his greatly informed essays on Beat times and author-
ship. Born of comfortable New England WASP vintage, an aspirant
writer from the start, Holmes's own jazz-savvy life took him close
but not too close to the Kerouac, Ginsberg, Cassady and Huncke
cadre. He saw himself as much the engaged observer, typically in his
keenly eyed portrait of Times Square as city milieu:

> It was a world of dingy backstairs 'pads,' Times Square cafete-
> rias, be-bop joints, night-long wanderings, meetings on street
> corners, hitchhiking, a myriad of 'hip' bars all over the city, and
> the streets themselves. It was inhabited by people 'hungup' with
> drugs, and other habits, searching out a new degree of craziness;
> and connected by the invisible threads of need, petty crimes of
> long ago, or a strange recognition of affinity. They kept going all
> the time, living by night, rushing round to 'make contact,' sud-
> denly disappearing into jail or on the road only to turn up again
> and search one another out. They had a view of life that was
> underground, mysterious, and they seemed unaware of anything
> outside the reality of deals, a pad to stay in, 'digging the frantic
> jazz,' and keeping everything going. (36)

Within this backdrop he positions the 'ceaseless movement' (10) of his
Beat cast, prime among them Pasternak (Kerouac), Stofsky (Ginsberg)
Kennedy (Cassady), Ancke (Huncke) and Dennison (Burroughs).
Talk, drink, partying, affairs, breakups, the will-to-art, and women's
lover-muse presence like that of Kathryn, Christine, May and Estelle,

all play into the choreography of the 1940s–1950s as countercultural theatre. The presiding note is alienation, an America of Spenglerian dark. Yet at the close of the novel, and as they gaze precisely at twilight upon Manhattan from the Hoboken shoreline, Paul speaks to Estelle of 'labyrinths of the underground' (259). He sees possible redemption in a new season of energy, beyond conformity and by implication Beat.[4] The novel, much as it offers an ample register in its own right, also gives a bridge into Holmes's *The Horn* (1958) as Beat-jazz tour de force.

No doubt on grounds of its more explicit Beat configuration, *Go* has tended to eclipse *The Horn*. That does a disservice. For Holmes's insider purchase on jazz musicianship leaves no doubt of his grasp of African American creativity, the symphonic blues and bop in the face of colour-line history and empty mainstream consumer glut. In the on–off playing of the main figure, Horn, pseudonym for the legendary Edgar Pool, he creates a Lester Young/Charlie Parker fusion, prodigious talent yet fractured by drugs, bars, underpaying gigs and travel, and, not least, the often fake mythologisation of beatnik followers:

> In Edgar's furious, scornful bleat sounded the moronic horn of every merciless Cadillac shrieking down the highway with a wet-mouthed, giggling boy at the wheel, turning the American prairie into a graveyard of rusting chrome junk; the idiot snarl that filled the jails and madhouses and legislatures: some final dead-wall impact. (19)

This is jazz as figurative counter-relief, an anti-America heard and played in musical acoustics.

Edgar, sick, losing ground, hustles drunkenly for the dollars he hopes will return him to his birthplace in Kansas City. But it is a path into decline and death as witnessed by the jazz fraternity in which he has been a leader – horn-men like Walden Blue, Wing Redburn, Metro Myland and Kelcey Crane, the keyboarders Cleo and Junius Priest, the officious arranger Curny Finny, and the blues mama and one-time Edgar mistress, Geordie Dickson. Holmes alternates their witness in chapters headed Chorus and Riff, with epigraphs drawn from Herman Melville and Charlie Parker ('If you don't live it, it won't come out of your horn', 180).

The prose, at times, can risk becoming over-fervid, a veer into exaltation. But it can also hit the right note. 'Jazz was a kind of

growing Old Testament of the Negro race' (10) it is said at one
point. 'Bird dead, Horn dead . . . Once they blew the truth' (242) it
says at another. As Holmes recognises, along with Kerouac in texts
like *Mexico Blues*, jazz gave Beat its own in-house music, its access
to Afro-America's language of sound.

William Burroughs: A banquet you will never forget

Burroughs holds a paradoxical place in Beat history, in one way
joined at the hip yet in another insistently, and darkly, unjoined. In
interview he addresses the relationship with considerable precision:

> I don't associate myself with (the Beat Movement) at all, and
> never have, either with their objectives or their literary style.
> I have some close personal friends among the Beat movement:
> Jack Kerouac and Allen Ginsberg and Gregory Corso are all
> close personal friends of many years standing, but were not
> doing all the same thing, either in writing or outlook. You really
> couldn't find four writers more different, more distinctive. It's
> simply a matter of juxtaposition rather than any actual associa-
> tion of literary style or overall objectives.[5]

Opinion, over time, has increasingly elevated Burroughs beyond
Ginsberg and Kerouac for his insights into modernity as simula-
crum or constructed grid and line matrix. To that end, his uses
of disordering cut-up or fragmentation have won their following
as a means to contest hegemony actually as much on as off the
page.[6] The upshot, on both counts, has been his accreditation as
postmodern, his refusal of all institutional or mediatic ownership
of how those with power exploitatively broker reality. That allies
with his hostility to all Grand Narrative and either-or thought sys-
tems. His resolve was always to disrupt, even break, the language
of normative consensus and to turn it challengingly inside out and
back on itself.

Portraiture, given the various early outcries and alarums about
obscenity, for the most part has been celebratory, but on occasion still
cautious, un-adulating. Jack Kerouac's fond memoir of Burroughs as
Old Bull Lee in the New Orleans of *On the Road* sees him as mari-
juana farmer but also 'a teacher' spending 'long hours with Shake-
speare' and 'Mayan Codices on his lap' (129–30). He could well have

added Spengler, T. S. Eliot, Wittgenstein or even scientology's L. Ron Hubbard. For her part, one of the so-called 1980s bratpackers, Kathy Acker, argues for Burroughs as a figure of prophecy:

> In his novels, Burroughs saw the society around him so clearly, he announced the future. Writing what seemed radical when it appears today looks like journalism. In other words: today in the United States, we are living in the worlds of Burroughs's novels.[7]

Outside of immediate Beat ranks, Norman Mailer was quick to speak of genius. As defence witness in the 1965 Boston Supreme Court trial of *Naked Lunch* he designates Burroughs 'possibly . . . the most talented writer in America'. The British novelist Will Self, however, describing Burroughs as 'Janus-faced . . . like some terminally cadaverous butler', offers less willing approbation:

> Burroughs was the perfect incarnation of 20th century western angst precisely because he was an addict. Self-deluding, vain, narcissistic, self-obsessed, and yet curiously perceptive about the sickness of the world if not his own malaise, Burroughs both offered up and was compelled to provide his psyche as a form of Petri dish, within which were cultured the obsessive and compulsive viruses of modernity.[8]

Allowing for early novel-documentary like *Junky* (1953) and *Queer* (unpublished until 1985), it is *Naked Lunch*, with its anatomy of a monstrously controlled supply-and-user human order including and beyond actual drugs, that fully launches the Burroughs trajectory. The follow-through, his multi-novel mythography, overwhelmingly construes power as the ultimate addictive 'fix' in genres that transpose *roman noir*, science fiction and the Western. These are to be met in the cut-up trilogy of *The Soft Machine* (1961), *The Ticket That Exploded* (1962) and *Nova Express* (1964) and in their selective recombination in *Dead Fingers Talk* (1973). So vigilant, often coruscating, a vision extends forward into the more formulated sequence of *Cities of the Red Night* (1981), *The Place of the Dead Roads* (1983) and *The Western Lands* (1987), the interwoven narrative of cosmic origins, rituals of authoritarian and religio-sexual practice, and descent into atavism.

Still later published work in turn repatterns these interests. *Inter-zone* (1989), stories gathered from across his career, refracts Tangier as Maghreb labyrinth, drugs, boys, dealers and an early blueprint of *Naked Lunch*. *My Education: A Book of Dreams* (1995), cut-up in form, yields a log of sleep scenarios from cats to masochism, friend-ships to narcotics, an 'interior' Burroughs to contrast with the often punctilious, formally besuited self he so often presented in readings and interviews. *Last Words: The Final Journals* (2000) acts as an epilogue and as a poignant tribute to Ginsberg, Huncke, Leary and others, assortments and fragments and might-be plotlines, and his ruminations on outlawry and love.

Within so voluminous an output, *Naked Lunch* remains the linch-pin, Burroughs's own unique counterfactual mosaic or action paint-ing written as though in the voice of an addict undergoing withdrawal ('a nightmare interlude of cellular panic') and for which he supplies intermittent *Habit Notes*.[9] 'A banquet you will never forget', from the introduction penned by J. G. Ballard for a 1993 reissue of *Naked Lunch*, summons notable overlaps.[10] It shadows Allen Ginsberg's poem 'On Burroughs's Work' in *Reality Sandwiches* ('The method must be purest meat / and no symbolic dressing') and Burroughs's own debt to Kerouac for his title ('The title means exactly what the words say: NAKED lunch – a frozen moment when everyone sees what is on the end of every fork').[11] For Burroughs that means over-whelmingly systems of control, actual and subliminal, each under the custodial remit of the Nova Mob or The Board. These signify gov-ernment and medical bureaucracies, corporate business, CIA, FBI or KGB surveillance agencies, and the Pentagon, along with media and advertising, penal systems and the double-standard 'war on drugs'. To be included is the imprisoning sameness of every suburban norm and all organised religion (Buddha 'a metabolic junkie', Mohammed 'invented by the Chamber of Commerce of Mecca').

Burroughs's novel thereby doubles as fever-chart but also riposte, unsparing, often brutal and brutally funny. His emetic passwords have taken on their own familiarity: for example, *the algebra of need, the sexuality of power, wouldn't you?, word virus, cancer at the door with a Singing Telegram*. Even 'the word' as linear semantic unit, and its regulatory syntax of subject-verb-object and binary I–you, can be challenged as pre-emptive, not least in the light of the pictographic Mayan, ancient Egyptian and Asian codices. Non-Aristotelian logic like that proposed by the semanticist Alfred Korzybski beckons. The goal, thereby, indeed becomes end-of-the-fork clarity, a way through and out of pre-emption and homogeneity.

'A word to the wise guy' reads his 'Deposition: Testimony Concerning a Sickness', often used to preface the main text of *Naked Lunch* (14).[12] 'I can feel the heat closing in, feel them out there making their moves' (17) opens the text proper, a near ectoplasmic response to the encirclements of authority with its enforcers, agents and hidden persuaders.[13] The faux-intimate savvy, terse, ironic, takes the novel beyond Chandler or Hammett into territory more that of the pre-Renaissance dystopia of Hieronymus Bosch or of the Augustan Age satire of Jonathan Swift's *Gulliver's Travels*. Louis-Fedinand Céline, whom Burroughs visited with Ginsberg in Paris in the 1950s, would also be of the company in the assault on any agreed liberal consensus. A wholly different kind of private-eye novel is on offer, one of riffs, fade-outs, serio-comic black pantomime, or, in another phrase favoured by Burroughs, 'routines' ('I am a recording instrument,' he insists, 'I do not presume to impose "story," "plot," "continuity",' 194).

In exploring as he perceives it the 'broken image of Man' (136), and the world's infected and manipulative power systems, *Naked Lunch* offers Burroughs's rogue visitation to the world of the Control Room and its writ (61). This is an in-a-mirror-darkly world, one of 'sex and pain' (73), conditioned need and its control, the unyielding graphics of host, supplier and virus, hypodermic, vein, ejaculation, jism, blood, faece, pain-pleasure, and manipulated anxiety and de-anxietisation. Above and throughout there rules 'the black wind sock of death . . . smelling for the crime of separate life' (176). But the effect is far from solemnity, mere grimness.

A wondrous carnivalesque cast presides. Dr Benway under his sobriquet of The Lobotomy Kid runs Freeland's Reconditioning Center. His companions in spirit include The Vigilante, Bradley the Buyer, Placenta Juan the Afterbirth Tycoon, The Paragoric Kid, A.J., Dr 'Fingers' Schaefer, and Hauser and O'Brien as cops who the narrator acknowledges may be figments of his febrile imagination. Burroughs himself makes his entrance under the surrogate mask of Agent Lee. The Liquifactionists and Mugwumps, as against the Factualists (in whose number Burroughs counts himself), add their own George Grosz or Francis Bacon grotesquerie, alien but exploiter-exploitee humanoid life forms.

The novel was never for the feeble-hearted, especially the 'Gentle Reader' (44) mock-courteously appealed to in the novel's 'Atrophied

Preface'. Scene upon scene ('You can cut into Naked Lunch at any intersection point', 176) certifies Burroughs's deconstructive and rarely other than scabrous wit ('As one judge said to the other: "Be just and if you can't be just, be arbitrary"', 9). The repertoire has become infamous, whether 'talking assholes' as purveyors of political or bureaucrat-speak, fashionista society women impregnated by water pistols, medical student *espontáneos* running wild with scalpels in Benway's operating room, clinic, or the Mark–Johnny–Mary hanging scene as blue-movie indictment of capital punishment. Homosexuals are chemically reoriented to 'heterosex' and heterosexuals the reverse. A.J's restaurant serves grotesque platters and aphrodisiacs in emulation of haute cuisine. Southern sheriffs, whether in 'Coon County, Arkansas' (46) or Texas, relish their good old boy race hangings. Jelly and metamorphosing flesh, cockroach and other insect-forms, genitalia and body vents, give the narrative at-speed hallucinatory currency.

Each vignette, within the phantasmagorical landscapes of Mexico-like Annexia ('No one ever looked at anyone else because of the strict law against importuning', 32), 'Scandinavian' Freeland ('clean and dull by God', 36) or 'Moroccan' Interzone ('The City is visited by epidemics of violence', 93), serves Burroughs as counter-writ. His cinema of disgust takes full aim at the pornographies large and small of control and the effect upon those being controlled. Mastery of drug and street vernacular, vaudeville dry eddies of wit, and the insistent force of his vision or rather anti-vision, make the *Naked Lunch* an instrument-board for, as he terms it figuratively, 'what I can pick up without FM on my 1920 crystal set' (180). Beat, if *Naked Lunch* qualifies as such, has known no greater combative mythology.

Gregory Corso: Yaks, Bombs and Marriage

Corso long has been assigned supporting-player status: Beat's fourth Beatle. Ginsberg was not alone in recognising that so lowered an estimate did serious disservice. In his introduction to *Gasoline* he writes advocatingly, 'Open this book as you would a box of crazy toys ... Such weird haiku-like juxtapositions aren't in the American book.'[14] Ted Morgan, author of *Literary Outlaw: The Life and Times of William Burroughs* (2012), takes a leaf out of Alexandre Dumas: 'If Ginsberg, Kerouac and Burroughs were the Three Musketeers of the movement, Corso was their D'Artagnon.'[15] From either vantage-point Corso gives reason to occupy his own ground. His poetry carries shelves of often extravagantly inventive image, devotion to Shelley, penchant for the visual arts (Uccello, Botticelli, Vermeer and Rembrandt notably), a keen sense of historic place, long commitment to Thomist Catholicism, and, always, genuine reaches of wit. It can hardly surprise that Ginsberg's Introduction, written in evident affection and with flourish, goes on to call him 'a scientific master of mad mouthfuls of poetry'.[16]

Given that the fuller repertoire is to be met in *Mindfield: New and Selected Poems* (1989), the best-known collection remains *Gasoline* (1958), thirty-plus pieces in all and not out of print since its first issue as No. 8 in the City Lights Pocket Poets Series. Corso's other collections, starting from *The Vestal Lady on Brattle and Other Poems* (1955) and extending through *Happy Birthday of Death* (1960), *Long Live Man* (1962), *Elegaic Feelings American* (1970) and *Herald of the Autochtonic Spirit* (1981), indubitably yield their returns. *Gasoline*, however, and as Ginsberg highlights it, carries Corso's especial flavour, his talent for situating the world within loops of unique Beat–Dada observation.

The two epigraphs that introduce *Gasoline* hold both for the poems within and for the wider arc of his other poetry collections. The one epigraph gives acknowledgement to prison library reading, Dostoevsky to Stendhal, Chatterton to Shelley ('books of illumination'), which he says saved him during cell-time served in New York's Clinton Prison after parental abandonment and street-rough Manhattan youth fostering and delinquency. The other echoes Gary Snyder's celebrated short poem 'How Poetry Comes to Me' ('It comes blundering over the / Boulders at night'). For Corso the poetic process resembles mysterious collage, a species of alchemy: 'it comes, I tell you, immense with gasoline rags and bits of wire and old bent nails, a dark arriviste, from a dark river within.'[17] A sheaf of poems from across his range does duty.

'The Whole Mess . . . Almost', first published in *Herald of the Autochthonic Spirit* offers a key Corso paradigm, his symptomatic penchant for play, seeming extemporisation.[18] The operative metaphor is one of cleaning out his apartment ('I ran up six flights of stairs / to my small furnished room / opened the window / and began throwing out / those things most important in life'). 'Out', repeated throughout, twice capitalised as 'OUT', and several times with exclamation mark attached, acts as initial hinge. 'Those things',

however 'important', are serially given mock-notice. The impact as
the piece unfolds is that of a near pattern-poem yet cannily varied
by each droll interjection or commentary.

   'Truth' is first to go, 'squealing like a fink'. 'God' follows, 'glow-
ering & whimpering in amazement'. 'Love' is dispatched 'on her fat
ass' while 'cooing bribes'. 'Faith Hope Charity', however plaintiff
and 'all clinging together', is next. 'Beauty' come under accusation
of being murderous ('Beauty kills') even as the speaker runs down-
stairs and catches her fall. 'Money', if diligently searched for, is
noticeable only by its absence. Death, 'hiding beneath the kitchen
sink', receives the heave ('Kitchen sink and all'). The final 'all that
was left' is 'Humor' which elicits the elliptical turn-about of 'Out
the window with the window'. Engaging to a fault the poem gives
funny-sardonic resistance to the idea that Big Themes always make
Big Poetry. Corso indeed wants a clear-out, a winnowing, of heavy-
duty abstraction. The ludic impulse as voiced in his poem brings
just the right subversion to bear, deftly antic yet serious.

   This emphasis holds throughout the writings, the poet's hall-
mark. In *Gasoline* 'The Mad Yak' offers an absurdist yet unmis-
takably compassionate vision of death ('I am watching them churn
the last milk they'll ever get from me, / They are waiting for me to
die').[19] The milk signifies a she-yak, one from whose bones buttons
will be made and whose 'sisters and brothers' have previously gone
to their deaths. The executioners are not mad Nazis but a single
likely Mongolian monk accompanied by his muffler-wrapped stu-
dent, who load up the yak-speaker's tired yak-uncle. His bones, too,
are up for exploitation. The closing couplet ('And that beautiful
tail! / How many shoelaces will they make of that?') might conjure
Hamlet's Yorick or lines from Samuel Beckett. Yak milk, bones and
tail succinctly conjoin as fantasy, Corso's engaging but also disturb-
ing contemplation of mortality.

   'Bomb', written in Paris at the Beat Hotel, printed as a City
Lights Broadside in 1958, and included in the collection *The Happy
Birthday of Death*, stirred controversy from the outset.[20] Could
Corso actually be endorsing atomic warfare? From the bomb-
shaped opening layout through to the four or so pages that follow,
Corso positions himself as serious jester. He takes up the unex-
pected stance of situating the bomb within the larger trajectory of
human life and death. A challenging thesis is so built into the poem,
namely that, however gravid, the A-bomb serves as but one more

increment in the cycle of historic violence and warfare running from the stone age (and behind it the Big Bang) through to Hiroshima and Nagasaki and to include disease ('it is no crueler than cancer'), capital punishment ('a man dying in the electric chair'), dead births, and all other military 'bomb death'.

Corso calls the Bomb 'the final Pied Piper' and recognises that 'all man hates you'. But he also suggests that other modes of death have been quite as momentous. The poem thereby assaults the standard piety about thermonuclear destruction, neither advocating not simply condemning its place in humanity's generic fear of death's darkness. In reality the Bomb indeed may act as a 'budger of history' and 'a brake on time'. But its blast is also to be imagined stirring a surreal aftermath – 'turtles exploding over Istanbul', a 'flying jaguar', 'penguins plunged against the sphinx'. The Bomb so almost beckons as apocalyptic love affair ('I sing the Bomb / Death's extravagance / Death's jubilee'). It invites being thought 'The spitball of Buddha', 'Planetarium Death'. Within the galactic sum of things there might even be life-after-Bomb, a kind of bomb cemetery where 'more bombs will arise'. The imagery could not be more provocative, the violent, and quite arguably inevitable, zigzag of life's entrances and exits. When Corso read the poem at Oxford in 1957, a shoe was thrown at him by anti-nuclear campaigners no doubt without an ear for the fuller irony being put before them.[21]

'Marriage', the other best-known poem of *The Happy Birthday of Death*, carries a full menu of tease, a shy at society's presiding institution.[22] The opening lines leave no doubt of the riffs ahead ('Should I get married? Should I be good? / Astound the girl next door . . . Don't take her to the movies but cemeteries / tell all about werewolf bathtubs and forked clarinets'). The speaker can imagine himself called to bourgeois right behaviour and couture ('hair finally combed, strangled by a tie'), a fright to prospective parents-in-law ('He wants our Mary Lou'), and bound for the cliché of a Niagara Falls honeymoon ('I'd sit there the Mad Honeymooner / devising ways to break marriages, a scourge of bigamy'). He parodies himself as model spouse ('God what a husband I'd make'), drooling paterfamilias ('For a rattle a bag of broken Bach records'), lover bemused by love ('I see love as odd as wearing shoes') and, finally, aged bachelor ('all alone in a furnished room with pee stains on my underwear'). Corso himself, belying this persona, in fact, had three marriages. The closing refrain ('Everybody else is married! All the universe married but me'), however, hints of a frame of reference wider than domesticity. The poem, figuratively and with the usual Corso loops of metaphor, shies at all forms of fixity, the closing down of life-appetite, spirit, openness.

Wit, assuredly, offers but one route into Corso's range. A short manifesto poem like 'I Am 25' in *Gasoline* makes for tongue-stuck-out bravura with its proclaimed 'love, a madness for Shelley, Chatterton and Rimbaud' and yet resolve to move on from them and 'steal their poems'.[23] A jazz tribute like 'For Miles' with its 'Your sound is faultless / pure & round / holy / almost profound' shows his agility in having the verse re-enact the measure of a late-night riff between Miles Davis and Charlie Parker ('some wondrous / yet unimaginable score').[24] 'Weird Happenings in Haarlem' ('Four windmills, acquaintanceships, / were spied one morning eating tulips', 19) and 'Paris' ('Childcity, Aprilcity . . . Poets, worms in hair, beautiful Baudelaire, / Artaud, Rimbaud, Apollinaire', 48), typically envision the inner within the outer site. The gnaw of metropolitan loneliness, the poet dunking his croissant as he fantasises Parisian love with Cosette, heroine of *Les Misérables*, holds for a poem like 'The Sacré-Cœur Café' in *The Happy Birthday of Death*.[25] This willingness to find unexpected metaphor for personal feeling or place presses into each subsequent collection.

His Kerouac obituary in the extensive title-poem of *Elegaic Feelings American* ('Alas, Jack, it seems I cannot requiem thee without / requieming America'), with its affection for his 'dear friend, compassionate friend', summons comparison with Whitman's eulogy to the slain Abraham Lincoln in 'When Lilacs Last in the Dooryard Bloom'd'.[26] An accompanying work of serious fellow compassion in *Elegaic Feelings American* lies in 'Spontaneous Requiem for the American Indian'. Throughout Corso gives compendious historical and geographic sweep to the 'Indianic earth', Muskegee to Iroquois, Mohawk to Choctaw, and the settler dislocations visited on the tribes.[27] To his credit he avoids Vanishing American mawkishness but rather celebrates energy, survival against odds, closing with the Beat counter-image of a very much alive motorcyclist Blackfoot barrelling down the highway. The 'spontaneity' of the poem reminds not only of Beat poetics, but the enduring spoken and chant legacies of the Native American tribal tradition.

Few Corso poems better summarize his Beat calling card than 'Columbia U Poesy Reading – 1975' in *Herald of the Autochthonic*

Spirit in which, with typical bravura, he identifies himself as belonging to the 'Revolutionaries of the Spirit':[28]

> 16 years ago we were put down
> for being filthy beatnik sex commie dope fiends
> Now—16 years later Allen's the respect of his elders
> the love of his peers
> and the adulation of millions of youth . . .
> Peter has himself a girl so that he and Allen
> Hermes willing might have a baby . . .
> Bill's ever Bill
> even though he stopped drugging and smoking cigarettes
> Me. I'm still considered an unwashed beatnik sex commie
>   dope fiend . . .
>
>   (1–2)

Dates, names, memory of the cultural antagonism that Beat encountered, are perfectly historic but as so often given in terms of calculated travesty. Beat at times could risk solemnity, mission statements close to tripping over themselves. The unique tilt of Corso's poetry keeps matters on the right side of pretension.

Lawrence Ferlinghetti: Poems, Mirrors, Painting

Debate has also long joined as to how Ferlinghetti best comports with the Beats. Custom holds him to be at least co-participant, or as he himself frequently insisted, publisher of Beats if not himself a paid-up member of the movement. That, in turn, needs to be situated within his standing as creative all-rounder. His poetry has been one of wide-angle pictorialism, wit and radical political temper (seeing Nagasaki after the bomb left an indelible impression). He has the impressionist novel *Her* (1960) to his name, and lifelong interests as painter and travel writer. He also brings to the table his navy veteran years as a submarine commander during the Normandy landings, his French and translator skills honed through early family years in France and in writing a Sorbonne dissertation on the city and modern poetry, and though Yonkers-born, the career that among other achievements led to his appointment as San Francisco poet laureate (1998–2000). His role as City Lights publisher is incontrovertible, its own unfinished legend.

Were route-way into his poetry called for then it can readily be found in 'Populist Manifesto' which rounds out the collection *Who Are We Now?* (1976).[29] The poem's plea, energetically playful and allusive throughout, is for 'open' form, free of 'workshop poets', 'poets writing poetry / about poetry', and the 'Poetry Police'. His tease takes aim at 'All you house-broken Ezra Pounds' and 'All you pre-stressed Concrete Poets', not to mention 'cunnilingual poets' and, with a glance to Robert Frost, 'A-train swingers who never swing on birches' (61–4). To go along with his joshing of 'freaked-out cut-up poets', an explicit, even irreverent, touch of Beat affinity surfaces in the lines: 'We have seen the best minds of our generation / destroyed by boredom at poetry readings' (63). Poetry, again in Beat vein, he avers, 'falls from the skies / into our streets still open'. The beckoning goes out to the poetry-makers he remembers Whitman designating 'wild children'. At once manifesto and versatile skit, the 'Populist Manifesto' displays not only Ferlinghetti's characteristic readability but his own version, shall we say, of Beat measure.

The hallmarks were recognisable from the start. The *flâneur* pose has about it both breeziness and shrewdness. The insistence on openness of form shapes his many works of image-and-word, his taste for ekphrasis. Image-and-word texts like *When I Look at Pictures* (1990) and *How to Paint Sunlight: Lyric Poems & Others, 1997–2000* (2001) emphasise the interest in visuality, not only of the ekphrastic compositions but his reflexive drawings, canvases and jazz-verse recordings.[30] Other career-marking collections like *Endless Life: Selected Poems* (1983), *These Are My Rivers: New & Selected Poems, 1955–1993* (1993) and *San Francisco Poems* (2000) confirm a poet fluently also self-reflective in his offerings of eye and observation. The political disposition, always undogmatic, can be sighted early in his acclaimed eight-page Golden Mountain Press broadsheet 'Tentative Description of a Dinner Given to Promote the Impeachment of President Eisenhower' (1958). The taunts look sportive, playful. But the collocations take on disturbing point, Ike-as-golfer and nuclear cliff-edge, the 'brilliant military mind' and the 'irradiated vegetables'.[31]

Pictures of the Gone World (1955) and *A Coney Island of the Mind* (1958), his perhaps most 'Beat' collections and which launched his career, leave no doubt of Ferlinghetti's composite motifs of seeing, mirror and painting. The centrifugal fifth poem of *Pictures*, untitled and unpaginated like the rest of the collection and set out in suitably accessible line divisions, offers guidance. The emphasis upon picturing, the dynamic human pictureliness of the world, is patent, a calling-card that will run throughout his work. Adapting Stendhal he puts in uppercase the line: 'A POEM IS A MIRROR WALKING DOWN A STRANGE STREET.' Ostensibly, this is a sign carried by a stroller who 'claimed to be / a painter'. In truth it does duty for Ferlinghetti as poet, equally 'taking it all "in" / and reflecting / Everything in his great big / Hungry Eye'. The poem broadens to then 'take in' as though in one crowded rush the panorama of 'one hundredandsixtythreepeople all talking and / waving and laughing and eating and drinking . . . etc'. Dense ordinariness fills the vista. Sight becomes word. There can be little doubt of a poetics that chimes considerably with that of Ginsberg, Kerouac and Corso. Whether Ferlinghetti is fully, or only partly, to be enlisted in Beat's author ranks, his name continues to win associate status. The very word 'gone' in the title of *Pictures of the Gone World* appropriately bears its Beat trace, the poet en-captured by the sight and sound within life's horizons.

Accompanying poems in the volume give support. Number 1 sees in a 'wetly amorous' woman hanging rooftop sheets the linkage to sky and 'kingdom come'. Number 4, with its vistas of France, speaks of 'an algebra of lyricism / which I am still deciphering'. Number 18 uses a metaphor of striptease, artist and model to catch at art's processes of metamorphosis. 'Dada would have liked a day like this / with its various very realistic unrealities' begins Number 23, reality and unreality joined in 'not so accidental analogies'. Number 28 can serve as encapsulation for the overall sequence that invokes the visual languages of painters and sculptors like Praxiteles, Brancusi, Sorolla and Picasso, along with writers from René Char to Jean Cocteau and W. B. Yeats and which follows the open spacing of verse like Jacques Prévert's *Paroles*, a work Ferlinghetti himself translated:

> And each poem a picture
>   at an exhibition
>   upon a blank wall
>   made of concrete chaos

A Coney Island of the Mind yields poems that with each successive reprint have become Ferlinghetti touchstones. In Number 1 ('In Goya's greatest scenes . . .') he installs the fatalistic Spanish master as tutelary spirit of an America 'spaced with bland billboards / illustrating imbecile illusions of happiness' (9). Number 3 continues the prospect ('The poet's eye obscenely seeing / sees the surface of the round world . . .') with America's 'immigrant dream . . . mislaid among the sunbathers' (13). For Number 5 Ferlinghetti waggishly uses mock Beat-beatnik argot to retell the crucifixion of Jesus ('Him just hang there/on his Tree / looked real Petered out', 16).

Few poems more bespeak Ferlinghetti in Beat-similar mode than Number 15 in which he gives figuration to makers of poetry:

> the poet like an acrobat
> > climbs on rime
> > > to a high wire of his own making
> and balancing on eyebeams
> > > above a sea of faces
> > paces his way
> > > to the other side of day. . . (30)

These acrobatic poetic feats, along with 'other high theatrics', take their course 'all without mistaking / any thing / for what it may not be' (30). North Beach literary veteran of an age and spirit with Kenneth Rexroth or publisher-writer with Ginsberg and Kerouac, Ferlinghetti evidently has had his own furrow to plough. For him, as he says, the poet is best thought a 'charleychaplin man' (30), an allusion that goes with the very naming of City Lights. Beat, however, has also been part of his aura, an affinity, a share in the circle, that persists.

Michael McClure: Fire is not made to die

The notion of 'a new era' arising out of the 1960s was immediately seized upon by Michael McClure. Long a Beat luminary as poet, playwright, visual artist, essayist, collaborator with Ray Manzarek and the Doors, and one of the poets who read at the 6 Gallery in 1955 when Ginsberg delivered 'Howl', his output has been both considerable and bracing. His editing of *Arc II / Moby I* and *Journal for the Protection of All Beings* not only responded to environmental interests but provided an outlet to much Beat creative voice. In 'Letter to Georg Büchner', with which he opens *Meat Science Essays* (1963), he is early to discern a period change:

A new era is at hand and it must be joyfully struggled for in full awareness and enjoyment of life. The change is not only inside myself. In all men there is a new consciousness. A new combat for freedom and happiness and pleasure is beginning everywhere – I see signs of it in the continents and peoples of the earth.[32]

These touchstones assume a widespread urge but there can be little doubt they derive from the countercultural matrix in which Beat's commitment to release of the senses, a changed regime of feeling, plays a major part.

The controversies that arose in connection with McClure's *The Beard* (1965), his theatre piece in which Jean Harlow and Billy the Kid unpeel their mythic personae to reveal imperfect lives and engage in graphic sex, has long threatened to eclipse his poetry. Bans, police raids, jail-time for the play enter the story. But a compilation like *Huge Dreams: San Francisco and Beat Poems* (1999) serves to remind of the poet overall and of his Beat affiliations in particular. 'I was interested in the poem being alive in the air as well as on the page' he writes in 'After Thoughts' (169). His spacings and length-variations of line, and each deliberate capitalisation, he has said, are calculated to give tantric effect, one aimed not just for guided reader-listener collaboration but sympathy.[33]

A short poem like 'For Thelonious Monk', replete with references to Avalokiteshvara, the guardian Buddha and Kwannon, the Japanese mercy goddess, gives an instance. The speaker's goal, enacted as if a series of perceptual steps or jolts, is Buddhist-Beat-jazz transcendence and fear of its loss:

> ALL IS COOL, AND BOUNDLESS AS A ROLLING
>   LAMB OF
>   JAZZ, I SEE
> the shades slipt behind me, Avalokiteshvara!
>   I am blessed and protected. I hear the beauty
>   of the tossing notes. I am safe!
>   It does not matter. Love. Avalokiteshvara, Kwannon,
>   love you pale beauty;
>   see my twisted head and face grow thin again . . .
>   . . . happy,
>   for an instant.
>   OH! OH! OH! OH! Tired old fear. OH! OH! (43)

The endeavour to convey self-awakening, its jolts and stirs, is unmistakable.

In 'Ode to the Negative Universe' McClure writes 'THE HUMAN SPIRIT IS THE REAL/PHYSICAL ACTS IT MAKES' (85). He has long pursued the search to act upon this dictum. His sequence '13 Mad Sonnets' underscores exactly the idea of making the spirit act itself out in the body (he frequently uses the Buddhist notion of the body as meat). 'Mad Sonnet 13', expressly dedicated to Ginsberg, speaks of walking 'THE EMPTY VALLEY OF WALL STREET' (75) and of being 'inspired / by the moving beauty of their (own) physical figures' freed of 'the-vibrations-of-money' (75). 'The Answer' addresses planes of human suffering in which 'Money and Politics are a universe of discourse / entrapping physiques' (100). 'The Human Face' invokes 'real flesh, of rose and brown and pink' (101) as the outer form of a might-be best inward grace ('But the human face is a meat jewel / and I love the face / as much / as / hands! / We *are* perfect' (101).

McClure's verse does not always come over easily. It requires an ear and eye attentive to his jumps of metaphor, the tantric role of capitalisations, and on-page patterning as a way of entering the flows and contra-flows of consciousness. But, unremittingly, he writes verse that gives expression to his Whitman–Ginsberg resolve to meet and explore all turns of body and spirit. He so writes, uppercase again, in 'Liberation': 'I DEDICATE MYSELF TO BE SENT A MULTITUDE OF NEW WAYS' (162). The Beat vector is clearly indicated.

Neal Cassady: Chaplin's Tramp Walking into the Future

Partnering Cassady with Charlie Chaplin, or rather Chaplin's immemorial silent-screen tramp, was an idea that belongs to Lawrence Ferlinghetti in his brief Editor's Note to the decade-later reissue of *The First Third & Other Writings* (1972, 1982). Ferlinghetti goes on to speak of 'homespun, primitive prose', a text 'at once antic and antique, often awkward and doubling back upon itself'.[34] Carolyn Cassady's Afterword ('He knew he was neither trained nor equipped to think of writing in terms of literary merit', 140) likewise implies the underwhelming prospectus.[35] Doubtless *The First Third* will continue to stir reservation, lockstep autobiography, moribund styling. But if the work does not shake the literary rafters, that far from closes the case, not least its actual flourishes and, however passing, the alert touchstone mentions of Proust, Céline, Burroughs and Kerouac.

It would be disingenuous to think that interest in Cassady's writing does not connect to his historic Beat persona, none more so than Kerouac's Dean Moriarty in *On the Road* and Ginsberg's 'N.C., secret hero of these poems' in 'Howl'. Each incarnation has taken on mythic proportion, whether Denver street boy, car-thief and joyrider, brakeman and hopper of rails, relentless pria-pic adventurer, San Quentin jailee, or the LSD-fuelled driver of Ken Kesey's Merry Pranksters bus whose adventuring Tom Wolfe chronicles with New Journalist élan in *The Electric Kool-Aid Acid Test* (1968). The description of the bus's practice-run ahead of the trip from California to the New York World's Fair in 1964 has Cassady 'driving and barreling through the burning woods wrenching the steering wheel this way and that way to his innerwired beat'.[36] Stephen Y. Kay's movie *The Last Time I Committed Suicide* (1997), based on Cassady's relationship with Natalie Jackson which ended in her death in November 1955 in the wake of the 6 Gallery read-ing, gives emphasis to his ambition of becoming a writer. Yet Kesey himself maybe comes closest in the observation 'I saw that Cassady did everything a novel does, except he did it better because he was living it and not writing about it.'[37]

Both the main text of *The First Third*, and the 'fragments' that accompany it, to include several spontaneously run-on letters to Kerouac and Kesey, even so invite careful degrees of attention. The plain-style Cassady genealogy that serves as prologue, from the nineteenth century to the Depression and on through generational Irish–German wedlock and the family's Iowa farmsteading and shifts of geography within the West, supplies a hinterland. But the family splits and bruises, the passed-down bullying, the silences, might almost signify dynastic pathology. These antecedents, at least implicitly, carry into the denser narrative of Cassady's Oliver Twist-like childhood in 1930s tenement Denver. Here, if anywhere, lies the making of Cassady as urban cowboy, the embryonic figure of the Beat hero-renegade.

In Neal Cassady Sr., however, the 'drink susceptible' father (37) of stop-start barber work who breaks with Cassady's well-meaning mother and her no fewer than half-dozen other children, the account has its presiding spirit. Yet if 'wino' (46) and 'Saturday Night drunk' (70), Pap Finn slum dropout and hustler, he can also win over his offspring: 'I really loved the old boy' (49). The world recalled of downtown Larimer Street, single room occupancy in cheapskate hotels like the Metropolitan and Snowden, thereby evolves into the double focus: the fond but unfatherly miscreant father, the life-apprentice son. The one belongs to the 'shattered souls' (53) of alcoholic cronyism, the other, despite endless makings-do and infant urchinry, to the creative fellowship of those 'consciously amazed at life' (65).

Cassady as both incipient and actual writer takes on a number of forms. His eye for Denver city life is sharp throughout, whether the school-route starting from 'the busy 16th and Market Streets intersection' (54), his gunnysack trash rummaging, the street life of 'Larimer's brigade of bums' (59), the food bank at the Citizen's Mission, the Zaza movie theatre, the South Platte freight yards, or 24th Street's 'Negro shanty' (119). The hoboing and freight-hopping to California and back with his father ('our zig-zag of the west', 123) yields a full helping of story-drama. His portrait of Shorty, begrimed street veteran cut off at the legs, and with whom he finds himself obliged on occasion to share one of the Metropolitan's sleeping-cell rooms, again hints at Dickens.

Childhood as both substance and vantage-point includes boy-gang life aplenty, the schoolyard, the fights, the escapades and always braggadocio. Sexual awakening has its reference in the pubic chalk drawings with Beverly Tyler and childhood sexual fumblings with Vera Cummings, then in the threat of the shadowy Curtis Street pederast. But with other street seven-year-olds like Bobby and Sonny it also serves as the filter through which to give ground-level particularisation to 'the frenzy of . . . life about us' (207). These drawn-upon experiences, as the rest of the busy catalogue, summon the remembrance of Cassady's nascent literary calling, the stir he feels for the film and then the book versions of Dumas's *The Count of Monte Cristo* and H. G. Wells's *The Invisible Man*. 'There was no ebbing in the love of literature that had sprung forth' (76), he recalls, a declaration, albeit that it addresses only the opening increment of his life's timeline, and whether as prologue to Beat or otherwise, Cassady dutifully folds into *The First Third*.

Herbert Huncke: They were all so very intellectual

Like his Beat fellow passengers Herbert Huncke has long passed into celebrity, the fabled underworld guide to the Times Square of drugs and thievery and the begetter of the word 'Beat' as beaten-down which in Jack Kerouac's fashioning would combine with beatitude.

'Intellectual' was Huncke's word for Burroughs and Ginsberg espe-
cially, as against his own hustle, thieving, sexual opportunism, drug
supply, heroin addiction, and considerable jail-time in Riker's Island,
Sing-Sing, The Tombs and other penitentiaries. Yet, as *Huncke's
Journal* (1965), the short-fiction and poetry collection brought out
by Diane di Prima in her Poets Press, the pieces in *The Evening Sun
Turns Crimson* (1980) and *Guilty of Everything* (1990), his full-
blown autobiography for all its account of life in the lower depths,
also confirm his will to authorship ('I had three dreams as a kid, act-
ing, dancing, and writing', 67–8).[38] He would further confirm these
ambitions in his many eventual campus, radio and TV appearances,
Beat's celebrity crook turned exceptional raconteur.

'My ultimate destination' (21) Huncke says of Times Square
in the wake of his Massachusetts birth, Chicago upbringing and
drifting existence in the 1930s and 40s that saw him linger in New
Orleans and other cities and en-ship to the Caribbean, Honolulu
and Wales. Drugs featured early ('I was a natural for it', 24). Cross-
sexuality was a forte ('I have had relationships with both men and
women my entire life', 72). The serial 'burglary scene' (113) would
notoriously involve stashed goods at Ginsberg's apartment and the
poet's court-ordered dispatch to the Columbia Psychiatric Presbyte-
rian Psychiatric Institute. 42nd Street, the Lower East Side, bars like
the Bucket of Blood and the Cedar Tavern, become home territory.

Huncke's life increasingly resembles theatre. Jail educates him.
Alfred Kinsey interviews (and pays) him for his sexual history.
William Burroughs becomes a drug client ('I gave him his first shot',
70). A Hogarthian cast of characters fills his life and eventually his
page. The giant Luxembourg-born hermaphrodite Elsie John crosses
his path ('I tell you she was something else', 30). His pal and fellow-
thief Johnny is shot by Treasury men. Vickie Russell and Little Jack
Melody, prostitute and grifter, make for satellite players. These,
and a roll-call of fellow miscreants involved in break-ins, purloin-
ing, arrests and narcotics, he forges into the one narrative roll. Yet
he was never vicious, and not unreasonably, Irving Rosenthal in
Sheeper (1967) can say of Huncke 'his tales light up with compas-
sion the most blighted and bizarre personalities'.[39]

Writing in *The Evening Sun Turns Crimson* he has little hesita-
tion in exploiting his Beat connection, at once protégé and avatar
('We were a strange group . . . we were the people who formed
the inner circle', 146). The circle he celebrates, besides Ginsberg,

Burroughs and Kerouac, will reach to Lucien Carr, John Wieners, LeRoi Jones, Hal Chase, Ray and Bonnie Bremser, Alexander Trocchi and always di Prima. He has a major love in Janine Pommy Vega ('absolutely beautiful', 127), lauds Peter Orlovsky ('His whole life is poetic in a way', 128), and mourns the death of Elise Cowen ('It was just a shame, because she wrote extremely well', 154). He shows great respect for Joan Vollmer Adams, writer and den-figure who later becomes common-law wife to Burroughs. Manhattan underworld or Beat page, Huncke offers his distinctive passport into both.

Front Row

The Beat, or Beat-related, septet of this chapter all extend the remit of America's post-war counter-voice, writings and their begetters unwilling to settle for the median. Holmes does jazz and literature cartography. Burroughs unfurls unique dystopia. Corso displays antic and serious Shelleyism. Ferlinghetti blends word and picture, his ekphrastic flair. McClure aims to turn poetry to tantrism. Cassady tries valiantly to turn the dysfunctions of his early life into functioning narrative. Huncke brings the subterranean above ground. Each, uniquely, and always to his own drummer, gives grounds for membership in Beat's front row.

Notes

1. Michael McClure, *Scratching the Beat Surface: Essays on New Vision from Blake to Kerouac*, San Francisco: North Point Press, 1982. Reprinted New York: Penguin Books, 1994.
2. Bookstore photograph reproduced in Maria Anita Stefanelli (ed.), *City Lights: Pocket Poets and Pocket Books*, Rome: Ila Palma, Mazonne Editori, 2004, 6. See, in this connection, Nancy J. Peters, 'The Beat Generation and San Francisco's Culture of Dissent', in James Brook, Chris Carlsson and Nancy Joyce Peters (eds), *Reclaiming San Francisco: History, Politics, Culture*, San Francisco: City Lights Books, 2003, 199–215.
3. John Clellon Holmes, Introduction, *Go*, New York: Thunder's Mouth Press, 1952, 1976, xvii–xxiii.
4. I offer a fuller account of *Go* in *Modern American Counter Writing: Beats, Outriders, Ethnics*, New York: Routledge, 2010, 27–9.
5. William Burroughs, *The Job: Interviews with Daniel Odier*. New York: Grove Press, 1970, 52.

6. For a helpful overview of cut-up and its connection to avant-gardism, see Rona Cran, '"Everything is permitted": William Burroughs's Cut-up Novels and European Art', *Comparative American Studies: An International Journal,* Special Issue: 'The Beat Generation and Europe', 11:3 (September 2013), 300–13.
7. Kathy Acker, 'William Burroughs's Realism' (1990), *Bodies of Work*, London: Serpent's Tail, 1997, 3.
8. Will Self, 'William Burroughs: The Original Junkie', *The Guardian*, 1 February 2014.
9. William Burroughs, *Naked Lunch*, London: HarperCollins/Flamingo Modern Classics, 1993, 56. All quotations are from this edition.
10. J. G. Ballard, 'Introduction', in William Burroughs, *Naked Lunch*, London: HarperCollins/Flamingo Modern Classics.
11. *Reality Sandwiches*, San Francisco: City Lights Books, 1963, 40. William Burroughs, 'Deposition: Testimony Concerning a Sickness', in *Naked Lunch*, London: HarperCollins/Flamingo, 7.
12. William Burroughs, *Naked Lunch*, Paris: Olympia Press, 1959; London: John Calder, 1964. *Naked Lunch*, London: HarperCollins/Flamingo, 1993.
13. The phrase derives from Vance Packard, *The Hidden Persuaders*, New York: Penguin, 1957. Packard diagnosed, not uncontroversially, subliminal techniques in advertising, corporation practice and politics.
14. Gregory Corso, *Gasoline*, Pocket Books Series, Number 8, San Francisco: City Lights Books, 1958, 7.
15. Ted Morgan, *Literary Outlaw: The Life and Times of William Burroughs*, New York: W. W. Norton, 2012, 242.
16. Allen Ginsberg, 'Introduction', *Gasoline*, 7.
17. *Gasoline*, frontispiece. Corso puts the words in quotation marks as if spoken and appends a reference, maybe mock-scholarly as it were, of 'page 1369'.
18. Gregory Corso, 'The Whole Mess . . . Almost', *Herald of the Autochtonic Spirit*, New York: New Directions, 1981, 48–9.
19. Gregory Corso, 'The Mad Yak', *Gasoline*, 42.
20. Gregory Corso, 'Bomb', *The Happy Birthday of Death*, New York: New Directions, 1960, interleaved and folded into pages 32–3.
21. Gregory Stephenson offers the following pertinent summary: 'The poet suggests that much of the modish opposition to the bomb has its origins in the fear of death which is an inevitable component in the human situation. He enumerates other forms of death which he sees as far more likely and equally or even more terrible . . . In the fiery wind of thermo-nuclear blast all human vanities will be revealed in their ultimate triviality, and surreal, absurd juxtapositions and metamorphoses will occur.' *Pilgrims to Elsewhere*, Roskilde: EyeCorner Press, 2013, 88.

22. Gregory Corso, 'Marriage', *The Happy Birthday of Death*, 29–32.

23. Gregory Corso, 'I Am 25', *Gasoline*, 36.

24. Gregory Corso, 'For Miles', *Gasoline*, 44.

25. Gregory Corso, 'The Sacré-Coeur Café', *The Happy Birthday of Death*, 66.

26. Gregory Corso 'Elegaic Feelings American (for the dear Memory of John Kerouac)', *Elegaic Feelings American*, New York: New Directions, 3–12.

27. Gregory Corso, 'Spontaneous Requiem for the American Indian', *Elegaic Feelings American*, New York: New Directions , 1981, 13–17.

28. Gregory Corso, 'Columbia U Poesy Reading – 1975'), *Herald of the Autochtonic Spirit*, 1981, 1–5.

29. Lawrence Ferlinghetti, *Who are We Now?* New York: New Directions, 1976, 'Populist Manifesto', 61–4.

30. For an assiduous account of poet-to-picture in Ferlinghetti's writing, see 'William T. Lawlor, 'When He Looks at Pictures: Lawrence Ferlinghetti and the Tradition of Elphrasis', Cornelius A. van Minnen, Jaap van der Bent and Mel van Elteren (eds), *Beat Culture: The 1950s and Beyond*. Amsterdam: VU University Press, 1999, 195–208.

31. Lawrence Ferlinghetti, *Tentative Description of a Dinner Given to Promote the Impeachment of President Eisenhower*, San Francisco. Golden Mountain Press, 1958, distributed by City Lights Books.

32. Michael McClure, *Meat Science Essays*, San Francisco: City Lights Books, 1963, 13.

33. He writes of wanting his poetry 'to have a body language on the page, and with the voice when spoken aloud . . .'. See Michael McClure, *Huge Dreams: San Francisco and Beat Poems*, New York: Penguin Books, 1999, 168.

34. Initially City Lights published the book as *The First Third: A Partial Autobiography*, San Francisco: City Lights Books, 1972. The full Chaplin paragraph, summoning the 1930s, reads 'Cassady's descriptions of that pre-war world has the quality of the old silent movies – so quintessentially the somehow lonely Western experience of that vanished time – Chaplin's Tramp walking into the future.' City Lights Editor's Note, n.p.

35. Carolyn Cassady gives cameos of Cassady's resolve to become a writer and his efforts to compose *The First Third* in *Off the Road: My Years with Cassady, Kerouac, and Ginsberg*, New York: Penguin Books, 13, 93. She underlines his notion of bop prosidy, to be fleshed out in his letters to Kerouac, the need for prose to be spontaneously transposed from life.

36. Tom Wolfe, *The Electric Kool-Aid Acid Test*, New York: Farrar, Straus and Giroux, 1968, 61–2.

37. Quoted in Mark Christensen, *Acid Christ: Ken Kesey, LSD, and the Politics of Ecstasy*, Tucson: Schaffner Press, 2010, 112.
38. Herbert Huncke, *Huncke's Journal*, New York: Poet's Press, 1985; *The Evening Sun Turns Crimson*, Cherry Valley, NY: Cherry Valley Editions, 1980; and *Guilty of Everything*, New York: Paragon House, 1990.
39. Irving Rosenthal, *Sheeper*, New York: Grove Press, 1967, 113.

CHAPTER 5

Gallery: Outrider Beats

What do you think about the Beat Generation?
What point of view do you want?

Gregory Corso, 'Variations on a Generation' (1959)[1]

After one look at this planet any visitor from outer space would ask to see the manager.

William Burroughs, *The Adding Machine: Collected Essays* (1985)[2]

Outriders

However often used the 'Beat Generation' as term goes only so far, familiar by repetition, a working abbreviation. For beyond the literary centre of gravity in Kerouac, Ginsberg and Burroughs and Corso and Ferlinghetti as their fellow travellers in verse, story and the arts, Beat from the outset has actually possessed differing thoroughfares, a dense net of individual freebooters. Down the timeline, and adjacent or not so adjacent, there can be little doubt in Corso's phrase given in the heading above of Beat's considerable 'variation'. In this regard, text and life, the extended fuller gallery invites recognition.

Like Burroughs, always assuredly each in their own manner, the writers who come under the Beat flag might all have seemed to be asking 'to see the manager' if not quite of the planet then at least of America and the modern world in general. Together, and in a medley of respective gradients, their 'point of view', and what invites being thought their 'outer space' ways of looking, extends the ambit of the Beats.

Gary Snyder: Nature is not a place to visit. It is home.

Zen, Earth, Mountain. The terms virtually adhere to Snyder. His relationship with Beat has been undeniable, but it has also been kept at arm's length. An interview in 1974 lays out the connectedness that still continues while insisting upon keen individual direction:

> I never knew exactly what was meant by 'The Beats,' but let's say that the original meeting, association, comradeship of Allen, myself, Michael (McClure), Lawrence (Ferlinghetti), Philip Whalen, who's not here, Lew Welch, who's dead, Gregory, for me, to a somewhat lesser extent (I never knew Gregory as well as the others) did embody a criticism and a vision which we shared in our various ways, and then we went our own ways for many years.[3]

The balance of Beat connection yet separate pathway comes across quite succinctly.

Riprap (1959), Snyder's inaugural, un-numbered and delicately cover-stitched volume of poems from Origin Press, and the thirty-nine-poem *Mountains and Rivers Without End* (1996), which evolved over four decades from 1956 to1996, offer nodal points from within a voluminous career. Titled for a breakwater or embankment, *Riprap*, scroll-like in appearance, gives sight and image to a run of meticulously fashioned memory-sites and travel. As iconic American topographies, Snyder invokes Sourdough Mountain in the Northern Cascades as though haiku ('Drinking cold snow water from a tin cup / Looking down for miles / Through high still air'), Piute Creek and Pate Valley in Yosemite, and Nooksack Valley in Washington. Looking across the Pacific, Japan for Snyder calls up Kyoto's Shingon Temple with its 'Cool Bodhisattva – maybe Avalokita' and 'cynical curving round belly' and other Kyoto sites. A tanker en route to the Middle East he sees crewed by 'the blood of the Pacific' and by men from the Cartagena of Colombia.[4] Each poem moves at meditative pace, encounters of inner as much as outer register across mountain, land, wilderness, sea. The title poem 'Riprap' sets the presiding vision:

> Lay down these words
> Before your mind like rocks.

In 'The Making of *Mountains and Rivers Without End*' Snyder explains his source in the beauteous Sung Dynasty scroll painted by Lu Yüan Ch'ing while at the same time tracking his own literal and imaginative voyaging from the Pacific Northwest to temple Kyoto.

Rightly interpreted as an ecological epic of earth and its elements, *Mountains and Rivers Without End* pursues a span that traverses the Cascades, Alaska, California and New York, the Japan of encompassing Zen, the China of painted landscape tradition, and the India of sutra and dharma.[5] Indigenous myth, animal and avian life, sightlines of rock and water, prehistories and geologies, ghost worlds and his own profound Buddhist spirituality all are enrolled into the overall poem, one of inter-hemispheric time and reach.

'Endless Streams and Mountains', the opening poem, invokes a Ch'i Shan Wu Chin scroll of hills, cliffs, trails, boulders and ravines. That then links the poet's pilgrim-self to the turning natural order:

> *Walking on walking,*
> *Under foot   earth turns* (9)

'The Mountain Spirit', the closing poem, picks up on this dynamic, Nature as life always in motion:

> *Streams and mountains never stay the same* (152)

This sense of Nature's kinetics runs throughout the four sequences of the collection, the earth as life-energy both beneath and about all human existence. The 'walking' is Thoreauvian in its American Transcendentalist commitment to Nature as outward show of inward spirit and akin also both to that of the classic figure of Bashō in his *haibun* travel-diary *Narrow Road to the Interior* (*Oku no Hosomichi*; 1689) and to Snyder's admired contemporary Nanao Sakaki in collections like *Break the Mirror* (1987) and *Let's Eat Stars* (1997). These all tell actual yet at the same time spiritual journeying. Snyder's poems do likewise, at once Beat and Asian in their freight and implication. They clearly arise out of the resolve to express open life, and open landscape, within open poetics.

'Night Highway 99', typically, offers a visionary 'road' from the Northwest to San Francisco. The components might suggest Kerouac as much as Asian traveller: hitchhiking ('We're on our way', 11), food ('Dried, shrimp / smoked / salmon', 13), transport ('All night freezing in the back of a truck', 17), and topography ('Snow on the pines & firs around Lake Shasta', 21). 'The road that's followed goes forever' (21) insists the poem. 'There IS no 99' (24) says a closing voice. Snyder directs his reader perfectly to the duality of the journey being undertaken. 'Bubbs Creek Haircut', set partly in San Francisco and partly in its surrounding geography, likewise calls up a personally lived outdoor west of trail crews, treks, trout, canyon, mountain and 'the memory of smoking pine' (38). Pollution is anything but ignored, any more than the racist anti-Indianism of the Barber College where he goes for his haircut ('sat half an hour before they told me / white men use the other side', 34). Memory, indicatively, looks back also to shared truck-travelling with 'Allen in the rear on straw' (37), at once dharma bums and Beat companions.

'Journeys' offers a touchstone, a trip undertaken with Lew Welch into Washington Mountains 'back country' (56). The encountered terrain ('peaks stony and barren, a few alpine trees', 55) transposes into a vision of life-and-death, each transcendentally equal and seamed into the other. It gives cause, by design or otherwise, to be thought Snyder's elision of ecology, Buddhism and his own distinctive variety of Beat.[6] The Pulitzer Prize in 1975, the American Book Award in 1984, and the Bollingen and each other award, could not have been better merited.

Peter Orlovsky: Me a Russian American on a big white ship

'Our cultural inheritance is diminished without him.' So Ann Charters, who famously went on a date with Peter Orlovsky to the 6 Gallery reading, gives a warm hurrah to him in her Foreword to *Peter Orlovsky, a Life in Words: Intimate Chronicles of a Beat Writer* (2014).[7] The tribute is considerably deserved. In one respect Orlovsky can be considered the consummate insider, Ginsberg's lifelong American lover-partner, participant in a thousand readings and co-traveller to Europe, India, the Maghreb and beyond. His eventual sad decline into mental instability, drugs and alcohol does not erase the handsome ephebe who first entranced the author of 'Howl'. Nor does it undo recognition of the family devotee and farm cultivator who took scrupulous care of his psychologically damaged brother Lafcadio. Equally, however, it underplays Orlovsky as a writer, his poetry and his lively diary and correspondence, as born out in *A Life in Words*.

When City Lights took it upon themselves to publish *Clean Asshole Poems & Smiling Vegetable Songs: Poems, 1957–1977* (1978), Pocket Poets Series #37, they were not out simply to deliver

some off-the-shelf shock-horror title. Ferlinghetti had long pressed
to have Orlovsky gather his poems into a single collection. He also
understood that the anatomical and alimentary references were
metaphoric: a life best lived clean of detritus and under regimes
of 'nutritional' good faith. 'Frist Poem', written in Paris in 1957,
gives an early taste of Orlovsky's flavour – the spelling's metathesis
playfully deliberate as in many of his poems:

> A rainbow comes pouring into my window, I am electrified.
> Songs burst from my beast, all my crying tops, mistory
> fills the air. (9)

A fantastical listing ensues. 'Ten children' sit on the speaker's lap.
'A fat colored woman' becomes his mother. He wants 'everybody to
speak to me'. In surreal fashion he meets the Czech modernist Franz
Kafka who flees his presence. He sings in the elevator thinking him-
self en route to heaven. These observations, and those that accom-
pany them, might almost suggest a perambulation by New York
poet Frank O'Hara, working filaments in what Orlovsky terms 'my
gay jubilation' (10).

Similar formulations run through his verse. In 'Another Day' he
writes 'Silence can also be a poem' (20) and 'A pillow for a hello'
(20). He offers sex poems ('Jerked Off', 70, or 'Out at Sea', 79–82),
Manhattan poems ('Poems from Subway to Work', 59–60), and
literary credos like 'Writing Poems Is a Saintly Thing' (53) and
the prose-verse of 'How I Write Poetry & Who I Learned From'
(123–4), with its acknowledgement of debts to Ginsberg, Kerouac
and Corso, the French modernist poetry of Arthur Rimbaud and
Guillaume Apollinaire, and the 'fast funney wit lines' of Kenneth
Koch. In 'Peter's Jealous of Allen' he dreams of his love–hate at
Ginsberg's pre-eminence among the poets ('I wanted to bleed to
death slowly in front of them – / for here I would be the centre of
attention / & not Allen', 26).

Two longer poems, travel at their centre, bear out Orlovsky's
ability to sustain his poet's vision beyond any one immediacy. 'Dear
Allen: Ship will Land Jan 23, 1958—' (27–37), written at sea as he
nears New York and the Statue of Liberty after a year's absence,
ponders his relationship both with Ginsberg ('this is the weirdest
letter I ever wrote to Allen or / anybody', 29) and America ('Oh
my Liberty dont step on toes . . . Oh Devel Librity Kiss me', 33–4).
'Lepers Cry' (105–10) summons India, his own morphine addiction

and scenes of street leprosy near the riverside steps of Dasadsumed Ghat. These conditions, western and eastern, look to tell contrastive experience yet both are offered by Orlovsky across a vista of compassion and under the one Beat voice.

Tram Combs: Secret Beat

In Tram Combs, Beat has another of Beat poetry's veteran co-workers beginning from *Pilgrim's Terrace: Poems American West Indian* (1957) about which William Carlos Williams writes in his introduction 'They are all short, seized at a moment's observation . . . It is amazing how the pictures are filled with life' (7).[8] A steady output ensues, the writings collected in *But Never Mind: Poems, 1946–1950* (1961) and, in sequence, *Artists-Boys-Cats-Lovers-Judges-Priests: Ceremonies in Mind* (1959), with its varieties of portrait, *Saint Thomas: Poems* (1965), as set in the Caribbean of the Danish-founded American Virgin Islands, and *Briefs* (1966), given over to love and sexual close encounter. He took some pleasure in calling himself the Secret Beat.

San Francisco has an active presence in Combs's poetry: the city features variously as Combs's bookstore, his connection to Kenneth Rexroth and North Beach counterculture literary circles, and his early gay activism and affiliations, along with the bouts of nude modelling that have continued into his nineties. The ready acquiring eye, sexual openness, and poetics of open measure, spacing and lack of capitalisation, all point to Beat as aesthetic.

The prospectus Combs sets for himself is to be met in 'captain o captain' in *Saint Thomas, Poems*:

> the poet
> sits there
> waiting to be raped
> by the muse
> & hoping
> It won't come out a bloody mess
> again, like the last time
>
> once a year?
> he can bring it off
> howling in
> the breath of life. (62)

Beat, or its resonance, is yet more distinctly to be heard in poems from *Pilgrim's Terrace* like 'America' with its Ginsberg echo ('America / I love you / broad dawns over the silty Missouri / the electric spires of Manhattan/and filth and sunlight sifting down/into its grand canyons', 54) and 'towards balls for Jack' with its Kerouac-Buddhist patois: for example, 'if you can't kill dandelions / learn to love them / they are like yellow elves / perfect-ly themselves' (41). Combs can be uneven, as his poetry has hits and dips, but he gives grounds to join Beat's register.

Jack Micheline: Carrying Mattresses through the Street

The bow Jack Micheline made with *River of Red Wine* (1957) famously bears the introduction by Jack Kerouac, penned when he, too, was full of wine. The preface is nothing if not enthusiasm ('he has the swinging free style I like and his sweet lines revive the poetry of open hope in America') and to which Micheline pays reciprocal homage in 'Chasing Jack Kerouac's Shadow' (1982). In the twenty or so collections that would follow, to include *67 Poems for Downtrodden Saints* (1997), *North of Manhattan: Collected Poems, Ballads and Songs, 1954–1975* (1976), a slew of *Beatitude* and other pamphlet and small-press publications, and collections like *In the Bronx and Other Stories* (1965), it could hardly be said that Micheline was always quite exactly pledged to hope. But there can be no mistaking the improvisational energy, the edge of a self-dubbed street poet unwilling to settle for easy compromise with his society. It is also no doubt in keeping that he decried being called a Beat poet, classic Beat contra-Beat statement.

To come on to his poetry is to also meet a life of some eventfulness: Jewish birth in the East Bronx in 1929 as Harold Silver (the Jack he assumed from Jack London), a stint in the US Medical Corp in 1947–8, a kibbutzer in 1949, winner of the Village's 'Revolt in Literature Award' in 1957, and publication in the first issue of LeRoi Jones and Hettie Cohen's magazine *Yugen* (1958–62), led on to an almost unbroken life on the road. That includes 1961–2 in Mexico where he developed the art study that would continue through to the word-and-image graphics he left on the walls of San Francisco's Abandoned Planet Bookstore long after the eventual full-time move to North Beach. No doubt he was a roustabout, at times a ranter and barfly who several times ended up in jail or hospital, but like his writer friends Charles Bukowski, Harold Norse, Bob Kaufman and A. D. Winans he kept up a steady output of fiction and poetry and even theatre as in his play *East Bleeker* (its origins the Bowery poem 'East Bleeker').

In the footfalls of Ginsberg's *Howl* and Burroughs's *Naked Lunch*, his story 'Skinny Dynamite' with its uninhibited portrait of the sexual adventuring of a young woman bohemian, led to prosecution of his publisher in 1968. His work so joins a notable Beat litany of work, ritually thought obscene, brought before the courts of justice. Micheline may well have chosen the street as his bailiwick, but he inhabited ambits well beyond as his readings to Charles Mingus's jazz and the Naropa Prize for 'Most Valuable Performance' give witness. With good reason his Memorial in Los Angeles in March 1998 drew a list of Beat notables to include Orlovsky, Jones-Baraka, Pommy Vega and Ira Cohen. It was justice for a writer perhaps too infrequently feted, or given full place in Beat and allied ranks. Under the rubric of 'Poet of the Streets' (1960) he had, after all, announced himself 'unconquered with the legacy of Whitman and Lorca / a poet unconquered by stone, by glass, by greed, by madness'.

When Micheline is in symptomatic Beat mode he can rarely be bettered: for example, in 'Chasing Jack Kerouac's Shadow', composed as he himself indicates 'on a bus from San Francisco to Santa Rosa, March 1987'. Writing as though in confessional persona the landscape and curriculum vitae it details bespeaks a poet of margins. Society is seen from below – 'Streets, poems, nuthouses, paintings, con men and time / My twenty years of poems and paintings stored away in houses and cellars / relentless with anger and love / I ponder at life and the world around me'. The voice to hand remembers an artist's indigence, etching out a living, 'years spent begging and hustling / carrying paintings on buses / carrying mattresses through streets'. Each of the 'evictions' and 'lost loves' yields to the speaker's own actual body with its 'hangovers, rheumatism, hemorrhoids'. And yet, beatifically, there persist light and warmth, a prospect of human warming: 'We are all the sun / You are the sun / We are one'.

Almost any selection of Micheline's poems plays upon these Beat-like antinomies, the poet at lower-depth, the poet fortified by the energies of imagination. 'Poem for a Dead Pigeon', set in London, contrasts the expired bird with his 'sunlit' kiss of its wing. 'Poem for the Children of the World', co-written with Bob Kaufman, bespeaks a special tenderness towards infancy as stellar and an eternity of invention and fable ('A child walks in a dream / Her eyes dance in the night of stars'). 'Blues Poem' draws these Beat threads into a single composition, the poet street-farer unsmiling because 'down' yet able to contrive a 'solo riff' on his blues horn through which to find 'life', 'dance', an as yet 'unborn sun'. In that prospect is to be discovered 'a song', 'a poem', 'some paradise of mind'. Human kindness returns, beatitude over despair ('I got to smile now / I'm feeling good / The city street / The palace of my mind'). The upshot is Micheline's call to wellbeing, nothing if not in shared spirit with Beat's encompassing wider good faith.

Ed Sanders: Peace Eye

In 'A Book of Verse', the chapter he appended to the reissue in 1990 of *Tales of Beatnik Glory* (1975), Ed Sanders gives memory to the impact of reading Ginsberg as teenager. Keeping his story in the third person, 'He read *Howl* and was stunned . . . *Howl* ripped into his mind like the tornado that had uprooted the cherry tree in his backyard when he was a child' (281). The upshot could not have been more decisive, as he took leave from his Kansas City home to enrol at the University of Missouri with the resolve, as he told his best friend, that 'I'm going to New York to become a poet'. In doing so he launched a career as activist and as countercultural as it was literary; yet, almost discrepantly, underwritten by the degree he took in Classics from New York University in 1964. Homer, among other Greek influences, threads through his life and writing, as does Beat. Not a few times, the prankster in him never far beneath the surface, he has taken to describing himself as 'the only Beatnik who can yodel'.

His activism and writing, and their connections with Beat circuits of friendship and frequent co-publication, began early with the move into the Village. His 1961 incarceration for trying to board the warship *Ethan Allen* in protest at Polaris missiles led to *Poems from Jail* (1963), his first verse-collection, which was published to his great delight by Ferlinghetti under the City Lights imprint. In 1964 his founding of the Peace Eye Book Store at 383 East Tenth Street created a landmark gathering place for Beat-bohemian culture – books, readings, mimeograph and small-press publication, happenings, improvisation, and the centre for the Campaign to Legalize Marijuana. It was from there that Sanders published *Fuck*

You! A Magazine of the Arts with its repertoire of Beat and coun-
tercultural contributors. Copies, almost by duty, went to Ginsberg,
Burroughs, Ferlinghetti and Charles Olson, but also, audaciously,
to Castro, Khruschev, Picasso and Beckett. Kerouac, often the
worse for drink, was known to phone in poems to be transcribed
by Sanders. The 2 January 1966 New York City police raid on the
store for holding obscene material, Sanders's 9th Precinct arrest and
a protracted court case with the American Civil Liberties Union
(ACLU) in defence (to include Kenneth Koch and John Ashbery as
witnesses), invites being thought a virtual Beat rite of passage.

His long-time mobilisation against America's military–industrial
complex, anti-nuclear and anti-Vietnam War stance, Civil Rights
commitment, and aid to draft refuseniks heading to Canada, finds
an apotheosis in the formation in 1965 of the folk-rock satire group
the Fugs. Fug had been Norman Mailer's not a little tongue-in-cheek
euphemism for fuck (and so used to get round censorship) in *The
Naked and the Dead* (1948). The group pledged itself to 'fierce
pacifism' and has continued to be remembered whether for live per-
formances like those initially at the Players Theatre and then other
venues, or the recordings first contracted with Reprise Records (its
principal stockholder Frank Sinatra) and the different tapes, CDs
and videos many of which now available on the web.

In *Fug You: An Informal Memoir of the Peace Eye Books Store,
the Fuck You Press, the Fugs & Counterculture in the Lower East
Side* (2011) Sanders writes of becoming enmeshed with Beat cul-
ture and of the Fugs 'as found in Greenwich Village bookstores, in
the poetry readings in coffee houses on MacDougal street, in New
York City art and jazz, and in the milieu of pot and counterculture
that was rising each month' (xiii). Given his book's overall contrar-
ian posture, and contextual proliferation of detail, it perhaps little
surprises that William Burroughs offered the cover endorsement of
'eight years of total assault on the culture'.

If radical communitarian and anti-war politics always weighed on
Sanders's life, so equally has authorship, to range from his documen-
tary *The Family: The Story of Charles Manson's Dune Buggy Attack
Battalion* (1971), with its chronicle of hippiedom turned murderous,
to *Let's Not Keep Fighting the Trojan War: New and Selected Poems
1986-2009* (2009), with its 'page become history' in the words of the
Introduction by Joanne Kyger (xiii). This output edges towards the
voluminous, whether a City Lights manifesto like *Investigative Poetry*
(1976), his poet's vision of the 1960s as change-era in *Thirsting for*

Peace in a Raging Century: New and Selected Poems 1961–1985 (1987), or the ambitious multi-volume poetic chronicles inaugurated with *1968: A History in Verse* (1997) and continued unremittingly in *America: A History in Verse* (Volumes 1-9, 2000–16).

Not the least in this regard has been Sanders's *Woodstock Journal*, from the same terrain as the historic Woodstock Festival of 1969 with its considerable Beat associations. The *Journal*, having moved from print to online, continues his chronicle of region, culture, politics and natural-grown food. Likewise his span includes the audio-volume recited to the music of Mark Bingham, *Poems for New Orleans* (2007), a verse-panorama of the city's history in the wake of Hurricane Katrina and spanning Vodoo, Dixieland, Andrew Jackson, Mark Twain and a host of contemporaries caught up in the catastrophe. In each of these multiple activities, Beat and its ligatures and ripples is unmistakable.

Two texts make explicit Sanders's connection to Beat. *The Poetry and Life of Allen Ginsberg: A Narrative Poem* (2000), fond, dense, assiduous in detail and date, offers what he calls in the Afterword 'a kind of pathway through the Forest Ginsberg' (245). The affiliation is to be heard, typically, behind each vignette, as in the view of Ginsberg's relationship with Naomi ('Ginsberg/with a crazy mother/ was very sensitive/to craziness/Crazy Wisdom/Crazy Times/& Vision', 4). Equally pertinent would be the angle of vision given to Ginsberg's lifetime love tryst with Kerouac ('On way back from seder in Paterson/(at Louis's house)/Allen and Kerouac/parted at 125th Street/Allen demanded Jack hit him – I wanted attention from him/any kind of attention', 20). The cancer that killed Ginsberg in 1997 affords a quite special poignancy in Sanders's account, the dying of the light for Beat's pre-eminent bard amid Orlovsky and others of the cadre and under the gaze of his evident poetic forerunner:

> They brought him home on Wednesday, April 2
> to the light-wood-hued/loft with his books & paintings/&set
> up his
> final encampment
> They placed a hospital bed near the
> white-bearded photo of Whitman
> on a brick wall
> between two windows that looked
> upon 14th Street (236)

'Ode to the Beat Generation', a banner piece in *Let's Not Keep Fighting the Trojan War* (230–1), leaves nothing to doubt of a legacy summoned, a time's flowering. Styled as a 'wild dance' it presses also as a memory-theatre using retrieved graphics, mimeographs and canvases. To de-solemnise matters there is the wry remembrance of Chianti bottles and their candles, sandal-wearing, bongo drums, even midnight crossings on the Staten Island Ferry. Lead players get their mention in the text, whether it is Creeley stenciling 'Howl' on Rexroth's typewriter, Ferlinghetti's leftist verse, Di Prima writing 'Revolution', or the differently hues in identity of Burroughs, Ginsberg, Corso, Snyder and Kyger. 'Weaknesses', even, can be forgiven ('Kerouac's voting for Nixon') in the hope of Buddha-like 'Eternity'. Quest, voice, and the exhilaration of beauty are imagined to fuse into a single continuum: 'The art of the Road and the art of the Word is the art of the Rose'. Beat, on Sanders's evidentiary reckoning, continue to exert serious call but as always not without whim: for example, 'Ecstasy Fondue! Sax Clover! Tire-Sandal Soup!'.

Ray Bremser: Scatting related to Monk Coltrane Taylor Charles

This run-on tag of four jazz names provided by Allen Ginsberg in the preface to Ray Bremser's *Poems to Madness & Angel*, dated 27 May 1964, also provides a perfect entry into *Blowing Mouth: The Jazz Poems 1958–1970* (1978). The earlier volume is given over to the 'holy madness' of life at the city margins, drugs, crime, and the Angel who as Bonnie Bremser would in turn write him into being in *Troia: Mexican Memoirs/For Love or Ray*. The later collection, Bremser's sequence of riffs and talking blues operates in more improvisational free form.

The compositions in *Blowing Mouth* Bremser teasingly alleges in one of its main poems, 'Heart of Texas Blues', all have led to his 'BEING ARRESTED AGAIN FOR POETRY' (38). The Beat inflection for a life led much on the lam, drawn into drugs, at odds with conformity and if full of mishap then also his own irresponsibility, is unmistakable. The opening poem 'backyards & deviations', a memoir of being drawn incestuously to his sister, looks back to 'the scrawling, violent/unbroken poet in my head' (9). That poet, typically, can be heard both in 'FRANKENSTEIN',18–23) , a museum fantasia of humanity left soulless and rough-stitched by computers

and consumer trademarks, and in 'follow the east river' (40), exist-
ence seen as though Egyptian mummified history.

By contrast, 'Heart of Texas Blues' turns to jazz for its 'round
midnight/straight no chaser' (30) as redemption for his incarcera-
tion in the Lone Star State. Monk plays 'mystery blues' (30). John
Coltrane, Sonny Rollins, Art Blakey all contrast with the 'Texas' of
cowboy minutemen, sheriffs, pursued 'wetbacks', guns and spurs.
Jazz so offers the counterpoint to the 'painted-desert winds of
doomsday' (35). 'Funny Lotus Blues' derides muzak as sound and
listening, Dial Soap music as he calls it. Thelonious Monk meta-
morphoses into 'Melodious Thunk', 'astounding even hisself/with
the density of tongue/he transforms in the cheek of the piano' (51).
'Blues for Harold,' written for a black one-time inmate in Trenton's
New Jersey State Prison who died of an overdose, remembers their
talk of the sublimity of Miles Davis and Coltrane. Harold's own
'solo' has been his life, his 'unholy communion' with hate and each
race-line act of 'utter malice' (56). Jazz poems they assuredly are,
as evidenced in the line spacing, measure, run-ons and breaks. But
equally they bear a Beat banner of arms: Beat in Bremser's written-
up spoken register.

Tuli Kupferberg: Is there life after birth?

To summon Tuli Kupferberg almost obliges allusion to *Howl*'s 'best
minds of my generation' (9). There, amid hipsters and visionaries,
Ginsberg lists the un-named Kupferberg as the figure 'who jumped
off the Brooklyn Bridge this actually happened and walked away
unknown and forgotten into the ghostly daze of Chinatown soup
alleyway & firetrucks' (14). That the bridge was the Manhattan
Bridge and that Kupferberg was treated for serious spinal injury
at Gouverneur Hospital in Lower Manhattan perhaps ranks in
lesser significance than that he had in fact suffered a nervous break-
down. Few Greenwich Villagers can more lay claim to the role of
countercultural and luminary. Anarchist, pacifist, Yiddish-speaker,
Brooklyn College graduate, his would be a lifetime of dissent
('I had intended to be a doctor, like a good Jewish boy' he liked to
proclaim). His magazine *Birth*, launched in 1958 and lasting only
a few issues, was early to publish Ginsberg, Di Prima, LeRoi Jones
and Ted Joans. But given his street performances, anti-war rally-
ing, blizzard of pamphlets and poster-poems from Grove Press and

other avant-garde publishers, nothing quite became him like the co-founding with Ed Sanders of *The Fugs* in the mid-1960s. Beat-anarchist energy, poetry as hex or incantation, had found an apotheosis. Composed by Kupferberg alone, or with Sanders, song upon song (which he called *parasongs*, a neologism in kind with his *perverbs*) took aim at Corporation and Pentagon, Vietnam and Market. He found radical co-spirits in Students for a Democratic Society (SDS), the Panthers, each anti-war alliance, and never least, Beat-beatnik-hippie and punk culture formations. With the issue of *The Village Fugs Sing Ballads of Contemporary Protest, Points of View and General Dissatisfaction* in 1965, their first album, the compass was set. No quarter was to be given to militarism, FBI control, free-for-all Wall Street any more than to nine-to-five office or cocktail-hour custom. Rather, in verse and cartoon, and subsequently YouTube witticism (typified in 'Is there life after birth?'), this satiric marauding, irreverence towards all the shibboleths of capitalism and the allures of middle-class conformity. In an online interview with Richie Unterberger in 2000, Kupferberg proffered the view that 'I guess I was the urban commie kid, Ed was a kind of Mark Twain . . . a Mark Twain of rock and roll.'

Rereading and listening to Kupferberg is to be reminded of a kind of inspired Bad Behaviour, Beat or Beat-style art angled to amuse yet discomfort. Pattern series like *1001 Ways to Live without Working* (1961), with Robert Bashlow, *1001 Ways to Beat the Draft* (1967) or *1001 Ways to Make Love* (1969) carry typical satiric punch. *3000000000 . . . Beatniks: or The War against the Beats* (1961) issued a mock-warning. The solo albums *No Deposit, No Return* (1961) and *Tuli & Friends* (1989) offer him in storytelling mode. Cable TV broadcasts his *Revolting News*. The final CD under the title *Be Free: The Fugs Final CD Part2* contains song-poems like the send-up 'I Am An Artist for Art's Sake' and 'Backward Jewish Soldiers'. He could ever be relied upon to come through with tactical shock-parody, not least given labelling like *I Hate Poems about Poems about Poems* (1994) and pastiche of self-help in *Teach Yourself Fucking* (2000).

Ginsberg or Corso could exhibit their own Bad Behaviour moments, but Kupferberg brought a unique anarchist sensibility to his output, Beat's cousinly jester. The debts are there to early-century Dada, and even more evidently to Yiddish humour. Best-known Kupferberg 'Beat' compositions have long passed into legend, few more

so than 'Kill for Peace' (*Fugs Second Album*, 1966) as an accusation
and sardonic turn-about chant ('Kill, kill, kill for peace / Kill, kill, kill
for peace / Near or middle or very far east / Far or near or very middle
east . . . / If you don't want America to play second fiddle / Kill, kill,
kill for peace').

'Greenwich Village of My Dreams' acts as both a spiritual call
to affirmation and memorial post-war geography leavened by typi-
cal jags of wit. If there was 'Blues in the Soviet Union', there were
'Onions in times square'. Was not this a time, the poem asks, could
there not again be a time, to encounter a 'Japanese in Chinatown',
'A soup sandwich', 'The Battery of startling sunlight'? How to resist
the tableau of 'Charlie Parker & Ted Joans talking / in Sheridan Sq.
Park' or the fantasy of 'Lionel Trilling kissing Allen Ginsberg / after
a great Reading in the Gaslight' (the Gaslight Café in Greenwich
Village, closed in 1971, a major Beat venue).

The run of paradox that follows adds impetus. 'Civilians' are
imagined 'telling cops to move on'. 'Walt Whitman cruising on
MacDougal' echoes the opening of Ginsberg's 'A Supermarket
in California'. Edgar Allan Poe is to be thought 'a dentist / in the
Waverly dispensary & giving / everyone free nitrous oxide high'.
The Eisenhowers, 'Ike & Mamie', become improbably drunk in
the Minetta Tavern. Taken overall, history and invention, 'Green-
wich Village of My Dreams' celebrates Beat and its panorama as
'world of art', 'joy', 'the village come to life again'. For the writer
no punches are pulled. With footfalls again of Whitman as Homeric
bard ('I wake up singing') and Ginsberg ('How beautiful is love /
And the fruit thereof. /Holy holy holy / A kiss and a star'), time and
place cannot but continue to signify. Kupferberg's temper is agile
and full of curve as a form of Beat outrider remembrance of 'world'
and 'dreams'.

Clive Matson: I wake up blue and a little sick

The name Clive Matson rarely enters the Beat index. Yet his *Main-
line to the Heart and Other Poems*, published in 1966 by Diane di
Prima's Poets Press with an introduction by his admired mentor John
Wieners, and reissued in 2009, gives reason to be harboured there.[9]
That it was seized by British customs as borderline pornographic
adds a touch of daredevilry, the glamour of notoriety. The poems he
recalls coming out of his 'neo-Beat' years – Beatdom he would later

reject as too male-centric and even elitist.[10] Albeit raised in Southern California, he came of age in New York's Lower East Side, the aspirant writer who quickly threaded into Village bohemia. Acquaintance with the Beat circle of Ginsberg, Corso and di Prima followed, as it did with writer-editors like Irving Rosenthal. In Herbert Huncke he found his father-figure and drug supplier. His ten or so poetry collections, ranging from the short but bracing chronicle *Heroin* (1972) to his myth-woman monologues in the *Chalcedony* series (2007, 2009), includes the widely successful literary instruction manual *Let the Crazy Child Write* (1998).[11] Return to the West Coast in 1968, eventually to be full-time in Oakland, and rehabilitation from drugs, has allowed him to sustain not only the continuing poet but the literary workshop guru.

Love as drug, love of drugs, presides throughout *Mainline to the Heart*, poems that probe need and fulfilment, the quest for the authentic 'high' of experience. The characteristic turns and about-turns Matson locates within bold flows of breath-line, the addiction spiral the novelist Al Young in his endorsement calls the poet's 'season in hell'.[12] Perhaps best indicative of the search for the exhilaration of finding life-within-life can be found in the lines of 'I Put Her Thru Changes':

> I've a disease called life
> and its aching, what to
> do with it. (44)

What the poet-speaker 'does with it' is test life's promise of fulfilment, its consummation. Poem upon poem turns upon love as key denominator yet whose bluff he is moved to call ('Can't it keep me / high every night' it is asked in 'Talk about Love',18). In 'The Goodbye Scene', love takes on a John Donne-like voice of erotic demand and attraction and yet antagonism: 'All right, split . . . make me sad . . . Your eyes stare someplace else . . . So Go! / I won't take any more of this', 22–3). Sexual love, the anatomical rapture of the body, gives 'Nighttime' its theme, each climax and yet built-in temporariness: 'I lay back tired and drowsy / in the boredom of nothing to desire' (42).

Matson's writing in *Mainline to the Heart*, Beat-confessional as it were, enacts an unyielding theatre of need, whether love, heroin or the will to authorship. His metaphors assume their own edgy salience: 'Our bodies lean from conflict' in 'Talk about Love' (19)

or 'I burn to out shine the sun' in 'Psalm' (28). The poetry's coor-
dinates, which seek the reader as welcoming ally, he encaptures in
'Millions Come Haunting' (49–51):

> Only the shape of these four walls
> is mine, luxury contains the bare room
> where I stand alone thinking
> of the exquisite torture. & of words,
> >   words
> someone will take as a drug and discover
> a friend inside. (51)

Matson's association in life with di Prima, Huncke and Ginsberg
gives one kind of Beat emphasis. His querying maps of self articu-
lated in open verse and line forms gives another.

Harold Norse: Parapoems, Cosmographies, Cut-up Magic

In common with Burroughs and Ferlinghetti, Harold Norse let it
be known that Beat was nomenclature he did not unduly welcome.
Yet his writing and artwork, by default or otherwise, gives out any
amount of Beat resonance. That holds for the direct, open-form
'parapoems' as he terms them and which won early praise for their
authenticity of American idiom from William Carlos Williams and
with whom he maintained a lifetime's correspondence.[13] These,
and Norse's 'cosmographies', meticulously tantric map drawings
given exhibition and then published as a six-page catalogue with a
text by William Burroughs in *Librairie anglaise* (1961), contribute
to the career of *Hotel Nirvana: Selected Poems, 1953–1973* (1974)
from City Lights, *Carnivorous Saint: Gay Poems, 1941–1976*
(1977) with its unblinking erotica, and *In the Hub of the Fiery
Force: Collected Poems, 1934–2003* (2003) as the overall contour
of his life's verse.

*Memoirs of a Bastard Angel: A Fifty-Year Literary and Erotic
Odyssey* (1989) reveals Norse circling a variety of authors from
W. H. Auden to Charles Bukowski, Anaïs Nin, Gore Vidal, Paul
Bowles and James Baldwin. He recalls his intensely lived residence
in the Beat Hotel Paris of rue Gît-le-Cœur where he took a room
in 1963, Italy, and subsequent life in San Francisco. His overlaps at

the Beat Hotel and elsewhere with Ginsberg, Burroughs and Corso, and in North Beach with Ferlinghetti, were frequent and not least in the appearance of their work in *Evergreen Review*. No connection, however, better serves than his novel *Beat Hotel*, first published in German translation in 1975 and at once story-round, cut-up apotheosis (complete with manifesto-guideline 'Cut-up Magic') and the postscripts of 1963 and 1982.[14]

Norse's accounts of the literal hotel under the baton of Mme Rachou describes a house of rooms each in its shabby sparseness variously scriptorium, painter and music studio, exhibition wall, arts and word experiment chamber, and drug retreat. Invoking *Time* magazine's disdain for the hotel as 'a flea-bag shrine' in a Paris 'where passers-by move out of the way for rats', he counters:

> After living there nearly 4 years the only rats I ever saw, and moved out of the way for were from TIME . . . In the fleabag shrine Burroughs wrote *The Soft Machine* and *The Ticket That Exploded* after assembling *The Naked Lunch*, Corso wrote BOMB, Allen wrote *At Apollinaire's Grave*, Brion Gysin's cut-up technic (*sic*) and MINUTES TO GO were conceived (the first cut-up texts) and I wrote SNIFFING KEYHOLES in the BEAT HOTEL . . . Ian Sommerville developed the Dreamachine there . . . (58)

Norse's quite canny prophecy that 'the flea-bag shrine will be documented by historians' carries the justified comment of 1982 that 'This . . . has already come true' (59).

'Cut-up Magic' throws necessary light on *Beat Hotel* and in so doing also conveys with great exactitude the impetus behind the creative work of Burroughs, Gysin and Sommerville. Assemblage, disordered word and page alignment, broken clustering, and random association, are the means by which to subvert manipulated constructions of 'the real'. The aim is always breakout from authority's ownership of norms:

> CUT-UPS and PARAPOETRY are a new emphasis on what have always been poetic ingredients . . . Like the walls of the Beat Hotel, CUT-UPS and PARA-POETRY destroy barriers erected by authority and tradition . . . In an age of robot activity true inspiration is to beat the machine at its own game, taking the trouble to climb over, or filter through, the walls of conditioning. (64–5)

The dozen or so elliptical vignettes in *Beat Hotel* act on these cues to a fault, fact-fantasy, disassociative, often acerbically comic. 'Sniffing Keyholes' has become the best known, a send-up sex graphic which gothicises and hyper-flamboyantly inflates the couplings in play at the hotel. 'Queen Z. Z.' and 'Chief Mello', white woman painter and African macho lover, enter and perform every which way as though sexual acrobats of Priapus, vent, mucus and membrane. Their bodies are 'royal horsemeat' (24), 'vegetable consciousness' (26), 'roulette orgasm squirts' (27), in all a 'movie montage floor show' (24). The very irreality of their sex practices seeks to push language beyond itself ('All words were made flesh', 26). This is to free sensation from any enclosing shell of conventional vocabulary or syntax. The piece's final line, in the manner of cut-up, so opts for seemingly unmediated graph ('Nothing but flow change lust desire flame', 27).

Norse's other stories show similar bravura, self and world projected diagonally and through the most oblique of lenses. 'Strength & Health Circuit', in the form of Bob's dissonant junk fantasy which traverses Radio Cairo to Rimbaud's *Une saison en enfer*, Gaullist France to Tangier, takes collagist aim at a world order steeped in homophobia, anti-Semitism and 'nuclear junk' (9). Epigrams abound ('Rigid heterosexuality is a perversion of nature', 7). Stories are said reflexively to be 'dry leaves in echo chamber', 8). 'Half-Clad Apparition Kids' etches gay life, loves and intimacy against persecutors with their mantra of 'WIPE OUT THE FAGS' (16). These and accompanying hate campaigns Norse spoofs as 'We want a nation of *real* men and *real* women . . . under God . . . the Flag . . . the Leader . . . who OBEYOBEYOBEYOBEY', 18). 'Alarm' offers a psychedelic stock-take of human life not only endangered by 'Roulette Bomb' but manipulated 'mind blank' (42-3).

'Take a Chance in the Void', which closes *Beat Hotel*, pulls the threads together, the author as 'HAROLD NORSE NORSE PARIS ORACLE' in his call to rally against the world controlled into cliché and sameness: 'Current language so impotent-thinking-habit-fixated on abuse – cut-wordsshatter groove think' (54). Beat and Norse's cut-up perhaps do not seamlessly cohabit. Each, however, in their renegade ways, run close one to another.

Gallery

Varieties of Beat experience, to adapt the title of William James's classic *Varieties of Religious Experience* (1902), serves as greatly apposite phrasing. The range has been wide, Snyder's Zen ecology to Norse's antic cut-ups. An unfeigned multiplicity holds. Orlovsky offers all-to-purpose wordplay, Combs his observational close eye, Micheline his street register. In Sanders, Beat has verse biographer and historian. Bremser's poetry overlaps jazz, heroin and penitentiary. Kupferberg brings comic-anarchist irreverence to bear. Matson write of love under duress and needle. All of these create texts within Beat's considerable 'variations' or 'lookings', the one and several kinds of flag.

Notes

1. Gregory Corso, 'Variations on a Generation', *Gemini*, 2:6 (Spring 1959), 47–51. Reprinted in Thomas Parkinson (ed.), *A Casebook on the Beat*, New York: Thomas Y. Crowell, 1961, 88–97.
2. William S. Burroughs, *The Adding Machine: Collected Essays*, London: John Calder, 1985, 125.
3. James Mackenzie, 'Moving the World a Millionth of an Inch', Interview with Gary Snyder, University of North Dakota Writers Conference. Reprinted in Arthur and Kit Knight (eds), *The Beat Vision*, New York: Paragon House Publishers, 1987, 2–27.
4. This pattern of alternating Far West/Far East, West Coast America/Japan and India, is earlier used by Snyder in *The Back Country*, New York: New Directions, 1968. 'Back country' is also Snyder's metaphor for location of consciousness.
5. See, in this respect, Mark Gunnerman, *A Sense of the Whole: Reading Gary Snyder's Mountains and Rivers without End*, New York: Counterpoint, 2015.
6. For a helpful analysis of Snyder in this regard, see Josh Michael Hayes, 'Being-at-Home: Gary Snyder and the Poetics of Place', in Sharin N. Eklholy (ed.), *The Philosophy of the Beats*, Lexington: University Press of Kentucky, 2012, 47–61.
7. Ann Charters, 'Foreword', in Bill Morgan (ed.), *Peter Orlovsky, A Life in Words: Intimate Chronicles of a Beat Writer*, Boulder: Paradigm Publishers, 2014, xix.
8. 'Secret Beat' is Combs's own phrase for himself and which Bent Sørensen cites in a recent conference presentation at Aalborg University, Denmark. My thanks to him for this and other information on Combs.
9. Clive Matson, *Mainline to the Heart and Other Poems*, Berkeley: Regent Press, 2009.
10. See, in this connection, the Matson website in which he writes: 'My neo-Beat poetry begged to be expanded beyond its hip ethos.'

11. Clive Matson, *Heroin*, Berkeley, Neon Sun, 1972; *Chalcedony's First Ten Songs*, San Francisco: Norton Coker Press and Port Townsend: Minotaur Press, 2007 and *Chalcedony's Second Ten Songs*, Port Townsend: Minotaur Press, 2009; and *Let the Crazy Child Write: Finding and Freeing Your Creative Voice!*, Novato, CA: New World Library, 1998.

12. The fuller comment by Al Young is wholly apropos: 'In essence a helpless and passionate romantic, Matson and his poetry zeroed in dead center on what pop-vernacular sang and was calling "The Big Hurt." In every direction the world you looked, the world as in flames . . . with a mentor like Herbert Huncke, junkie raconteur and Beat icon, to inspire him, how could Matson not sing to the pitch-memory and funkiest of blues: the death-wish blues?' Frontispiece, i.

13. William Carlos Williams and Harold Norse, *The American Idiom: A Correspondence*, San Francisco: Bright Tyger Press, 1990.

14. All page references are to Harold Norse, *Beat Hotel*, San Diego: Atticus Press, 1983 (first American edition).

CHAPTER 6

Beat's Women. Women's Beat.

I write this book to try to understand what message I got about being a woman. What that is. How to do it. Or get through it. Or bear it. Or sparkle like ice underfoot.

Diane di Prima, *Recollections of My Life as a Woman.*
The New York Years (2001)[1]

Are you a Beat Poet?
No, I'm my own Poet
Joanne Kyger (1998)[2]

I'm the multiple-universes woman
Anne Waldman, 'Fast Speaking Woman, Part II' (1996)[3]

Multiples

Beat's women. The phrase likely conjures up the familiar configuration of Beat-era lovers and wives, black-garbed muses, silent listeners, homemakers and childminders, and, in all too frequent past regard, simply facilitating extras. After all, was not Beat, as Ann Douglas suggests, a bid to 'transform and *masculinize* American cultural expression just after World War II'?[4] Debate, and not just feminist debate, has understandably chafed at chauvinist marginalisation in life and publication along with the under-reporting of Beat literary accomplishment by women. *Women's Beat*, to a degree, redirects the weathervane. The better recognition of Beat or Beat-inclined writing by women may have been culpably slow, texts written as early as the 1950s and 1960s and assuredly in the decades to follow. But recognition over time has taken hold and grown. Nor has it come about as mere ideological riposte, your turn and now our turn. For in the language of di Prima, Kyger and Waldman in the opening quotations, there has indeed been long-time reason to think the authors in however different measure to 'sparkle' and to be their 'own' and 'multiple' selves.

Each of these writers, like others across Beat, has her respective affiliations: imagism to confessional writing, Black Mountain projective verse to the $L=A=N=G=U=A=G=E$ circle. The work equally invites being situated in a line of antecedent women's voice in America: Emily Dickinson through to a modernist pantheon of H.D., Marianne Moore and Gertrude Stein, then Helen Adam, Jane Bowles and Denise Levertov. The geographies involved also have their spread, whether the New York of Manhattan, the Village and the St. Mark's Poetry Project, or Boulder and the Naropa Institute, or the West Coast of North Beach, City Lights and Bolinas, or even abroad in Europe, Japan and India. But whichever the genre, or the legacy and mooring, Women's Beat earns standing for how in its own right it creates new pathways of imagination – Beat and beyond Beat. In the process, life writing and verse, fiction and discourse, the further effect has been to fundamentally help retilt Beat's towards an attentiveness to the gender across issues of subject voice and choice of theme.

The exponential growth of Beat anthologies and scholarship by, and about, women has led to better established maps, a gathering of archives, and timely rounds of salute. Were sample voices sought they inhabit the pages of Brenda Knight's *Women of the Beat Generation: The Writers, Artists, and Muses at the Heart of the Revolution* (1996) and Richard Peabody's *A Different Beat: Writings by Women of the Beat Generation* (1997). Substantiating horizons, under the dual editorship of Nancy M. Grace and Ronna C. Johnson, follow in *Girls Who Wore Black: Women Writing the Beat Generation* (2002) and *Breaking the Rule of Cool: Interviewing and Reading Beat Women Writers* (2004). To take on a selection of single texts both confirms this aggregation of tracks and particularises the Beat female page.

Life Writings: Autobiography, Memoir

'I'm in such a hurry at nineteen to finally be the heroine of my own drama' recalls the Joyce Johnson, née Glassman, of her young womanhood in 1954 in her eloquent, enduring *Minor Characters: A*

Young Woman's Coming-of-Age in the Beat Orbit of Jack Kerouac (1983).[5] The 'drama' she recounts thirty years on, without apology and full of alertness about herself as Kerouac, deservedly ranks in flair with Beat's classics. For, however drawn into love of Kerouac, the 'Zen pilgrim in Salvation Army clothes' (112) with his creative writer intensity and first-encounter looks ('I keep stealing looks at him because he's beautiful', 128), she also, reflexively, is about the literary emergence of herself from the chrysalis of her staid Jewish parental home in Upper West Side Manhattan ('we existed in a kind of cultural loneliness', 20). In one of several swerves into the historic present she recalls 'I long to turn myself into a Bohemian' (31). Clandestine teenage trips to the Village, and the adventure of its café arts and poetry readings with always the prospect of 'the crime of sex' (102), leads on to seeing herself, life and writing, silhouetted in Françoise Sagan then newly famous with *Bonjour tristesse* (1954). As though to shadow the F. Scott Fitzgerald evident in her fiction, which she began with *Come and Join the Dance* (1962) with its Village-bohemia coming-of-age of Susan Levitt, she says of the 1950s: 'There was restlessness in everyone I knew' (117).

The auguries were good for the entrance of Kerouac (even their blind-date meeting in Howard Johnson's arranged by Ginsberg) and indeed the Beat orbit of which she again offers greatly affecting remembrance in *Door Wide Open: A Beat Love Affair in Letters, 1957–58* (2000). Barnard College comes and goes with a doleful backward glance at the two decades later Class of 1955 reunion amid the suburban matrons she was meant to be. The early expeditions to the Village yield countercultural citizenship ('the sweet slum of Bohemia', 208). Literature and art beckon. Affairs include the novelist Fielding Dawson. Contraception, and an abortion in Brooklyn-bleak Canarsie, mark out biological status. Jazz at the Five Spot and in Harlem, the Cedar Tavern and the loft parties, signal the rhythm of the times. The transition from the MCA Literary Agency into a consequential editing position with the New York publisher Farrar, Straus folds into her career in authorship. In giving memorable spotlight to the Millstein review of *On the Road* ('the next morning . . . he was famous', 185), she remembers with justice her own first novel being taken on by Random House ('Joyce Glassman the author paused dizzily on Madison Avenue and wondered if the hour that had just passed was the best one of her life', 172).

Minor Characters evidently gives Kerouac in his many con-
tradictions, his inspirational intensity but sexual guardedness, the
'good times' (132) but also the absentee road intervals and seago-
ing, his shows of affection but also the 'woman-hatred' (133) she
discerns in *Desolation Angels*, and the sadness and anger at the final
breakup. The brushstrokes range widely, contextual other loves,
other writers. The friendship with Elise Cowen ('my Crazy Jane',
58) whose doomed addiction to Ginsberg, stark imagist poetry
and 'dread of lovelessness' (77) she also memorialises, accrues any
amount of poignancy. Hettie Cohen, later Hettie Jones, early and
then lifelong friend, she characterises both for 'her unexpected
future' (213) in interracial marriage to LeRoi Jones ('the brilliance
and the fire in him', 215) and as a sister author with her boxes
of then unpublished sheaves. The canvas embraces Ginsberg ('All
his life, Allen had been familiar with madness', 76), Carl Solomon
('a large, alarmingly gentle man', 64), Neal Cassady ('A joy-riding
car thief, a yea-saying delinquent', 23), and visual art and music
names like Franz Klein, Jackson Pollock, Robert Frank and David
Amram. But, above all, in her refusal of being assigned to the Silent
Generation as it was labelled in 1951 and her talent and emotional
generosity, it is the Glassman/Johnson of the 1950s ('the sixties
were never quite my time', 261) who engages as quite among the
foremost in Beat articulacy.

Carolyn Cassady's twice-over accounts, written more than a
decade apart, meticulously fill out the evolving circumstance of
woman artist and wife-mother within the undoubted androcentrism
of the canonical Beat writers. Both *Heart Beat: My Life with Jack
& Neal* (1976), with its spin-off in which she becomes Marilyn in
the Nick Nolte/Sissy Spacek 1980 film, and its later rewriting as *Off
the Road: My Years with Cassady, Kerouac, and Ginsberg* (1990),
work as a fusion of biographies. Hers lies within that of her often
hyperventilating spouse, his within that of the durable, responsible
guardian of their three children, and that of Jack Kerouac within
their love triangle. A 1952 photograph reproduced in *Off the Road*
shows her in Neal Cassady's clasp but appearing to hold back, a
wary look of distance to his smiling exuberance. Her gloss aptly,
and cryptically, reads 'a rather typical illustration of our relation-
ship'. The note speaks volumes, the 'web' (10) of her experience
of Beat life-and-art to be reworked into procedural documentary
with its mixed report on their history. Yet throughout, and against

odds of largely single-parenting ('a lonely road', 260), desertion ('my suffering', 249), making-do ('It was up to me to find a way of survival', 321), she resists descent into victimhood ('There were lovely evenings, too', 196). She so manages to keep spirit with both the Denver fine arts graduate capable of a considerable portfolio of graphics, portraiture and costume design and the life writer in waiting.

Event borders on the operatic once the demure Carolyn Elizabeth Robinson finds herself drawn to the kinetic Cassady. If her hoped-for family partner, at his best actually solicitous and even the doting father, he also embodies the liar, erratic, serially unfaithful, perhaps incipiently bipolar. The mix, for Carolyn, was clearly a trial but also compelling. She finds herself obliged to share Cassady sexually not only with other women but Ginsberg and urged, not that unwillingly, to take Kerouac as a lover which serves her also as an act of reprisal. Neal's sex-addictive liaisons brim with drama: LuAnne Henderson, his sixteen-year-old ex-waitress wife who becomes Marylou in *On the Road*; Natalie Jackson, whose suicide in 1955 arises out of cheating Carolyn of cash to finance his horse-betting; Diana Hansen, whom he married bigamously in 1950; and Anne Murphy, companion of the later years (whose autobiography *Living with the Viper* remains unpublished) when he drove the Merry Pranksters bus under the baton of Ken Kesey and ingests LSD with Timothy Leary. Despite divorce in 1963, and the Cassady death in Mexico in 1968, Carolyn never remarries. Wistfully, whatever her reproaches, she can observe in a late interview 'There wouldn't be anybody to match Neal.'

Among its different claims *Off the Road* acts as Beat de-mythologisation. This is Kerouac for all his 'magic words' (197) in need of a home, Ginsberg playing with the Cassady children (243), Corso seen with 'a permanent scowl' (281). It remembers the Neal of his myriad highway drives, cross-country and into Mexico. But this is also the roustabout nursing the broken thumb from hitting LuAnne, frittering on the horses the $16,000 compensation for his broken foot when a brakeman on the Southern Pacific, cooking family pasta, and unglamorously serving time in San Quentin and elsewhere on marijuana charges. It also calls up their shared interest in Edgar Cayce as spiritual self-help occultist and Neal's struggle to write *The First Third*. The cumulative effect becomes one in which the popular image of Beat, whether the exaltation, the turn to the visionary, or the earthly road, sex and jazz escapades, take their course against Caroline Cassady's round-the-clock grounding and her own creativity in art as in family.

'My first wild man and my first drunk' reads one of Helen Weaver's formulations for Jack Kerouac in *The Awakener: A Memoir of Kerouac and the Fifties* (2009).[6] Her Buddhist-tinged title for the book gives praise but also tempering regret to the remembrance of her enraptured passion for him in the Village of the 1950s. She, like Kerouac's other paramours, gave far more than she received. 'He was so beautiful' (55) she says in one of several uncanny parallels with Joyce Johnson (to whom Kerouac decamps after one drunken spiral too many). But much as he was a cynosure for her, the object of her 'mad love' (80), the life she chronicles involves a full cast, a range of other drama.

Following her Scarsdale suburban upbringing and Oberlin College degree in English literature there is early same-sex romance with Lili Chan and the alliance with her Manhattan flatmate Helen Elliott ('The Helens' as they became known, 49). Kerouac has fellow-bidders for her affections in Gregory Corso ('a finer sort of Caliban', 74) and Lenny Bruce ('hipster priest' who 'gave us language for our age and alienation', 148) and whose 1964 trial for obscenity she helps protest. Beat friendships embrace Ginsberg ('Allen said they were all poets', 12), Lucien Carr ('witty, sarcastic, a brilliant talker, and a devout drinker', 54), and the Orlovsky brothers: Peter, also 'beautiful' but 'with the sad Russian face', and 'tall, silent' Lafcadio (12). Kerouac's fellow Canadian Frenchman, Henry Cru, cures her of a body rash with Epsom salts. She moves into yet other relationships, but, unlike Johnson, identifies 'with the hippies who were the natural heirs to the Beats' (104).

Much as Kerouac offers the lodestone, and whose epitaph on his Lowell gravestone she quotes approvingly ('He honored life', 178), she does not lose sight of her own strengths of creativity. Her literary prologue takes on momentum when mentored by the poet Richard Howard. Farrar, Straus becomes her employer, another overlap with Johnson, and as French translator she co-fashions with Susan Sontag the landmark *Antonin Artaud: Selected Writings* (1976), a figure of consequential Beat influence.[7] No less than fifty other translations issue from her desk. Her later years based in Woodstock, with its emblematic place in Beat history, see her campaign with Ginsberg to legalise marijuana, reconcile with Johnson (whose *Minor Characters* she lauds for its 'grace, wit, and an ironic edge', 109), move into astrology, and reflect upon herself as Dulouz's lover Ruth Heaper in *Desolation Angels*. History or fiction, Helen Weaver's presence within Beat is not to be doubted.

Looking back in *How I Became Hettie Jones* (1990) to the publication of *Yugen*, No 8, the last in the journal's series-run with cover-work by Franz Kline and containing Burroughs's 'The Cut up Method of Brion Gysin', the author ponders her billing as her 'Asst. Editor' in the name 'H. Cohen-Jones' (168). Well she might as she explores her life as inveterate Manhattanite, self-nominated 'Yankee Jew' (119), and partner to LeRoi Jones/Amiri Baraka in a celebrated cross-racial marriage and divorce in 1965. The move from Brooklyn and Laurelton in the Borough of Queens into the centrifuge of the West Village and 14th Street was short in distance but long in creativity. For the narrative gives a busy cast: Ginsberg, Kerouac, Ed and Helene Dorn, di Prima and Gil Sorrentino make up one literary column. Jazz affords Thelonious Monk ('master inventor' 34), John Coltrane ('a main attraction' at the Cedar Tavern in succession to Monk, 46), Sonny Rollins and Billie Holiday.

Inevitably, LeRoi Jones has his sway. 'I liked Roi too much to trifle with him' (32) she remembers on first meeting him. 'His quirky intelligence, his good humor, his stride' (41) disarms her. The frequent perception of them as 'blackman/whitewoman couple, that stereotype of lady and stud' (35), and the several street jeers at them and their children, hurts but is resisted by both. She charts his rise to fame, the launch with work like *Preface to a Twenty Volume Suicide Note* (1961), *Cuba Libre* (1961), *Blues People* (1963), *Dutchman* (1964) and *The Dead Lecturer* (1964), and therein the deepening call to the politics of what one of his best-known poems will call 'BLACK DADA NIHILISMUS'. She writes without recrimination of his abrupt departure for Harlem, the Black Arts Theatre and a new 'black' marriage. [8] The omni-activity of poetry, magazine editing, parties, bebop, liaisons, fellow-artist talk, the lesser drugs and drink, and homes often the way-stations for fellow artists she captures as a world of velocities. She alights on Beat exhalations with an especially keen eye ('To be beat you needed . . . a saintly disaffection', 46), with allusions to Kupferberg, Micheline, Ted Joans and A. B Spellman along with the Ginsberg, Kerouac and Corso cohort.

But this remains Hettie's story, her resolve amid the breakthroughs and tethers 'to find the person I was in the one I'd become' (194).

Pertinently she invokes her friend Rena Rosenquist, North Carolina wife to the Black Mountain/New York School poet Joel Oppenheimer. 'Becoming an artist's wife', she observes, 'hadn't stopped her either' (82). Like Joyce Johnson, another necessary ally, she relishes the Village in its pomp ('a young time, a wild, wide-open, hot time . . . I tried to get my share', 71), yet she also recognises prices paid. Her marriage to LeRoi Jones veers over a brief half-dozen years from intimacy and literary coupledom, and each hand-to-mouth financial challenge, into 'lies, infidelities, and other large and small betrayals' (166). In copyediting for *Partisan Review* and the editorial work for *Yugen* she gains witness to New York's intellectual ferment while hoarding her own writing.

If Black Power and Vietnam, the Malcolm X and Martin Luther King Jr. killings, fill the air, she also recognises how 'race', despite resistance, fatally adds its bruise to her life with Jones. She gives a touching salute to the support she receives from the Jones grandparents even as her own parents keep distance and as she virtually single-nurtures her daughters, Kellie and Lisa. That she finds ways to hold to her own centre ('LeRoi Jones has left his white wife' declares one column, 226) is born out in the launch of her children's books and the fuller authorship as poet which ensues. The gloss she gives *Big Star Fallin' Mama* (1974), one of her own favourite creations, bespeaks with a droll touch the fuller self to have emerged: 'this book was written by Hettie Jones, a relatively new person in America' (236). It confirms with an instinctive writer's poise the unknotting of author and wife-mother (and then ex-wife) who is both the Hettie Cohen and the Hettie Jones bound into 'H. Cohen-Jones'.

Dynasty

In *You'll Be Okay: My Life with Jack Kerouac* (2007), her posthumous memoir fondly reconstituted by its two editors, Edie Kerouac-Parker (born Frankie Edith Parker in 1922) writes a love-letter to her conjoined past with Kerouac ('All my wishes had been for him. He was the genius, the writer', 28).[9] Her account she tells in clear local detail, from affluent Grosse Pointe, Michigan girlhood to her eighteen-year-old New York wartime meeting and passion with Kerouac ('the exhilaration of being young', 117). She shares an apartment with Joan Vollmer Adams ('my closest girlfriend', 73). Lucien Carr hovers ('I was spellbound by him', 122). The very young Ginsberg 'seemed to have an intelligent tongue' (123). Of Burroughs she writes 'he was kind and soft-spoken like Lincoln' (125). Kerouac's merchant seaman intervals imposes waits and pauses in the relationship, but it burns for her like nothing other.

The culminating final sequence lies in the Carr–Kammerer murder, with Kerouac held as accessory ('All of our lives had changed', 173) in the Bronx jail, their City Hall wedding in August 1944, and the ensuing $500 bail from the Parker family trust. Cheerful forays into sailor-soldier Times Square, Broadway and the Village, and affinity with her new parents-in-law, Leo and Gabrielle Kerouac, and their daughter Caroline ('Nin'), however, does not halt drift between them. They file for annulment of the marriage in 1946. The story's backward glance from the Kerouac funeral in Lowell in 1969 to the no doubt emblematic entry of Neal Cassady into their lives (*'end of Edie's narrative'*, 255) supplies the frame, with an epilogue in the editors' update of Edie's life through to her death in 1993. She remains, devotion and script, integral to the Beat story.

For Joan Haverty Kerouac in *Nobody's Wife: The Smart Aleck and the King of the Beats* (2000), adulation comes lower in the scale. Her account offers more subtle self-query, a considered interplay of episodes. Kerouac, for his part, takes his place within a comparative chart of lovers, most notably the Columbia University physics graduate student Herb Lashinsky and the rumbustious mentor Bill Canastra, notoriously decapitated in a drunken subway stunt in 1950. Village marriage and loft life in Canastra's old home, despite better moments, the jazz and parties, increasingly grates ('To Jack I was a possession', 162). When, early in their liaison he asks what she is interested in, she replies 'Everything' (84). That has its accompanying expression in her seamstress skills, culinary flair shared with Gabrielle on moving into the Kerouac parents' home, and in her own writings which when read by Kerouac without permission she thinks a 'deep, traumatic sense of violation' (144).

She offers matching ripostes in their various gender discussions, marriage included, of which she observes to Kerouac, 'I don't know where you get the idea that it's my whole life' (143). Increasingly she refuses his demands to play listener 'to everything he had to say'(133) or 'the little wife' (174) as Cassady calls her and to whose 'giddy mannerisms' (175) she in turn calls attention. Finally comes refusal to perpetuate 'this disastrous marriage' (192). Pregnant with Jan Kerouac and refusing the abortion Kerouac asks for, she ends on a kindly farewell with Gabrielle and in the hope that her daughter-to-be will 'take the Kerouac legacy one step further' (211). Murmurs have been heard of bitterness, retribution. But *Nobody's Wife*, true to its title and Beat by association or otherwise, deserves better as her placard for shared independence.

'The Princess of the Beat Generation' was frequently to be heard as a nickname for Jan Kerouac.[10] It could flatter to deceive. Notoriously unacknowledged by her father (she met him twice and then briefly), hers was life lived a great deal less than royally. Both her semi-autobiographical novels, *Baby Driver: A Novel about Myself* (1981), the chronicle of poverty with her mother, Joan Haverty Kerouac, in Washington, DC, teenage miscarriage in Mexico, and the fractures of hippiedom, Haight-Ashbury, men and addiction, and *Trainsong* (1988), which continues the story into more drift and drugs and with Boulder a key stopping-off place, bespeak discernible talent, though it has to be said hardly genius. Her grandmother's no doubt innocent response in *Trainsong* 'A beatnik! Heavens to Betsy!' (121) in no small degree understates the case. As in William S. Burroughs Jr.'s novels of amphetamine and other drug use, *Speed* (1970) and *Kentucky Ham* (1973), she gives Beat filial legacy a bittersweet twist.

Trainsong, especially, records a history at once raw, itinerant across the Americas, Tangier and Europe, given to drink and narcotics, the occasional literary and Hollywood celebrity, but also jail-time and prostitution. Of her illustrious father she writes 'my memory of him is mostly visual' (6). She is fully capable of a sentence like 'locomotives clang past, deep into the jaw bone of Earth's heart, our hearth' (21). But she can at times edge towards the ordinary ('I barely missed becoming an alcoholic that summer', 19). Her different men – Bertrand, Bruce, Melvin, Malcolm – amount to on-off traffic, domestic war ground as much as redoubts of love or marriage. Geographies mount up, a bus fight in MacDougal Street, wanderings in Lima, cook's assistant in Seattle, or encounters with Nick Nolte and Sissy Spacek in Hollywood. Ken Kesey and LSD come her way in Boulder. She visits the Frankfurt Book Fair, Amsterdam and then Hamburg for readings. She remembers Richard Brautigan in California ('strange sweet fellow with so much unseen trauma inside', 155). She practises Buddhism and meditation at Naropa ('I needed direction', 136). Jan Kerouac's *Trainsong* gives voice to inveterate appetite, the peaks and lows, and yields its wholly distinctive addition as another story of woman's Beat.

En route

Few women's texts centred in Beat relationships bespeak a more precarious balance of self-surrender and yet emergence than Bonnie Bremser/Brenda Frazer's *Troia: Mexican Memoirs* (1969), republished in London as *For Love of Ray* (1971). 'All for love', in John Dryden's phrase, might wholly apply, a young woman's radiant willingness to take on the risks of court flight, travail in Mexico, even self-prostitution, to help her hypnotic but no doubt reprehensible husband-poet Ray Bremser escape sentence and jail for robbery. *Troia*, a term in Mexican Spanish meaning whore, yet also suggestive of some debased Helen of Troy, becomes the badge she wears almost with pride, her role in the wake of a middle-class upbringing of latter-day Beat-bohemian Eloise to his unlikely Abelard. Her body becomes literal currency, the price of love's ticket.

For inside their sadomasochistic pilgrimage she shares drugs, turns tricks, endures beatings and abandonments, panhandles for dollars, allows adoption of her daughter Rachel, and even writes pornography for Ray citing her own sale and use. In a style that consciously tracks Kerouac, and across geographies of Mexcity and Veracruz, Laredo and Fort Worth, and back to Manhattan, she juggles submission and dissociation ('I am somewhat ashamed at enjoying what I am paid for', 48). The upshot poses its challenges, one of complicit *troia* yet also proud sacrifice, object and yet her own subject. The account she arrives at offers unshaded truth to the terms of her own life, a disconcerting authenticity through to her return to Ray and their shared last needle. That one of the books she reads on her travels is Sade's *Juliette*, classic slave–master erotica, bears directly on her relationship with Ray. *Troia* troubles as a text on any number of gender grounds. But it also carries the merits of its powers of chronicle, Bremser/Frazer's wholly legitimate writer's writing.

Thinking back to working-class Catholic girlhood in Union City, New Jersey in *Tracking the Serpent: Journeys to Four Continents* (1997), Janine Pommy Vega recalls 'I had been reading Jack Kerouac's *On the Road*. All the characters seemed to move with an intensity that was missing in my life.'[11] Within a trice, and having upped from New Jersey for the Village with its Cedar Bar and literary round of Corso, Ginsberg, Kerouac and Peter Orlovsky, with whom she became romantically involved, she was quick to clamber aboard 'the bohemian life style' (3). That involved sharing apartments with

Elise Cowen, her affair with the artist, musician and heroin-dealer
Bill Heine, friendship with the Huncke who became her devoted
mentor, time in Hawai'i with Lenore Kandel, and the later years liv-
ing in Willow, New York, close to Woodstock. Her literary career
announces itself in *Poems for Fernando* (1968), poems of celebration
and mourning published by City Lights and written for her Jewish-
Peruvian painter spouse dead of a heroin overdose in Ibiza in 1965.
It extends to the Beat-spoken verse of *Mad Dogs of Trieste: New
& Selected Poems* (2000), notably recitative first-person poems like
'The Re-entry' and 'The Traveler', and to *The Green Piano* (2005), in
prison poems like 'Blind Numbers over the Hill'. Her P.E.N. writing
classes, conducted in penitentiaries from New York to San Quentin,
find a connecting and sardonic reflection in the jazz-text performance
composition 'Habeas Corpus Blues'.[12]

Janine Pommy Vega's *Tracking the Serpent* turns Beat's male-
iconic road trope to its own feminist and greatly imaginative
advantage. Here, there are grounds to believe, indeed lies Women's
Beat, pilgrimage under gynocentric flag and the quest to discern the
goddess-serpent creative principle of the world in both its deific and
pagan forms and as manifested through California, Celtic Britain
and Ireland, Andean Peru and Himalayan Nepal. 'The universe
loves devoted travelers' (10), she affirms while at the same time
tempering matters in the observation 'It wasn't the Mother I was
looking for, it was myself' (40).

Maui serves as Vega's beginning 'place of pilgrimage' (9). Britain's
Neolithic Cornwall bequeaths female deities. West of Ireland yields
'magic' (37), a plentitude of women creation and healer gods. Peru,
whose jungle Amazon she braves and explores by boat ('Only the
rivers were reliable highways', 69) and whose Peruvian moun-
tains of the Cordillera National Park she foot-treks as she explores
shamanism, yagé and the cults of La Señora and La Pachamama,
becomes a series of vitalist sites of self-transcendence. Nepal, with
its Himalayan mother statuary, fertility lingam–yoni emblems, and
Thorung La pass, blends into her own internal landscape ('I was part
of those mountains, and they were part of me', 184). Sexual encoun-
ters abound, her womanhood as both bodily and spiritual appetite
('A great sister spirit' Anne Waldman's obituary calls her).[13] These
she links inventively to trans-hemispheric mythic and sexual arche-
types of women. As much as a personal rite of passage, Pommy Vega's
circumstantial eye for terrain, cultural practice, belief system and

ritual mark out *Tracking the Serpent* as a Beat chronicle that is uniquely individual, uniquely crafted.

Diane di Prima: Nothing is foreign to me

No woman author more steadfastly holds centre-place in Beat than Diane di Prima, there at the starting-out 1950s with the verse of *This Kind of Bird Flies Backward* (1958), still there in her ninth decade with *The Poetry Deal* (2014).[14] The through-line could not have been busier. It involves both the multi-genre authorship in which Beat has been intrinsic and an adventurous pansexual life with motherhood of five offspring. Brooklyn Italian by birth, entranced by John Keats in her high school and student years at Swarthmore College where she majored in Greek, she took immediately to becoming writer-bohemian and arts-den figure in the Lower East Side of Manhattan. *Reflections of My Life as a Woman* (2001) calls to memory her career of poet, Ezra Pound correspondent, co-editor with LeRoi Jones of the newsletter *The Floating Bear*, dramatist and founder with her then husband Alan Marlowe of the Poets Theatre and Poets Press, friendships with Ferlinghetti, Ginsberg, Corso and Orlovsky, artist's nude model, libertarian and gender activist, and LSD proponent. Latterly her campaign instincts have turned against obesity shaming. Her work from the inaugural *This Kind of Bird Flies Backward* into the 1960s and beyond has always exhibited notably 'open' styles of voice. That holds whether the story-collage of domesticity and its boundaries in *Dinners and Nightmares* (1961), the bold lyric textures of love and death in *The New Handbook of Heaven* (1963), the Taos and Rio Grande topographies of 'New Mexico Poem' (1967) or *Earthsong: Poems, 1957–1959* (1968) with its ironic Beat-argot update of Christopher Marlow's 'The Passionate Shepherd to His Love' in 'The Passionate Hipster to his Chick'.

The Bay Area California that becomes her full-time residence from 1968 has seen little fall-away of appetite. Zen study with Shunryu Suzuki Roshi and then Tibetan Buddhism she regards as pivotal. Involvement with the community radicalism and street theatre of the Diggers leads to her sixty-three-part Beat-countercultural and anti-capitalist *Revolutionary Letters* (1971). With *Memoirs of a Beatnik* (1969) she writes Olympia Press sexual gymnastics yet actually soft porn discreetly mocked. In 1974 she

establishes Eidolon Press in Point Reyes with intervals teaching
at Naropa, New College of California, and Columbia College,
Chicago. Her one-woman shows of watercolours and collages run
from 2001 onwards. Each poetry collection confirms the unbroken
call to both human hope and critique, typically *The Calculus of
Variation* (1974), *Selected Poems, 1956–1976* (1977) and *Pieces of
a Song: Selected Poems* (1990). That in 2009 she can be appointed
San Francisco poet laureate pays deserved due. 'Poetry became the
guiding force in my life' (5) she affirms in *The Poetry Deal*, appro-
priately a publication in the City Lights laureate series.

Any number of her better-known poems act as a speaking-out,
whether city-smart, or coastal or religio-mythic and karmic in per-
spective. 'No Problem Party' bids almost to serve as Beat anthem. The
teasing repetitions of the laid-back 'no problem' (sex, arriving cops,
dope, wine and beer, Naropans, staying another day) and allusions
to Ginsberg's refrigerator, Waldman's cupboard and Kyger's peyote,
all picture Beat as alternative American revel reaching across 'Brook-
lyn streets', 'Chicano Texas' and the California of the *Berkeley Barb*.
'Wings of Speech' gives honour to Ginsberg, his bravery of stance
against authoritarianism. 'Brass Furnace Going Out: Song, After an
Abortion' gives sobering resonance to her gender politics of free choice
and anti-contraception ('forgive, forgive, that the cosmic waters do not
turn from me'). The elemental wolf-mythic poems begun with *Loba:
Part 1* (1973), and the sequence gathered in full in *Loba* (1998), likely
ranks as di Prima's most substantial work, the centring of 'femaleness'
in myth from Shiva, Isis and the Virgin Mary to modern lap-dancer
and working woman. The span is ambitious, 'multiple' in common
with the epics of Waldman and Kyger, even if for some readers too
unmediated by history. No cavil, however, detracts from di Prima's
contribution, Beat luminary and unyielding free spirit who in the title
poem 'The Poetry Deal' puts herself forward in the following terms:

> I stand before you: a piece of wind
> w/a notebook & pen
>
> which one of us is it dances?
> and which is the quasar? (21)

Poet and word, music and enlightenment, Diane di Prima here
speaks in characteristic counter-voice.

Joanne Kyger: I am elevating

Much as she disavowed Beat as affiliation, preferring to be thought more enfolded in the West Coast Renaissance of Robert Duncan and Jack Spicer, Joanne Kyger moved often enough inside Beat circles as did her one-time spouse, Gary Snyder (1960–65). But throughout her authorship she keeps tactical and even sly distance. Few of her writings, in fact, do not come over at oblique angle, full of lowered eye and with a Zen substrate. The signs begin in the dream-and-weave subversion of the Penelope myth in *The Tapestry and the Web* (1965) and persist through the sweeping career reflected in collections like *Going On: Selected Poems, 1958–1980* (1983), *Just Space: Poems, 1979–1989* (1991), *Again: Poems, 1989–2000* (2001), *As Ever: Selected Poems* (2002) and *About Now: Collected Poems* (2006). This considerable roll-call through to her death in 2018 has links redolent of Beat many times over even if, ineffaceably, it holds its ground as that of 'my own poet'.

'October 29, Wednesday', first published in *All This Every Day* (1973), reports a crowd milling around Ginsberg and Snyder even as clad in Tibetan bathrobe she experiences a seeming transcendental moment ('I AM ELEVATING! from a / cross legged position'). She teases their assumption of guru status, the fray around them applauding Beat celebrity, while herself attempting to get above it and also above Ted Berrigan's 'The trouble . . . with you Joanne, is that you're not intelligent enough'. The effect is of Beat under droll fellow-poet scrutiny while cannily including herself in some of the parade. 'Town Hall Reading with Beat Poets' in *Phenomenological* (1989) teases her own participation in the poetry-reading after Ed Sanders onstage phones Burroughs and she learns from the day-after *New York Times* review that she writes 'understated Buddhist influenced miniatures'. 'July 92 at Naropa', reprinted in *As Ever* in 2002, neatly undercuts Beat's male domain in lines like 'Allen Ginsberg has been busy / taking pictures for the last 30 minutes / of Amiri Baraka with the lens cap on his camera'. Her portraits of Beat-era poets, however, give respect as well as nudges, typically 'Philip Whalen's Hat' or 'Snapshot for Lew Welch 25 Years Later'. But, again, she equally and throughout holds firmly to her own centre as born out in 'Is This the Buddha?' (*All This Every Day*) when within the desideratum of egoless quietude she concludes 'Thank you. It's me'.

Two bodies of text especially give notice of Kyger as both connected to, and independent of, Beat. *The Japan and India Journals, 1960–64*, at once travel book, dream journal, photography and a meditation on 'the craft of poetry' does careful autobiographical duty. Life in Kyoto with Gary Snyder and spiritual disciplines at the Zen Institute spans to wider Japan, Ryoan-ji Temple to Osaka Castle and Japan's islands. India can be multi-faith, the culture of sutra and the Hindu pantheon but also street-wearying and excremental. A link to the overall account lies in 'Poison Oak for Allen' (*Again: Poems, 1989–2001*) where she offers another corner of the eye view of Beat male company. Addressing Ginsberg and based on her shared trip to the subcontinent she writes: 'Here I am reading about your trip to Indian again with Gary Snyder and Peter Orlovsky . . . Who took the picture of you three / With smart Himalayan backdrop. / The bear?' (102). If the *Journals* ponder whether a woman can indeed write epic she rallies herself in exhalations like 'I want to write the world upside down', 30) and '*Aim* for a whole new way of using language' (242). The proof, were it needed, lies in *The Tapestry and the Web*, her rewriting of Homer's Penelope and the conventional male gender focus of the *Odyssey*. Kyger's Penelope, to the contrary, bespeaks an adult sexual woman ('Refresh my thoughts again / Just HOW solitary was her wait?') and no passive connubial model. Subtle in its play of myth and dream it has been thought, for good reason, the mirror of Kyger weaving herself amid the male regimes of Beat and the San Francisco renaissance.

Performance Art, Art Performance

Anyone witnessing Anne Waldman in full incantatory flow, text in hand, shawls, silks, bangles and regalia, would have little difficulty identifying the author of 'Fast Speaking Woman', the title pattern-poem of her *Fast Speaking Woman and Other Chants* (1975), Number 33 in City Lights Pocket Poets, and expanded into the 20th Anniversary Edition of *Fast Speaking Woman: Chants and Essays* (1996).[15] Second or even third generation in relation to Beat, Waldman's provenance has been proverbial. Jazz and arts were intrinsic to her Greenwich Village upbringing. As Project Director of the St. Mark's Poetry Project in the Bowery from 1968 to 1978 she established a wide poetic circle. For Dylan's Rolling Thunder Revue in 1975–6 she became poet in residence. Having taken on the role of co-founder with Allen Ginsberg of the Jack Kerouac School of

Disembodied Poetics at the Naropa Institute in Boulder, Colorado in 1974, she has long been its keeper of the flame and archivist both as writer and peace and ecological activist.

Fierce performance reader though capable of lyric quiet as in her text-and-music CDs, her over fifty volumes and different editorships (to include *The Beat Book*, 1996 with both its standard and less familiar names) make for literary stockholding as expansive as any in the Beat or Beat-connected fold. To those who hear, as well as read her work, she wins repute as performance virtuosa from conference addresses to slam, panel appearances to recordings, often to the accompaniment of musicians like her son Ambrose Bye. Waldman's favoured self-namings as Outrider and, borrowing from medieval Occitan female poets, as Troubairitz, give bearings, as does her commitment to Buddhism.[16] Her credo has long been 'investigative poetics', the bid for liberationist poetry 'adequate to . . . the historical present, while aiding the future' as memorably formulated by Ed Sanders in 'Investigative Poetry: The Content of History Will Be Poetry' (1978). From first collections like *On the Wing* (1968), *O My Life!* (1969) and *Giant Night* (1970), through her co-editorship with Lewis Warsh of the journal *Angel Hair* begun in 1966, to compendia like *Helping the Dreamer: New and Selected Poems, 1966–1988* (1989), *Vow to Poetry, Essays, Interviews & Manifestos* (2001), *The Room of Never Grieve: New and Selected Poems, 1985–2003* (2003), and the monumental *Iovis* trilogy (1993, 1997, 2011), she has made her 'vow to poetry' that of shamanism, tantrism, a deep inwardness with female myth and lineage, and always the notion of poetry as much life as literary transaction with the reader-listener.[17] Beat-Buddhist implications clearly come into play, the belief in being available to all experience, the accompanying open prosody.

Waldman's ending to 'Fast Speaking Woman' ('I'm the woman who dreams / I'M THE ARTIST INSIDE HER MAGIC HOUSE', 34) allies the poem's iteration of plural first-person womanhood ('I'm a shouting woman / I'm a speech woman . . . / I'm a flesh woman', 3) with incarnational woman myths to embrace Hinduism's deity Kali, Buddhism's goddess of mercy Kwannon and Mexico's *curandera* Maria Sabina. The upshot is Beat-feminist litany, the 'magic house' of female creative principle. The same intensity threads through her writing: symptomatically in *Marriage: A Sentence* (2000) with its *haibun* interweave of historic and mythic human conjunctions; *Structure of the World Compared to a Bubble*

(2004) centred in Java's holy stupa of Borobudur and indicative of her commitment to Buddhism; and *Red Noir & Other Pieces for Performance* (2007) or 'libretti' as she calls them with shadows of Noh and Kabuki. The *Iovis* triad, a quarter-century in the making, serves as summa, at once Virgilian yet modernist/postmodern epic which Waldman has said bids to restore 'she' in its full creative diversity to the overwhelmingly male energy of historical world-making. Waldman remains bracingly investigative, a compositional force of nature and underlined in self-reflexive odes to creativity like 'Verses for the New Amazing Grace', 'Kill or Cure' and 'Born Again Blues'. She embodies Beat continuance yet always in terms of her own greater amplitude.

'Jazz-poet-performer' – Waldman's sisterly cover endorsement of ruth weiss's *Desert Journal* (1977, reprinted 2011), her best-known work, is a fair synopsis.[18] It would be right to add avant-garde filmmaker of *The Brink* (1961), based on her improvisational San Francisco panorama-poem of the same name, playwright, actor, screenwriter, distributor of poem-prints, and longstanding jazz and poetry name. Berlin born, raised in Jewish Vienna, Holocaust escapee, her flight to New York in 1939 eventuates in 1952 in full-time berth inside North Beach bohemia after education in Harlem and Chicago and sojourns in New Orleans ('it was in NEW ORLEANS that the repartee between my voice & the riffs of bebop reached a deeper dimension', she writes in *Desert Journal*, 205). Under the mantle of *ruth weiss* (always lowercase as an anti-institutional gesture against German's capitalization of nouns and in respect for the memory of Hitler's state murder of Jews), she has assumed the mantle of Beat-style performance poet. A mainstay not only in the West Coast literary constellation of Rexroth, Ferlinghetti, Micheline, Kaufman and Madeline Gleason, but also of the jazz of The Cellar, she has featured in venues and festivals well beyond. The life-pull into literature and the arts finds inaugural publication in the limited-edition poetry chapbook *Steps* (1958) and the elegant tribute volume to female predecessors *A Gallery of Women* (1959), with a reprise of her poems in *A New View of the Matter* (1999). Into her nineties, there has been no let-up.

Can't Stop the Beat: The Life and Words of a Beat Poet (2011), with its playful titling, offers assemblage, a quartet of long-form poetic life-diaries with accompanying photography.[19] 'Ten Ten'

(1990), the number of her first apartment in North Beach, gives remembrance to her newcomer's perception of the San Francisco of Broadway, Coit Tower, Kearny and the enlivening truth that 'ONE MORE STEP WEST IS THE SEA' (4). 'I Always Thought You Black' (1993), eighteen prose-poetry segments ranging from Vienna to North Beach, pays dues to black musical culture, late-1950s hang-outs like the Co-Existence Bagel Shop, and literary and art friendships (Kaufman 'never beaten, black & a jew', 48, and Edward Brooks, Vietnam and California landscape photographer, 'you are the light', 72). 'Post-card 1995' invokes Mexico as iconic Beat destination ('BOB KAUFMAN wanted to die in MEXICO / and so did JACK KEROUAC', 96). 'Compass' (1958), however, steps back into time, the spontaneous journal notes of her car trip in 1958–9 with her first husband, Mel Weitsman, and dog Zimzum into the Mexico of *campo* and 'mexico the city' (152), keen of eye, a poem-documentary.

With *Desert Journal*, written 1961 to 1968 but to await publication a decade later, weiss finds her best fulcrum, the reflexive map of the creative mind's weaves and descants. 'The internal desert' she calls it, emphasising 'her need to explore that place' while having 'never been to an actual desert' (207). The forty-day sequence, its numbering the echo of Moses and the Israelite exodus, Jesus in the Judaean wilderness, and the 'Ali Baba and the Forty Thieves' story, offers associational canvas, a refusal of fixed syntax, rules of linguistic and narrative order. Rather, as the Thirty-First Day declares:

> the city of oneself
> crawls over the desert
> looking for solid ground (152)

This modernist impulse, perhaps unsurprisingly, draws from influences to embrace Gertrude Stein, T. S Eliot, Tristan Tzara and Charlie Parker. The eschewing of any one pre-emptive narrative, actual or scriptural, for weiss has to be the guideline:

> without a plot
> the story has a chance
> make it
> on its own (123)

In one of the poem's several voices she speaks, indicatively, and as though through a Buddhist lens, of 'the illusion of substance' (189), the requirement that experience be met on open terms unfettered by ideology. Her wordplay, riffs, implanted quotations, page layouts, and the spatial graphics by her partner, Paul Blake, give added expression to registering the creative mind which 'holds all possibles' (29). 'The way is always open / in the desert' declaims the Fifth Day (29). Beat's jazz-poetry can rarely have managed more vivid calls to the awakening of consciousness.

Postscript: Elise Cowen and the Mind for Border

'I'll find the cat who's got my / tongue' (31) prefaces the second sequence in Elise Cowen's *Poems and Fragments* (2014).[20] That 'tongue' now has posthumous reality, elliptical, fine-hewn short poems rescued from title-less pencilled worksheets none of which saw publication in her lifetime. Cowen's fame hitherto has been as a Beat-circle Jewish friend to Joan Volmer, Joyce Johnson, Janine Pommy Vega, Herbert Huncke and Leo Skir, besotted lover of Ginsberg whose 'Kaddish' she typed, and Bellevue psychiatric patient and totemic suicide, flinging herself from her parents' apartment window in 1962. Poem upon poem, however, points up the writer, at times self-lost but fortunately also self-won as imagist doyenne. 'There should be a new / word for every new sight / unstringing of words' (99) she writes in 'I can't understand who/what I am'. 'Who will close my eyes / when / In death / They see' (98), she asks in 'Who will slap'. 'Two weeks of the month / I'm half mad & half free' (109) runs one of her important confessional gems. The elisions recall the Emily Dickinson she admired and wrote about startlingly in 'Emily white witch of Amherst' (60). 'No love' likely serves as epitaph, a farewell list-poem to parents and friends from within Beat. 'Let me out now please — / — Please let me in' (116), the couplet with which it closes, assuredly again resembles Dickinson, even the dashes. But the torque of life and death as it arises from within Beat and its circles remains poignantly Elise Cowen's own.

Written, Written-in, Unwritten

A wealth of further Beat or Beat-related women's texts assume place in the tapestry. Lenore Kandel, North Beach regular, one-time

partner to the poet Lew Welsh and Hell's Angel Billie Fritsch, and
1960s hippie queen, writes a poet's 'holy erotica' in *The Love Book*
(1966). In this counterweight to the homocentrism of 'Howl',
she allies anatomy of hetero-coupling and the sexual body with
ecstatic spirituality. Mary Fabilli, poet and illustrator, Dominican
sister, curator of the Oakland Museum, and once married to Wil-
liam Everson, creates a quiet Catholic-spiritual analogy to Beat
and its dramas of consciousness in her two *Aurora Bligh* collec-
tions (1966, 1968) and other verse. Mary Norbert Körte, ex-nun,
found herself spurred to poetry after attending the Berkeley Poetry
Conference in 1965. Long the eco-poet with a base close to the
California redwoods her considerable output includes the mem-
orable poem attaching one-time religious vocation with Beat in
'Eddie Mae the Cook Dreamed Sister Mary Ran Off with Allen
Ginsberg' (1988). Joanna McClure depicts her Arizona origins,
journeyings, and haiku and ecology interests in *Wolf's Eyes* (1974)
and in the retrospect of *Catching Light: Collected Poems* (2013).
Elaine Kaufman's 'Laughter Sounds Orange at Night' retells her
meeting with Bob Kaufman, his poetry and street revels and their
shared countercultural life. Elizabeth Von Vogt in *681 Lexington
Avenue: A Beat Education in New York City, 1948–1954* (2008)
offers the remembrance of her immediate post-war coming-of-age
in the Manhattan Beat ambit of her brother John Clellon Holmes
and the Kerouac circle.

Women based on life and then refigured in fiction or verse
refigured from life notably feature in both Kerouac and Ginsberg:
for example, Mary Caney transposes into the heroine of *Maggie
Cassidy*, and Carolyn Cassady becomes Camille in *On the Road*.
Others include Elise Cowen as Barbara Lipp in *Desolation Angels*,
Diana Hansen as Diane in *Visions of Cody*, Natalie Jackson as
Rosie Buchanan in the *The Dharma Bums*, and, cross-racially,
Alene Lee as Mardou Fox in *The Subterraneans* and Esperanza
Villanueva as the beauteous Mexican prostitute-drug addict
in *Tristessa*. In Ginsberg's case his mother Naomi has her sear-
ing reincarnation in the revelations of 'Kaddish'. Self-unwritten
but of major import to Beat history would be Mémère Gabrielle
Kerouac, Joan Vollmer Adams, the activist Helen Hinckle and the
Corso family women. Beat's women into Women's Beat not only
co-genders Beat, as does each LGBTQ text, it marks the altogether
larger rewriting of Beat's history.

Notes

1. Diane di Prima, *Recollections of My Life as a Woman: The New York Years*, New York: Penguin Books, 2001, 26–7.
2. Cited in Ian Dreiblatt, 'Joanne Kyger (1934–2017); "Crawl on Your Sorrowful Hands"', Melville House Digital, 24 March 2017.
3. Anne Waldman, 'Fast Speaking Woman II', *Fast Speaking Woman: Chants and Essays*, 20th Anniversary Edition, Pocket Poets 33, San Francisco: City Lights Books, 1996.
4. Ann Douglas, 'Strange Lives, Chosen Lives: The Beat Art of Joyce Johnson', in Joyce Johnson, *Minor Characters: A Young Woman's Coming-of-Age in the Beat Orbit of Jack Kerouac*, New York: Penguin Books, 1999, xiv. The italicisation of 'masculinize' is mine. Subsequent page references are to this edition of *Minor Characters*. The text was originally published as *Minor Characters*, Boston, MA: Houghton Mifflin, 1983.
5. Johnson, *Minor Characters*, 92.
6. Helen Weaver, *The Awakener: A Memoir of Kerouac and the Fifties*, San Francisco: City Lights Books, 2009, 103.
7. *Antonin Artaud: Selected Writings*, intro. Susan Sontag, trans. Helen Weaver, New York: Farrar, Straus and Giroux, 1976. .
8. LeRoi Jones, 'BLACK DADA NIHILISMUS', *The Dead Lecturer*, New York: Grove Press, 1964, 61.
9. Edie Kerouac-Parker, *You'll Be Okay: My Life with Jack Kerouac*, ed. Timothy Moran and Bill Morgan, San Francisco: City Lights Books, 2007.
10. She cites the soubriquet herself in *Trainsong*, New York: Henry Holt & Company, 1988, 132.
11. Janine Pommy Vega, *Tracking the Serpent: Journeys to Four Continents*, San Francisco: City Lights Books, 1997, 2.
12. A reading of 'Habeas Corpus Blues', with guitar accompaniment and given at the Gershwin Hotel, New York, in March 2008 two years before her death, is available as a video directed by Laki Vazakas.
13. Anne Waldman, 'Janine Pommy Vega 1942–2010 – A Remembrance', *The Poetry Project*, 23 December 2010.
14. Diane di Prima, *This Kind of Bird Flies Backward*, New York: Totem Press, 1958. *The Poetry Deal*, Poet Laureate Series Number 5, San Francisco: City Lights Foundation, 2014.
15. Anne Waldman, *Fast Speaking Woman*, San Francisco: City Lights Books, 1985; *Fast Speaking Woman*, 20th Anniversary Edition, San Francisco: City Lights Books, 1996.
16. Anne Waldman, *Outrider*, Albuquerque: La Alameda Press, 2006. 'The OUTRIDER holds the promise of imaginative consciousness. The OUTRIDER rides the edge . . .' 185. *Troubairitz*, Atlanta: Fifth Planet Press, 1993.

17. See Anne Waldman and Lewis Warsh (eds), *Angel Hair Sleeps with a Boy in My Head: The Angel Hair Anthology*, New York: Granary Books, 2001.
18. ruth weiss, *Desert Journal*, Boston, MA: Good Gay Poets, 1977. New Orleans: Trembling Pillow Press, 2012, 205. All references are to this edition.
19. ruth weiss, *Can't Stop the Beat: The Life and Words of a Beat Poet*, Studio City: Divine Arts, 2011.
20. Elise Cowen, *Poems and Fragments*, ed. Tony Trigilio, Boise: Ahsahta Press, 2014.

CHAPTER 7

Afro-Beat

Baraka had joined the Beat Generation because he regarded its members as spiritual outsiders who were against white middle-class America. Yet over the years he became disillusioned . . . Baraka wanted an alternative to bohemianism.

William J. Harris, *Preface*, *The LeRoi Jones/Amiri Baraka Reader* (1991)[1]

How and where can I start talking of Ted, who taught me that a poet's job was not just to write good poems out of life but to 'live a poem-life?' . . . Although he was considered one of the three black Beats along with LeRoi Jones (Amiri Baraka) & Bob Kaufman, he is the least known.

Yuko Otomo, *Let's Get TEDucated! Tribute to Ted Joans* (2005)[2]

Recognised early as a major figure of the Beat Generation of writers and Poets . . . [Kaufman was a]premier jazz poet, and a major poet of the black consciousness movement.

David Henderson, Introduction, Bob Kaufman, *Cranial Guitar* (1996)[3]

Blues, Black, Grace, Race (*Mexico City Blues*)

Jazz, juke, rock and roll. Cool, bebop, jive. Parker, Monk, Coltrane. Can the African American seams in Beat writing, etymologies and music ever be doubted? But if Kerouac, especially, admired and borrowed from African American music, that leaves the question of black authorship itself. A wholly consequential body of Beat verse and other texts by black writers invites recognition, reaching from Greenwich Village to North Beach and with Dixie and Harlem inextricably woven into the heritage. In LeRoi Jones/Amiri Baraka, Ted Joans and Bob Kaufman are to be met three pre-eminent spirits, each quite distinct the one from the other yet literary kin in their creation of Afro-Beat and its expression. If they have cross-figured in white 'New Bohemia' both East and West Coast, and helped texture Beat poetics, then from the 1950s onward they take their place fully and of necessity in the politics of articulating black redress. Jones/Baraka would move into increasing militancy, while Joans and Kaufman, albeit no less conscious of race and its politics, stayed more with Black Arts literary calls to awareness and protest.[4]

LeRoi Jones/Amiri Baraka: A country in black & white

LeRoi Jones, the name as he spelled it (originally Everett LeRoy Jones) before Islamisation to Amiri Baraka in 1965, was actually only ever halfway drawn to Beat and then during the phase usually dated as 1958–62.[5] Newark-raised, briefly a student at Rutgers (1951) and Howard University (1952–4) and US Airforce gunner based in Puerto Rico where he was discharged for reading Lenin and Trotsky and supposed communist beliefs, he had made his move to Greenwich Village in 1957. 'New Bohemia' beckoned for sure to the burgeoning poet, dramatist and music journalist, Manhattan's Lower East Side of poets, performance, jazz, its networks of tavern, bar, cellar, club and cheap-rent apartment.

Literally the Village could be University Place, Cooper Square, MacDougal, Bleecker and Tenth Street, and the West Village's Christopher Street and Sheridan Square. But the buzz, the creative fermentation, had its yet more active gathering-places in the Gaslight, Jazz on the Wagon, Limelight, Club Bohemia and, notably, the Cedar Cavern. The Bowery's Five Spot Café supplied a frequent further venue. Where better, daily, nightly, and whether one to one or in cohorts, to encounter Ginsberg, Kerouac, di Prima, Corso, O'Hara, Joans, Kupferberg, or the painter circle of Pollock, Willem and Elaine de Kooning, Klein and Rothko? The Off-Off Broadway theatre of Julian Beck and Judith Malina (under the name The Living Theatre) functioned as yet another creative hub as did the Cherry Lane Theatre which staged Jones/Baraka's Obie Award-winning play *Dutchman* in 1964. *The Village Voice* served as newsletter, with Norman Mailer among its founders in 1955, James Baldwin

an essayist, Nat Hentoff on jazz, and Jones/Baraka both frequent
contributor and subject.[6]

Jones, as then was, plunged in as to the manner born. Here lay
working coteries for his life as poet, essayist, reviewer, line-writer
of jazz records, editor of the magazines *Yugen* and *Kulchur* and
co-editor with di Prima of *The Floating Bear* as well as his work
with Corinth and Totem Press. Here, too, was talk, affairs, serious
exchange but also drink and roistering, marriage to Hettie Cohen
in 1958 and fatherhood of their two daughters with another child
from his affair with di Prima. Jones/Baraka lore has long recog-
nised the augmenting fame that came with his anti-Cold War essay
'Cuba Libre' (1961), the musicology of *Blues People: Negro Music
in White America* (1963) and *Black Music* (1967), and the cir-
cling black-subterranean play *Dutchman*, set in the bowels of the
New York City subway. Disenchantment with Beat and the Village
famously led on to his move to Harlem and the founding of the
Black Arts Repertory before his return to Newark, remarriage to
the Sylvia Robinson who becomes Amina Baraka, and university
appointments at SUNY, San Francisco State and other campuses.

Black politics, he saw with increasing conviction through the
1960s, required move-on from white liberal-progressive reform
(and with it Beat dissent) into clenched-fist activism. For Jones,
soon to be Baraka, the reprise led to his role in the Pan-African
Congress in Atlanta in 1970 and the National Black Political Con-
vention in Gary, Indiana, in 1972. His agitprop broadsides and
community protest, the court cases, even the brief jailings at the
same time caused no slow-down in his rates of authorship. *The
Autobiography of LeRoi Jones* (1984) gives a vivid account of his
transition through Black Cultural Nationalism and the Black Arts
Movement as influenced by the Kawaida philosophy of Maulana
Karenga (typically 'BLACK DADA NIHILISIMUS' in *The Dead
Lecturer*, 1967) with its exorcising 'murders we intend / against his
lost white children') into, by the early 1970s, Marxism and Third
World liberation politics.

This cited writer-activist life, whether poetry, theatre work,
fiction or discursive writing and speech-making, extends unflag-
gingly from the one century to the next. Out of the 1960s arise
consequential verse like *Black Magic: Poetry 1961–1967* (1969),
In Our Terribleness (1970), subtitled *Some Elements and Meaning
in Black Style*, and fashioned in collaboration with the Chicago

photographer Billy Abernathy (known as Fundi), and *The Slave* (1964), his one-act 'marriage' play of ancestral black–white conflict. *The System of Dante's Hell* (1965) fuses and re-fables the underworlds of the *Divine Comedy* and contemporary America. *Home: Social Essays* (1966) delivers 'weights and measures' as he calls them in his dedication, 'Cuba Libre' not least, but also 'City of Harlem' ('Harlem is the capital of Black America') and 'The Myth of a "Negro Literature"' ('a legitimate product of the Negro's experience in America . . . must get at that experience in exactly the terms America has proposed for it, in its most ruthless identity').[7]

Each yet further work marks his evolving stance, be it the neo-Marxism enunciated in *Hard Facts* (1975) and *Daggers and Javelins: Essays, 1974–1979* (1984), the eulogistic *Book of the Monk* (2005), or the experimental storytelling of *Tales of the Out & Gone* (2006). The *Reader* edited by William Harris in 1991 supplies a helpful mosaic, with in its train the posthumous Grove Press compendium *S.O.S: Poems, 1961–2013* (2016). Jones/Baraka entered the new century to no greater controversial effect than in his excoriating 9/11 poem 'Somebody Blew Up America' (2002), with its Palestinian sympathy and anti-Zionism, and which led to his removal as New Jersey poet laureate in 2003. In this wider perspective and quite prodigious output across the genres, Beat inevitably can seem a long way behind. It would be wrong, however, to think it deserves to get overlooked or somehow even erased from the overall body of Baraka's creative and political history.

The *Autobiography* especially avails as point of entry into Baraka's early Beat affiliation:

I'd come into the Village *looking*, trying to 'check,' being open to all flags. Allen Ginsberg's *Howl* was the first thing to open my nose, as opposed to, say, instructions I was given, directions, guidance. I dug *Howl* myself, in fact many of the people I'd known at the time warned me off it and thought the whole Beat phenomenon a passing fad of little relevance . . . I took up with the Beats because that's what I saw taking off and flying somewhat resembling myself. The open and implied rebellion – of form and content. Aesthetic as well as social and political . . . I could see the young white boys and girls in their pronouncements of disillusion with and 'removal' from society as being related to the black experience . . . Yet as wild as some of my colleagues and as cool as I usually was, the connection could be made because I was black and that made me, as Wright's novel asserted, an *outsider*. (To some extent, even inside those 'outsider' circles.)[8]

Clearly the liaison with Beat was made in provisional good faith, enthusiastically yet with caution and a number of cavils. The appeal lay in the overlap of what in later interview he indicts as 'the whole reactionary period of the 50s' with the countering open-field literary forms he advocates in his anti-New Critical contribution to the *Statements on Poetics* in Donald Allen's *The New American Poetry, 1945–1960* (1960). There he offers as credo 'MY POETRY is anything I think I am' ('Can I be light & weightless as a sail? Heavy & clunking like 8 black boots').[9] In other words, under Beat's awnings, creative and social (though as yet not black nationalist) dissidence entwine, quite the colluding parts.

No collection better serves Jones/Baraka's overrun with Beat than *Preface to a Twenty Volume Suicide Note* (1961). For all the allusions to his own quest for existential as well as creative bearings and to blackness and jazz, the near-thirty pieces recognisably echo the Beat playbook. 'Notes for a Speech' debates his own midways position, black amid not just white but 'mother Africa' other black culture:

> Africa
> is a foreign place. You are
> as any other sad man here
> american. (47)

Across the poems the poet, or his persona, names the contending imaginative forces he finds himself called upon to negotiate, whether T. S. Eliot as classical model to be overthrown and Rimbaud and Baudelaire as countervailing forces, or Coltrane and Nat King Cole as musicianship to be honoured as much as that of others in the classical tradition he names like Tchaikovsky, Prokofiev, Ravel and Debussy.

Beat reference can be explicit. Poems like 'One Night Stand' with its carnivalesque vision of black presence in the cities ('We entered the city at noon . . . odd shoes, bags of books & chicken', 21–2) is dedicated to Ginsberg. 'In Memory of Radio', with its search for usable self-identity in popular-culture figures like Lamont Cranston as The Shadow, carries the line 'Who has ever stopped to think of the divinity of Lamont Cranston? / (Only Jack Kerouac, that I know of: & me', 12). 'Way Out West', with its *flâneur* run of queries and Zen-influenced self-contemplation ('I am distressed. Thinking / of the seasons, how they pass', 24–5), has Snyder as dedicatee. 'The Bridge' (25–6), with its affirmation of the blackness of blues and jazz ('that music you know', 26), is 'for wieners & mcclure'. 'For Hettie in Her Fifth Month' adapts William Carlos Williams's iconic modernist poem 'The Red Wheel Barrow' to a quasi-surreal vision of still-in-the-womb Jones–Cohen first child ('A slit in the flesh / & one of Kafka's hipsters / parked there / with a wheelbarrow', 14). 'Symphony Sid' pays tribute to the jazz and bebop disc-jockeyed over the radio by Sid Torin, at once both healing and sex music ('A man, a woman / shaking the night apart', 36).

Acclaim increasingly would accrue to Baraka's writings overall but not without acknowledgement of those from his Beat phase. 'Hymn for Lanie Poo', his satiric-fantastical portrait of his sister Sandra Elaine's bourgeois habits, takes flight from the Rimbaud epigraph *Vous êtes de faux nègres*. Yet for all his send-up of her too ostentatious coming-out party and her race deference ('doesn't like to teach in Newark / because there are too many colored / in her classes', 11) he can doubt his own indecisive pivot as black artist ('Sometimes I think I oughta chuck / the whole business', 8). 'Look for You Yesterday, Here You Come Today' has the poet-speaker searching for touchstones in Federico García Lorca, Charles Baudelaire or Frank O'Hara, or a hero of the screen Western like Tom Mix ('dead in a Boston Nightclub', 16), or comic-strip figures like the Lone Ranger, Dickie Dare and Superman. 'My Captain Midnight decoder', the speaker discloses, has been lost (17). Superman, all powerful, has become unfathomable (17). The 'suicide' of youngster-time popular culture pathways, and the call of far older African American legacy, is to be heard in the final couplets:

> My silver bullets all gone
> My black mask trampled in the dust
>
> & Tonto way off in the hills
> moaning like Bessie Smith (18)

'Notes for a Speech' speaks of America as 'A Country / in black &
white' and of Jones/Baraka's need to negotiate better of existence in
matters of race and power in America. Time, clearly, had come for
him to move on from Beat.

Ted Joans: Black Jazz Smile

Tag-phrases of his own making, playful and/or sharp-edged, were
long a forte for Ted Joans. Blackness, black consciousness, quite
evidently was the first and necessary reference-point. In his poem
'Africa' (1970), reprinted like most of his work in *Teducation*
(1999), he writes 'Africa I guard your memory / Africa you are in
me'.[10] In 'A Few Blue Words to the Wise' (1969) he lays out his call
to and for black voice:

> We must fall in love and glorify our beautiful black nation.
> We create black images   give the world
>   a black education. (1)

'Passed on Blues: Homage to a Poet' (1969), his eulogy to Langston
Hughes as mentor and Harlem modernist of 'round midnight' jazz,
tenement and the creation in his story fiction of the Jesse B. Simple
everyman, ends in the chant 'BLACK DUES! BLACK BLUES!
BLACK NEWS!' (67). Activist and arts heroes likewise embody
the black figures that Joans admires most, whether it is Malcolm X
in 'My Aces of Spades' ('Malcolm X freed me and frightened you',
59) or the graffiti artist Jean-Michel Basquiat in 'The Ladder of
Basquiat' ('a Black Positive Power', 85).

Joans's salutes to Afro-America and Africa, the legacies of style,
music, history, talk, erotica, and even, on a number of occasions,
food (he was a committed vegetarian and teetotaller), thus could be
teasing and fond, full of live intimacy. But they leave no doubt of
how powerfully he also chooses to slap down colour-line bullying
and hate. Had not his father, a Mississippi riverboat entertainer,
been killed in a racist outbreak in Detroit in 1943? His indictments
run through pattern poems like 'The Nice Colored Man' (1972)
with its deafening paradigm of the word 'nigger' (89–90). 'Uh
Huh' as vernacular Afro-Beat sound poem takes on segregation in
the trope of the history and human cost implied in the label 'THE
COLORED WAITING ROOM' (107). 'God Blame America!'
might be a flyting, a cascade against white racial phobia ('America /

I do not want to be integrated with you').[11] Terse shorter poems
come often into play in kind with 'NO MO' KNEEGROW' ('I'M
FLYING OVER ALABAMA WITH BLACK POWER IN MY
LAP').[12] 'Hand-grenades' Joans calls them.[13]

Among the best known of Joans's other mottos, frequently spoken
and written by him, has to be 'Jazz is my religion, and Surrealism my
point of view'.[14] Not only is the first phrase several times repeated
in the poem 'Jazz Is My Religion' but augmented as 'a unique musi-
cal religion', 'a weapon to battle our blues!', and 'my religion but it
can be your religion too' (49). 'Jazz Is . . .', dedicated to Cecil Taylor
for his free jazz forte as pianist-composer, emphasises the music's
co-optive power ('black sound / leaps / or glides / into the ear', 48).
'The Black Jazz Smile' captures the glory and yet with it the sadness
borne by jazz. Its carefully open-spaced lines conclude:

> When he   the blackman smiles in jazz
> look for the sadness   in his eyes (82)

A jazz trumpeter himself it was Joans, who on the death in 1955
of his one-time roommate Charley Parker, inscribed the legend
'BIRD LIVES' on Lower Manhattan walls and streets and created
a canvas with the same title that hangs in San Francisco's De Young
Museum. 'Him the Bird' (167) also deploys the line, together with
accompanying celebration ('Those solos he took on borrowed
alto / Sax gave everybody their jazz-as-religious thrills'). The god
implication lies also in the line 'his earth name was CHARLES
PARKER'. Jazz at large, and jazz virtuosi, constitute the very wrap
of Joans's life. 'Jazz Anatomy' metamorphoses jazz into the male
body, head as trumpet, heart as drums, ears as clarinets, penis as
violin, and more, culminating blues-like in 'my soul is where the
music lies' (170).

Surrealism had drawn him first to Salvador Dalí but whom he
came to think put money before art. Overwhelmingly, however,
André Breton stirred his reverence, discipleship which had him
make his way in 1960 and subsequently to Breton's home at 42
rue Fontaine, Paris. 'Nadja Rendezvous' gives one measure of his
dedication. But Joans's poetry positively revels in Surrealist flare,
dream-sequences, contrarieties of image, and patterns of exotic ani-
mal reference that include the rhinoceros ('Sanctified Rhino', 72–3),
the aardvark ('Aardvark Paw', 119–21) as well as the okapi, tapir,
pangolin, echidna and platypus. 'Jazz Me Surreally Do' (173) nicely

ties both affiliations into one. 'Jazz wisdom' can be thought 'the image of an aeroplane', its propeller 'oxtail stew for aardvarks', if a biplane then its wings 'all B-flat minor', the windshield 'saxophone reeds', and the hangar 'made of sweet potato fried pies' (193). Jazz and surrealism, arts of ear and eye, sew together, indicative of Joans's verve.

Beat lies within, and alongside, all these several affiliations. Looking back to his Greenwich Village years where he arrived in 1951 and quickly took up with Ginsberg, Jones/Baraka, Kerouac and others, he is explicit. In 'Je Me Vois (I See Myself)', published in 1996, he writes 'I am the early Black Beat' and, trailing Ginsberg's 'Howl', 'I too have known the best Beat names of my generation'.[15] In this regard are also to be reckoned his cafe and club readings, salon birthday parties, Rent-a-Beatnik capers, and, with a BFA degree from Indiana University behind him, his many surreal collages and canvases. Even the international travel, which saw him resident for long stretches in the Europe of Paris and London, in Tangier, and in Mali's Timbuktu and other Africa, took on a Beat aspect, a species of black Kerouac-ism. The run of his books, by title if nothing else, gives register to these different affiliations: *Beat Poems* (1957), *All of Ted Joans and No More: Poems and Collages* (1960), *The Hipsters* (1961), *Black Pow Wow: Jazz Poems* (1969) and *Afrodisia: Old and New Poems* (1970, reissued 1976).[16] These, in their wealth of variety, all lie behind *Teducation: Selected Poems, 1949–1999* (1999) with its tribute to a half-century's output.

Beat's presence in Joans's writing again can readily invoke 'The Wild Spirit of Kicks' (97). It offers a captivating epitaph to Kerouac's death and not only on account of warmth of friendship but shared jazz listening and club visits ('J.K. says hello to J.C./John Coltrane that is!'). The poem's remembrance gives shrewd notation of Kerouac for his Beat figurehead standing ('In the midst of Black hipsters and musicians / Followed by a White legion of cool kick seekers') and an arresting road image for his legend ('Running across the country like a razor blade gone mad'). This Kerouac, now 'at rest', wholly actual yet mythic ('well-worn dungarees and droopy sweater of smiles') so becomes in memory the 'Pale-faced chieftain tearing past'. Joans deftly manages the double effect, unfeigned affection for Kerouac and matching Beat inscription.

'The Sermon' (93–6), written in 1955 and not without whiffs of the time's chauvinism, lays out yet more expressly how Joans envisions Afro-Beat. Addressed as it were to some white sister, it gives his 'hip' recipe for how to forgo 'antique anglo-saxon / puritanical philosophy'. Sexual liberation, with hipsters usually bearded, should involve diaphragm or condom and not mean being caught in adultery. Working orders are to 'SIT DOWN and LISTEN TO JAZZ', Jelly Roll Morton as one musician of many. Required reading summons Ginsberg's poetry and *On the Road*, Mailer's controversial 1957 essay 'The White Negro', Corso's 'Marriage', Whitman and Poe, full immersion in Dada and Surrealist literature, and the *Village Voice* and *Mad Magazine*. SQUARES (in the poem's capitals), like greedy landlords, are to be avoided. Bible, Koran, Torah and Zen all come into the reckoning, as should good schooling if only to use against miscomprehending parental generations. The ground-rule becomes 'You should love your life out and live by loving / every minute of it'. In setting forth these desiderata, Joans may well have his tongue firmly in cheek, to include the word inversions. The poem is given over to being 'cool' and at the same time, reflexively, its own 'cool', Joans's own unique signifying of Beat.

'Afrique Accidentale', a mainstay poem in *Afrodisia*, not only gives focus to Joans's insider experience of the African continent but redresses the use of Timbuktu in English and French as a species of joke nowhere.[17] Mali, rather, the tough sub-Sahara road and ferry voyaging to get there, its complex tribal histories, a holding-centre of scholarship, spiritual belief and mask and other art forms, is to be given counter-status to his own version of America ('I count African rhinos not American sheep'). The Niger river, he stresses, parallels the Mississippi. Mali women display cousinship to those of Harlem. Joans takes care not to sentimentalise: the threats range from ants, snakes and crocodiles to dysentery and malaria. Timbuktu, nonetheless, stirs love and imagination in him, an Africa of real-time arrival and real place. At quite the same time 'Afrique Accidentale' bespeaks Beat in referencing and argot:

> Greenwich village is a long way off, with its coldwater
>   flat & sink
> I have traveled a long way on the Beat bread I made
> now I'm deep in the heart of Africa, the only Afroamerican
>   spade . . .
> Timbuctu, Timbouctou
> I finally made you
> Timbuctoo
> Yeah!! (8)

To be sure Joans's poetry, whether blues or rap or fantasy, derives
impetus from black experience, black speech and, perhaps above
all, black music. But a poem like 'The Truth', which opens *Black
Pow-Wow*, clearly incorporates Beat as further resource:

> if you should see
> a man
> walking down a crowded street
> talking aloud to himself
> don't run
> in the opposite direction
> but run towards him
> for he is a POET!
> you have NOTHING to fear
> from the poet
> but the TRUTH[18]

Given the linking configurations of blackness, jazz, Surrealism, art,
play and voyage within Joans's work, Beat is not to be denied its full
place at the table. 'The Truth', symptomatically and with appropri-
ate spoken cadence as it were, invites just that recognition of his
contribution to Beat.

Bob Kaufman: African Jazz in Alabama Jungles

The often startling figure, both life and verse, Bob Kaufman has
attracted few epitaphs closer to the mark than that written by his
fellow San Francisco poet A. D. Winans. His 'Poem for Bob Kauf-
man' remembers with admiration the acuity of Kaufman's street
and coffeehouse jazz poetry, the commitment to Zen, and the fierce
morality of the stance against war, the atomic bomb or capital
punishment. This was not to deny, implicitly, recognition of the
affrays, drug and drink episodes, jail (he was reckoned to have
been arrested over thirty times), and lapses that led to Kaufman's
death of emphysema and cirrhosis in 1986. Winans gives vivid
memorialisation to both poet and poetry:

> he walked the streets of North Beach
> an ancient warrior with hollow eye sockets . . .
> his life measured in hot jazz and verse . . .
> poems blaring in his ears[19]

Kaufman's New Orleans birth to his Catholic Martinique mother and father of German Jewish background may or not have been wholly true to the case. Likely there was some invention of a persona. But, if mixed heritage, it left Kaufman in no doubt of his own cultural blackness even as he sought an identity that went beyond racial or ethnic category and indeed in later years tried to cultivate anonymity. He would be raised on the Lower East Side, spend several years in the US Merchant Marine with discharge in 1947, and become a committed Union activist and speaker who was eventually victimised by McCarthyist blacklisting. His dips back and forth into the Manhattan of Ginsberg and Burroughs led on from the mid-1960s onward to settling as a full-time presence in San Francisco's North Beach bohemia and the literary orbit of City Lights.

His poetry took form from inside an eclectic body of autodidactic and jail-time reading (Lorca, especially, Hart Crane and Langston Hughes), his then-rare interracial marriage to Elaine Kaufman in 1958, the Buddhism that led him as a gesture of despair and revolt to a ten-year vow of silence on the assassination of John F. Kennedy in 1963, and always the abiding call of jazz.[20] On many occasions his extemporised compositions were collected and written up by others. The answer that Duke Ellington gave when asked about dissonance in his musical scores likely holds for Kaufman's writing: it is a quality that reflects the nature of black lives in America.

The straddling of East and West Coast finds important expression in Kaufman's journal *Beatitude*, with Ginsberg in the editorial line-up, and which runs for a half-century through thirty-five issues starting in 1959. Its editorial banner proclaimed 'a weekly miscellany of poetry and other jazz to extol beauty and promote the beatific or poetic life'. His own poetry, across the three principal collections, *Solitudes Crowded with Loneliness* (1965), *Golden Sardine* (1967) and *The Ancient Rain: Poems, 1956–1978* (1981), with a recapitulation in *Cranial Guitar: Selected Poems by Bob Kaufman* (1996), lays frequent claim to the beatific, while at the same time often both accusingly dark or given to surreal flight and wordplay.[21] He maintains a hope for human benignity despite every descent into barbarism (notably for him the Japanese atomic bombings) or into the absurd.

Something of both comes over in 'Benediction' (1965) in *Solitudes*, its opening line a reference-back to Moses as Jewish liberator while at the same time a figure conjured from black spiritual or the blues ('went down to Egypt land / To let somebody's people go').²² In giving their tally on immediate post-war America the ensuing images interlay ironic exoneration ('America, I forgive you') with a charge-sheet of serial misconduct ('Nailing black Jesus to an imported cross', 'Burning Japanese babies defensively', 'Cars, televisions, sickness, death dreams'). The further kick lies in the elliptical last lines, America and its Dream seen to be lurching into default, even having become posthumous:

> You must have been great
> Alive. (9)

Solitudes, as his first collection, typifies Kaufman's poetics. Jazz offers both measure and reference but does so in confluence with Beat. 'Walking Parker Home' (5), in this respect, might be a Parker saxophone fugue ('Sweet beats of jazz impaled on slivers of wind'), a 'Blues Times' invoking Coleman Hawkins and Lester Young, and at the same time vintage Beat performance. The poem creates a series of counterpoints in imagery and line-rhythm ('Historical sound picture on New Bird wings' or 'pyramids of notes spontaneously exploding'). 'Dayrooms of junk' bring rot, pain, but are seen to do so in equal part with 'money cancer'. Cure, or at least hope, lies in the 'Jazz corner of life' out of which Parker's music bequeaths 'raging fires of Love'. Through this 'walking home' of Parker's genius (for whom he would name his son), his soaring harmonic flights and riffs, the poem acts out the conjunction of spoken jazz and written Beat.

Other Beat-jazz compositions work in shared vein. 'Blues Note' (20), centred in the piano and song of Ray Charles ('the black wind of Kilimanjaro') embodies 'Screaming up-and-down blues'. An 'African symphony' is said to be 'hidden in his throat. He sings from 'Bessie's crushed skull'. 'Raw soul' emanates from his playing as he leads the blues 'into the Promised Land'. A 'dangerous man' says the poem yet 'I love him' says the poem's speaker. Cannot Charles, the sway of his music, be heard in the poem's own versification? 'Jazz *Te Deum* for Inhaling at Mexican Bonfires' (32–3) creates a jazz-like summons to human creativity over alienation or death, the life of imagination itself imagined as Beat incantation. 'Let us write', 'Let us poeticize', 'Let us compose', act as opening injunctions, their follow-through an exuberance of creation: 'reeling sagas', 'twelve-tone prints of Schoenberg', 'Teutonic folksongs'. Each further call adds to the litany, 'solar boats' and 'forbidden Sanskrit', 'illegal requiems' and 'circumcision Jossanas'. The point of arrival lies in 'smoke-flavored jazz' and Kaufman's presiding Beat-jazz touchstone:

> Let us blow African jazz in Alabama jungles and wail
> savage lovesongs of unchained fire. (33)

Explicit Beat makes its own entrance. 'Ginsberg (for Allen)' (23) exhibits much of Kaufman's flair for the discordant trope, the striking quasi-surreal phrase ('Ginsberg won't stop tossing lions to the martyrs'). This is the Ginsberg who 'continues to smoke carnal knowledge', 'was Gertrude Stein's medicine chest', and who 'wears rings and hoops of longitude and latitude'. So transfigured, he wins the accolade 'I love him because his eyes leak'. No poem, however, more explicitly enlists Kaufman in the Beat agenda than 'West Coast Sounds – 1956' (11) and right from its opening couplet ('San Fran, hipster land, / Jazz sounds, wig sounds'). Thumbnail sketches project a miniature Beat assembly, whether Ginsberg 'giving poetry to squares', Corso 'on knees, pleading', Rexroth and Ferlinghetti 'swinging', Kerouac 'writing Neil', or Neil, in turn, 'booting a choochoo / On zig-zag tracks'. As 'New York cats' and 'San Franers' they have become too packed together, a mere in-crowd, and better served by getting back on the road or across the US–Mexico border south of the 'closing' John Steinbeck canneries in Monterey. Kaufman offers a droll, and wholly apt, ending:

> Sardines splitting
> For Mexico.
> Me too.

None of this is to sidestep how his poetry addresses personal fault-lines, depletion, life managed precariously at the margins of addiction, psychiatric shock treatment or jail-time. 'I Have Folded My Sorrows' offers a line like 'Blues have come like introspective echoes of a journey' (3). 'Would You Wear My Eyes?' draws from subsistence lodging in 'My body is a torn mattress . . . The whole of me / Is an unfurnished room' (40). The extended soliloquy of 'Jail Poems' (56–62) movingly, though not self-pityingly, bespeaks both his own and wider incarceration. The thirty-four verses loop from self-taunt ('I am apprehensive about my future; / My past has turned its back on me' to self-reflexivity ('I sit here writing, not daring to stop / For fear of seeing what's outside my head'). Literal imprisonment ('The jail, a huge hollow metal tube' or 'Wino in Cell 3') transposes into wider life-vision. Kaufman's question-and-answer irony gives the parameters: 'In a universe of cells – who is not in jail? Jailers'.

Golden Sardine, No. 21 in City Light's Pocket Books, and *The Ancient Rain* contain their quotient of poems addressed to this degree of setback or loss. But neither collection forgoes its Beat-jazz fashioning. A run of poems in *Golden Sardine* like 'Tequila Jazz' (40), 'His Horn' (43), 'Blue O'Clock' (49) and the Mingus-inspired 'Round about Midnight' seek to capture both the spiritual meaning of jazz and to emulate its very sound. The untitled opening poem (3–6), a jazz dream-fantasy on the trial of Caryl Chessman as the 'Red Light Bandit' and his gas-chamber execution in San Quentin prison in 1960 after nearly twelve years on death row, fiercely excoriates the supposed evidence in the case and its result in capital punishment. Poems like 'On' serialises the human cost of an America distracted by consumer kitsch, Hollywood image and 'static events'. In 'Night Sung Sailor's Prayer' (69–70) he veers close to Ginsberg's 'Footnote to Howl' in seeking redemption for America's 'born losers, decaying in sorry jails' (69). Beat sanctification, or Kaufman's version of the Beatitudes, is to prevail ('All that lives is Holy, / The unholiest, most holy of all', 70).

A shared compassion is evident throughout *The Ancient Rain*. Few of Kaufman's poems thread together Beat, jazz and spirituality with greater bravura than 'War Memoir: Jazz, Don't Listen to It at Your Own Risk'.[23] Jazz, which he also dubs 'secret jazz', assumes form as though an animate being in the face of human destructive power. The poem takes its bearings in the contrast of the music's 'sound of life' with the 'stereophonic screams' of Hiroshima. A humour, close to scorn, come into play in the seeming throwaway observation '"Just Jazz, blowing its top again"'. Jazz, for Kaufman as for Joans, harbours balm, the reminder of aliveness ('living sound') amid the 'blood-soaked garments' of war, pillage, infanticide and rape:

> We hear a familiar sound
> Jazz, scratching, digging, bluing, swinging jazz.
> And we listen
> And we feel
> And live. (33)

Too easily unheard, or thought mere pastime, jazz on this kind of hearing has the power to conduct its listener beyond willed cruelty or pain. Once again, in confirmation, Beat-jazz as measure holds the poetry in place.

Beyond the poetry, Kaufman in Beat persona inescapably has to take in his Abomunist compositions. Published as City Lights broadsides, and as an epilogue to *Solitudes* (77-88), they target society's shibboleths, its self-approval and deference to the one or another 'ism'. The upshot is loop upon loop of Beat-voiced 'rejectionary philosophy' (80), an anarchist compendium delivered with wit and considerable legerdemain. ABOMUNIST MANIFESTO, capitalised throughout and ostensibly under the authorship of one 'Bomkauf', sets the point of departure ('ABOMUNISTS JOIN NOTHING BUT THEIR HANDS OR LEGS . . .'). The penultimate entry offers textual mock-commentary worthy of Alfred Jarry or Artaud:

> ABOMUNIST POETS, CONFIDENT THAT THE NEW LITERARY
> FORM 'FOOTPRINTISM' HAS FREED THE ARTIST OF
> OUTMODED RESTRICTIONS, SUCH AS: THE ABILITY
> TO READ
> AND WRITE, OR THE DESIRE TO COMMUNICATE . . .
> (78)

Each further sequence adds its quota, verse-prose full of back-to-front maxims. NOTES DIS- AND RE-GARDING ABO-MUNISM offers 'Abomunists think . . ."If I were a crime, I'd want to be committed"' (79). The ABOMUNIST ELECTION MANI-FESTO, likely in a veiled allusion to drugs, reports 'Abomunists demand suppression of illegal milk traffic' (81). ABOMNEWSCAST, a compilation of headlines each typically edged in the absurd ('Cubans seize Cuba', 'UN sees encouraging signs in small war policy'), ends with a last-stop vision of atomic destruction ('when you see one small mushroom cloud and three small ones, it is not a drill, turn the TV off and get under it', 87). These Dada-like compositions can be compared with Carl Solomon's *Mishaps* or the song-poems of Tuli Kupferberg. Beat counter-stance may not cover all bases. But as becomes clear in Billy Woodberry's indie screen documentary of Kaufman, *When I Die, I Won't Stay Dead* (2015), it comes close.

Conductor and Chorus

Afro-Beat, of necessity, is a term of approximation for Jones/Baraka, Joans and Kaufman. Each has sailed under related other flags. But Beat has its unmistakable featuring in their authorship, both perspective and idiom. They also have fellow practitioners in A. B. Spellman (the early poetry of *The Beautiful Days*, 1965) and the jazz portraiture of *Four Lives in the Bebop Business* (1966), and in the poet and composer-saxophonist Archie Shepp. Yet others can lay claim to a degree of Beat signature, including Jayne Cortez in *Pisstained Stairs and the Monkey Man's Wares* (1969), Nathaniel Mackey's *Four for Trane* (1978) and Lorenzo Thomas's *The Bathers* (1981). The gathered weight of these writings presses doubly: to confirm the vitality of black creative presence within Beat and to take Beat authorship well beyond any single ring fence.

Notes

1. William J. Harris (ed.), *The LeRoi Jones/Amiri Baraka Reader*, New York: Thunder's Mouth Press, 1991, xxii.
2. Yuko Otomo, *Arteidiola*, Online platform, June 2005.
3. Bob Kaufman, *Cranial Guitar*, Minneapolis: Coffee House Press, 1996, 7.
4. My previous interpretations of Afro-Beat can be found in A. Robert Lee, 'Black Beats: The Signifying Poetry of LeRoi Jones/Amiri Baraka, Ted Joans and Bob Kaufman', in A. Robert Lee (ed.), *The Beat Generation Writers*, London: Pluto Press, 1996, 158–77, revised and reprinted in A. Robert Lee, *Designs of Blackness: Mappings in the Literature and Culture of Afro-America*, London: Pluto Press, 1998, 133–51; 'Black Beat: Performing Ted Joans', Jennie Skerl (ed.), *Reconstructing the*

Beats, New York: Palgrave Macmillan, 2004, 117–32; 'LeRoi Jones/ Amiri Baraka', in Kurt Hammer (ed.), *Encyclopedia of Beat Literature*, New York: Facts on File, 2007, 9–11; 'Tongues Untied: Beat Ethnicities, Beat Multiculture', in Sharin N. Elkholy (ed.), *The Philosophy of the Beats*, Lexington: University Press of Kentucky, 2012, 97–114; and 'The Beats and Race', in Steven Belletto (ed.), *The Cambridge Companion to the Beats*, 2017, 193–208.

5. The dates 1958–62 are those given in *The LeRoi Jones/Amiri Baraka Reader*.

6. Notable is *The Village Voice*'s obituary 'Amiri Baraka: The Village Voice Years' by Anna Merlan for 3 January 2014. She cites the *Washington Post* on Baraka as 'radical', 'polarizing', as a writer who more than almost all others extended 'the political debates of the civil rights era to the world of the arts'.

7. *Home: Social Essays*, New York: William Morrow, 1966. 'City of Harlem', 87; 'The Myth of a "Negro Literature"', 113.

8. LeRoi Jones/Amiri Baraka, *The Autobiography of LeRoi Jones/Amiri Baraka*, New York: Freundlich Books, 1984, 156–7.

9. Debra L. Edwards, 'LeRoi Jones in the East Village', in Arthur and Kit Knight (eds), *The Beat Vision: A Primary Sourcebook*, New York: Paragon House, 1987, 131. Donald M. Allen (ed.), *The New American Poetry, 1945–1960*, New York: Grove Press, 1960, 424.

10. *Teduction: Selected Poems, 1949–1999*, Minneapolis: Coffee House Press, 1999, 2. All page references, unless specified, are to this edition

11. 'God Blame America!', *Afrodisia: New Poems by Ted Joans*, New York: Hill & Wang, 1970, 79.

12. 'NO MO' KNEEGROW', *Black Pow-Wow: Jazz Poems*, New York: Hill & Wang, 1969, 26.

13. The phrase is used as subheading for the first part of *Teduction: Selected Poems, 1949–1999*.

14. The motto, among other places, appeared on posters and book casings on display at the Shakespeare and Company bookstore in Paris.

15. Ted Joans, 'Je Me Vois (I See Myself)', in Shelley Andrews (ed.), *Contemporary Authors Autobiography Series*, vol. 25, Detroit: Gale, 1996, 227, 242.

16. Ted Joans, *Jazz Poems*, New York: Rhino Press, 1959; *All of Ted Joans and No More*, New York: Excelsior, 1961; *The Hipsters*, New York: Corinth, 1961; *Black Pow-Wow, Jazz Poems*, 1969; and *Afrodisia*.

17. 'Afrique Accidentale', *Afrodisia*, 4–8.

18. 'The Truth', *Black Pow-Wow*, 1.

19. A. D. Winans, 'Poem for Bob Kaufman', *American Poetry Review*, 21 (May–June, 1990), 19–20.

20. Kaufman, in this respect, is one of the poets studied in T. J. Anderson III's meticulously informed *Notes to Make the Sound Come Right: Four Innovators of Jazz Poetry*, Fayetteville: University of Arkansas Press, 2004.

21. Bob Kaufman, *Solitudes Crowded with Loneliness*, New York: New Directions, 1965; *Golden Sardine*, San Francisco: City Lights Books, 1967; *The Ancient Rain: Poems, 1956–1978*, New York: New Directions, 1981; and *Cranial Guitar: Selected Poems by Bob Kaufman*, Minneapolis: Coffee House Press, 1996.

22. 'Benediction', *Solitudes Crowded with Loneliness*, 9.

23. 'War Memoir: Jazz, Don't Listen to It at Your Own Risk', *The Ancient Rain*, 32–3.

CHAPTER 8

Inter-Beat. Post-Beat.

The Beats were a community driven by three main motors. One of them was Allen Ginsberg himself and what some people called 'Allen Ginsberg Industries' ... The second, chronologically, was City Lights Bookshop as a literary meeting place and as a publisher... The third motor is the Naropa Institute's Kerouac School of Disembodied Poetics.

Lawrence Ferlinghetti, Interview, 1999[1]

we are the post beat poets ...

hip & classless
very primitive 20th Century
very well informed
we all have our specialities
our meanings
our personal styles
our beliefs
always changing &always the same
        we all have our time & our time has come

Steve Dalachinsky, 'Post – Beat – Poets
(We Are Credo #2)', 2008[2]

Legacy

Beat cultural impact, both of in its own time and as legacy, inevitably redounds to the names who first set its terms of reference: Kerouac, Ginsberg, Burroughs. Interviewed in 2012, Joyce Johnson speaks of Kerouac's undiminishing power:

I think it's a legacy of terrific, extraordinarily beautiful prose. I think that's the part of [Kerouac] that's going to last. His work is so alive on the page, it just quivers with life. It's so full of music and mood changes. It's like he's in the room with you. He has an immediacy that a lot of other writing doesn't have.[3]

The British poet Michael Horowitz in an obituary for Ginsberg in 1997 remembers generosity, a profound sense of poetic debt:

He leaves behind hundreds, maybe thousands, of poets who are his spiritual children, but no heir apparent. A poet of such embrace and expansiveness comes along once in a lifetime. I'm grateful it was during mine.[4]

Patti Smith, looking back in 2010, attributes to Burroughs the gift of writing text as revelation: 'He's like another kind of Bible.'[5]

These each remain Beat's trinity inscribed as plaque or headstone. With the publication of their voluminous journals it also has become clearer that the resolve of Beat's founding generation to forge a new worldview, a radical change of idiom, did not come about by serendipity.[6] Work and dedication, along with assiduous mutual support, were always involved. Subsequent critical literature, biographies, reprints, library author holdings, websites, and college syllabi – despite the frequent misgivings of the cultural Right at inclusion of Beat texts – all aid and abet. But if the best-known writing persists, there has been growing recognition of both within-its-time other Beat voice and considerable lines of Beat succession. Inter-Beat verse can mean Bob Dylan, Andy Clausen or David Meltzer, inter-Beat fiction Richard Brautigan, Lawrence Ferlinghetti or Jan Kerouac. Post-Beat verse holds for names like Steve Dalachinsky, Charles Plymell, Edith Dame or A. D. Winans, post-Beat fiction for Maxine Hong Kingston, Toby Litt, Larry Closs or Ali Eskandarian. Given these circuits John Tytell, writing in 1976, offers what looks to have been an understatement of some considerable proportion:

Once the Beats were a few Lears raging in the storm, obscured by the vastness of the system. Their transformation of literary form and the informing power of what they had to say aroused mounting interest.[7]

Whether or not the Lear image quite does the trick, that interest has indeed persisted and grown and in sometimes unexpected directions both within America and in international reach.

Beat Inter-texts: Poetry

En route to the broadly post-Beat tiers of poetry and fiction reside a number of overlapping inter-texts, Beat in spirit but not always recognised as such. A striking instance would be Bob Dylan's *Tarantula*, drafted in 1964–5 and published in 1971, and at times almost Joycean in its wordplay and run-ons.[8] 'Like the beats before him, [Dylan] liberated culture from academia's ivory tower' opines the Publisher's Note to a 1994 reprint.[9] The implication is that, beyond the monumental songwriting, *Tarantula*, too, belongs alongside if not inside the Dylan 'musical' repertoire. Favouring accounts see something of the conscious fragmentation of Burroughs's *Naked Lunch*, the whimsy of Corso's 'Yak' and 'Marriage' poems, or the nonsense-verse of Lennon's *In His Own Write* (1964). Counteropinion, it has equally to be said, suggests word-glut, closed circuits. It can, however, get overlooked that Dylan himself believed he had written poems, prose poems as may be, but indeed of a shared style with the collage of his longer ballads.

Essentially, the book offers stream-of-consciousness panels, Dada or Beat-surreal associative picturing. Aretha Franklin assumes a recurrent place of reference for Dylan, her blues and scat a pointer to the improvisational nature of the text at large. Letters enter the fray, each under invented moniker ('Toby Celery', 'Hector Schmector' and the like). The impact is one of free-association diary, dream, pop culture, the faux obituary for 'Bob Dylan', girlfriends and friendships, household paraphernalia, slithers of Spanish, Vietnam, and an intermittent cast from Lyndon Johnson to Mae West, Buddy Holly to Lee Marvin. A Beat broadcast precursor like Lord Buckley (one of his creations the beatnik Go Man Van Gogh) makes a bow, as does Sherlock Holmes. Reflexive turns enter about reading and writing ('you could start with a telephone book – / wonder woman – or perhaps catcher in / the rye – they're all the same & everybody / has their hat on backwards thru the / stories', 71). The phrasings themselves twist and shout ('the dada weatherman gets mailed to Monaco', 'a sheriff in the machinery', 'are you still in the keyhole business?'). Section titles like *Cowboy Angel Blues* or *Sacred Cracked Voice & the Jingle Jangle Morning* edge the collection towards a blend of music and Beat co-text. *Tarantula* may or not wholly qualify as fully paid-up Beat, but it runs close, a literary companion in spirit.

If populist Beat can be said to have a champion among its prime
contenders, it has to be Andy Clausen on the evidence of *40th
Century Man: Selected Verse, 1996–1966* (1997). 'Bardic populism'
is Ginsberg's useful abridgement in his endorsement. The reverse
timescale, the 1990s to the 1960s, might have risked gimmickry,
the sophomoric. But Clausen pulls off an attractive feat, a working-
class America charted from the reverse end of the telescope. As to
his allegiances, a poem like 'These Are the Ones' (1968) leaves little
to doubt:

> These are the people, Ma Joad's people, the blues
>   singer's people . . .
> These are the ones computer society will leave behind
> These are Blake's Sunflowers
> Guthrie's One Big Soul
> These are the people I love. (165)

Steinbeck, Blake, Guthrie. It would be hard not to enlist also Ginsberg
or Kerouac.

Clausen's Beat connection is made explicit in 'The Night I Heard
Kerouac Died' (1969), set in Thlinket country, an Alaskan bar, with
a drink raised to the deceased luminary ('Here's to reading *On the
Road* again / at my 9PM lunch', 159). The speaker thinks Lester
Young and Charlie Parker, imagines Desolation Angels who 'pass
through' (160), and give the toast of 'Timber' meaning not only
tree-felling but drinks-on-me in local parlance. The affection could
not be more palpable. 'Seeking a Fool Proof Riff' (1972) again
invokes jazz and Beat, among others Eric Dolphy and Bob Kauf-
man ('some notes I can call on & won't be failed', 136). Another
pairing is even more familiar, first Shig Murao of City Lights then
'Allen and Peter at Shig's / giving advice to forget bitterness /
towards the poetry powers, temper me' (137). 'Be-Bop=Attitude',
from 1974, looks to Beat-jazz wellbeing, a 'medicine' and 'music to
literally move people . . . a grace / hip to the other side of the moon'
(130). Beat, as jazz, for Clausen fuses with his politics, forces for
liberation of society and spirit even if the title poem '40th Century
Man', written in 1994, reminds that America still has its ongoing
lost highways.

David Meltzer's *Beat Thing* (2004) brings to bear the author-
ity of a career (1937–2016) lived amid the interactive stir of the

San Francisco Renaissance (he moved full-time to the city in 1959 from Los Angeles), the jazz-and-poetry movement and, if putatively, Beat. His inclusion in Donald Allen's *The New American Poetry, 1945–1960* laid down a marker for his deserved reputation as craftsman from *Ragas* (1957) to *When I Was a Poet* (2011). Collections like *No Eyes: Lester Young* (2000) give idiom to his jazz knowledge and guitar playing, as does *David's Copy* (2005) and the edited anthology *The Secret Garden* (1976, reprinted 1998) to his assiduous kabbalah scholarship. The range hardly stops there, whether co-editorship with Ferlinghetti and McClure of *Journal for the Protection of All Beings* (1961–78), the novels begun with *The Agency Trilogy* (1968), the essays on poetics of *Two Way Mirror: A Poetry Notebook* (1977), edited collections like *Reading Jazz* (1996) and *Writing Jazz* (1999), or the interviews in *San Francisco Beat: Talking with the Poets* from City Lights in 2001. There has also to be added his poet's voice in successive jazz-rock recordings from *Serpent Power* (1968) to *Two Tone* (2016). Meltzer's repertoire evidently takes him outside as well as inside Beat. But there can be little doubt his mark also belongs there.

With *Beat Thing* Meltzer does epic service, a World War II to 1960s Beat verse anatomy set diligently in both American and international historical context. Mock-titled from Howard Hawkes and John Carpenter classic horror movies, the three parts meld into a whole as comprehensive as seamlessly playful and serious.[10] Popular culture allusion, jazz, cinema, TV, sports and politics all make for the density of the overall text. 'The Beat Thing Looms Up' conjures up Beat's birth, Kerouac and Ginsberg as heading the Hall of Fame, fanship, food, drugs and passage into nostalgia ('beat's dead, 'nuff said / it's rotting in the tool shed with Dada / & Mamma bear despair *surrealisme*', 20–2). 'Beat Thing: Commentary' remembers Hitlerism, Shoah and its denials ('the holocaust but an invention of Jewish-controlled media', 70), and the anti-Semitism and colour-line racism implicit in McCarthyism and the fearful 1950s, even as the jazz of Parker and Monk or the stand-up riffs of Lenny Bruce proclaimed free creativity. 'Primo Po-Mo' insists that whatever the postmodern turn ('Uncertainty becomes a sure thing', 85–6), history's blight, and especially its Jewish catastrophe, for Meltzer remains centre and certain. 'History is the story of writing' (154) runs the concluding sentence, the perfect aphorism for a poem as articulate and wide-ranging as *Beat Thing*.

Beat Inter-Texts: Fiction

On the Road and *Naked Lunch* may well retain their pre-eminence as Beat prose narratives. A near-perverse due is paid them by texts far from usually thought Beat, notably John Updike's *Run Rabbit* (1960) as ironic un-Kerouac riposte to *On the Road* and with its main character Harry 'Rabbit' Angstrom's beleaguered flight from and then back into suburbia. But other shelves of story from within the inaugural years, Beat in inflection whether by design or not, also require due. These might start with Ferlinghetti's *Her*, composed in the 1950s during his Paris years and issued in 1960, and which for all of its imagist dexterity bears its implicit Beat hallmark. Painterly, full of playful touches, it exhibits a young author-artist's search for his archetype of female muse and lover, at once Virgin Mary and Scarlet Woman, within a city whose metropolitan textures brim and compel. Not the least of his rite of passage is the resolve to break free of the legacy of the 1920s Lost Generation in their move to Paris, the bid to perform an uncoiling new round of narrative. Andy Raffine, as he dubs himself, sets up an authorial persona that inter-mirrors self and text:

> I was looking for the main character of my life, blundering along, stopping for an absinthe here, a coffee there, following the day-light ghosts of myself through the continuous landscape, death and resurrection in a tongue alack. Perhaps I was merely a dumb member of the audience strayed onto the stage by mistake, look-ing for some printed program that has dropped under a seat. (10)

This self-monitoring comment is typical, the author looking over his own shoulder.

As narrator he speaks of his 'my sleeping, seeing eye' (31), Paris memorialised as though in equal part somnambulant and historic, dream as much as actual. The Seine, the squares, Notre Dame and the churches, the Place de la Concorde, Champs-Élysées and boulevard Saint-Michel, the galleries, Existentialist cafés like Les Deux Magots, his waiter friend Lubin, each *tabac* and *pissoir* amount to 'the whole pageant and caravansary' (60). He aligns 'the site of myself' (77) with a city that stirs his every sense, parallel locales, twin modes of being. One Beat-centred remembrance calls up 'a wailing wild ragged band of American poets from the Rue Gît-le-Cœur' (42). He mockingly invokes himself as the then writer-apprentice creating 'great blazing poems on unwinding toilet paper' (44) with his own 'cracked mirror' (123) as vantage-point. He fantasises 'Poetry Police . . . about to capture all libraries, printing presses, and automats' (43).

Above all, the power of desire, the pursuit of love embodied in woman as higher spirit, sexuality, caryatid, provocation and recourse, gives the text its main thread. For, throughout *Her*, Ferlinghetti's Paris, the journeying aboard the Orient Express, the Rome interlude, operates as a drama of quest. If the run-ons of consciousness, and the pivots and gyrations as to imagining the eternal woman, reverberate as though from Joyce, the novel insistently creates its own echo-chamber. Other narratives suggest themselves, among them William Demby's cubist novel *The Catacombs* (1965) which similarly has its narrator play an alter-ego author and character within Rome, as an actual yet shadowy European city. But *Her*, Beat or otherwise, wholly steers its own course, Ferlinghetti's early tour de force.

Gregory Corso's *The American Express* (1961), also a Paris-based venture and given over to expatriate American *beatnikisme*, ventures into farce. Part picaresque, fantasia, another send-up of the Lost Generation, and a detective story in the person of Horatio Frump, its Beat-like world benefactors seek earnestly if chaotically to redeem the 'human experiment' (28). Richard Fariña's *Been Down So Long It Looks Up to Me* (1966), set in 1958 yet also anticipating the campus and sex-and-drugs underground of the 1960s, spans Las Vegas, Cuba and Athene (a version of Cornell University) as worlds caught up in a changing global paradigm. Gnossos Pappadopoulis, the novel's over-testosteroned adventurer, serves as steersman through a comic itinerary of sexual revolution, dope and campus upheavals. Richard Brautigan long took umbrage at being called Beat or Hippie. Yet *Trout Fishing in America* (1967), a novel in the form of fragmentary-absurdist mosaic, bears its Beat signals. It operates as a Donald Barthelme-like multiple of author-surrogate, faux-Westerner named Shorty, a hotel and a stream. Its thrust, starting from the Ben Franklin statue in San Francisco's Washington Square and ranging through the Pacific Northwest to Manhattan and back, is angled towards an America of vitality over consensus and waste. Each emblematic creek and act of fishing, echoing Izaak Walton or the solitary pursuits of Thoreau's *Walden*, points up the re-finding of ecological health against consumerist disconnect.

Post-Beat Texts: Poetry

Legacies have been as many and as inherently various as the first tranche of Beat literary output. *Selected Poems of Post-Beat Poets* (2008), published first in Chinese translation and containing the work of twenty-plus poets, and from which Steve Dalachinsky's 'Credo' is taken, gives a fair sampling of the poetry and poetics that sail both East and West Coast under the title banner.[11] A 'loose network' (14) the editor Vernon Frazer calls it in his Preface and one which has 'advanced the work of the Beats into areas the Beats never explored' (266) according to his detailed and greatly helpful Afterword. This new 'culture of spontaneity' (263) so can address arenas of temporary work and homelessness, take place in poetry slams, develop new styles of picture-poems in the tradition of Kenneth Patchen and composition by field, or fuse with stand-up comedy and hip-hop. The poems, each with their respective post-Beat markers, range through Enid Dame's 'Night Shift' ('There's somewhere / I have to / get to / tonight / without leaving the room', 39), Jack Foley's 'Ginsberg at the Mall' ('Courage teacher, / old poet, have you become an owl of wisdom, / a hawk of power, a swan of beauty, / a sunflower, / a leaf, / a bit of sunlight, / worm burrowing in the earth?', 54), Bob Holman's 'After Li Po' ('I'm so full of wine and poetry / Laughing, my pen falls down, / ending this poem' 95) and Cheryl A. Townsend's 'The Things We Do For . . .' ('and we all wonder / if any of it's real /. . . pages white as fantasy', 210).

Post-beat, like Beat itself in many respects, has to be an approximate term. Jack Foley, for instance, besides his performance poems has long hosted literary radio for Berkeley's KPFA station. Bob Holman has worn a number of hats, variously with St. Mark's Poetry, the Nuyorican Poets Café and as inspiration for PBS's multiform series 'United States of Poetry' (1996) that embraces rap, sign language, cowboy and sound poetry. These, and other poetic compass, postmodern or confessional or slam, evidently play into or alongside any post-Beat aesthetic.

As indicative a poem as any from outside the Frazer anthology has to be Dalachinsky's own Kerouac memorialisation in 'the leaves are falling', written in September 1994 when he was en route by bus to the Lowell Celebration Kerouac Conference – the gathering that in fact led to *Selected Poems of the Post-Beat Poets*.

As befits a long-time free jazz and poetry performer and expert record-liner writer, his poem assumes a velocity modulated to spoken performance as in turn it ponders Kerouac, both live and posthumous. On the one hand is the Kerouac tired of celebrity and writing to Philip Whalen ('kerouac says to whalen / that he's gonna build / a big fenced in-out / door / library / in his backyard / he'll sit all day / read / write / &drink boilermakers . . .'). On the other, with a recall of 'the road', there beckons companionship into the future, a new prospect:

> let's blow
> together
> like the wind down the highway
> let's stop together on asylum street
> beneath the golden dome
> let's walk through the capitals of heaven
> like 2 naked trees that just won the jackpot
> and straight/talk our way into warmth . . .
>
> the leaves are changing
> for the first
> time
>
> the leaves are changing.

The cycle of Beat time past, for Dalachinsky, so renews into Beat time to come.

Other East Coast voices enter the fray. Dan Propper (1937–2003), jazz aficionado, alto saxophonist and 'second generation Beat poet' according to the obituary written by Mikhael Horowitz, fellow post-Beat and stand-up performer, for the *New York Times* in 2004, was early to win notice with the sixty-section pattern poem 'The Fable of the Final Art' which Seymour Krim included in *The Beats* (1960):

> In the 1st minute of final hour Walt Whitman was found
>   in an ancient
>   subway tunnel beneath 52nd st, where he had lain
>   in ecstasy since
>   the first bars of jazz filtered through. (27)[12]

Collections like *For Kerouac in Heaven* (1980) bear out Propper's continuing affinity with Beat. Herschel Silverman (1926–2015), Ginsberg ally and lifetime correspondent, spent a lifetime as poet but also a distance from any usual Beat-bohemian career as the confectioner / sweetshop owner of 'Hersch's Beehive' in Bayonne, New Jersey. Best described as a poet of neighbourhood, his quiet Beat turn of voice is to be heard in *The Hey-Baby Blues* (1993) and *Bookshelf Cowboy* (2001) and the sequence 'Nite Train Poems'.

Aram Sorayan, unlike his expansive novelist and playwright father, William Sorayan, takes his bow as a poetic miniaturist culminating in *Complete Minimal Poems* (2007). From early work like *Coffee Coffee* (1967), with its often page-action single-word poems, Sorayan through his career gives post-Beat a species of Mondrian or Rothko flavour. His alphabetic, four-limbed 'M' has long become iconic, one instance of many in his oeuvre of consciously fashioned visual poetry. Rhode Island born and raised, and having taken early to Kerouac, Dave Church (1947–2008) steered between Beat and street poet (his job as a cab driver gave him plentiful source material). Whether the Kerouac tributes in *Blueballs Revisited and Other Poems* (1997) and *Roadie* (1999), the latter from Silverman's Beehive Press, or the proliferation of chapbooks like *Eternal Hummmmm* (2000), or his CD *Bebop-Rebop* (2002), Church brings his own poetics of spontaneity to bear.

California Beat has long vaunted Charles Plymell, poet, publisher of *NOW* magazine in the 1960s, veteran hipster-Beat, and though Kansas born and raised (Ginsberg's 'Wichita Vortex' owes inspiration from him) becomes a Haight-Ashbury legend. His small-press Cherry Valley Editions, founded in 1974, includes not only Ginsberg but Burroughs (a major ally), Ray Bremser, Janine Pommy Vega, Clive Matson, Herbert Huncke, Robert Crumb and Claude Pélieu. From *Apocalypse Rose* (1967) to *Incognito Sum* (2016), he has created a huge experimental oeuvre, not least from City Lights his San Francisco countercultural novel *The Last of the Moccasins* (1971). In his Reality Studio online interview (2008) he speaks of his friendships with Cassady ('I called him the Fastest Word in the West'), Ginsberg ('he masterminded the Beat Generation'), Kerouac ('A great ear for Jazz. Though to me he remained a somewhat square Republican') and Burroughs ('the genius old man of a generation').[13] If West Coast Beat, and post-Beat, looks to a symptomatic spirit, it assuredly belongs to Plymell.

In Neeli Cherkovski the California tradition has the first-hand por-
traitist of Ginsberg, Corso and others in *Whitman's Wild Children*
(1989), the biographer of Ferlinghetti (1979) and Bukowski (1991),
the co-editor of *Beatitude*, and in 1996 the poet of the 106-page *Elegy
for Bob Kaufman* ('when he died North Beach / took a dive / and
didn't recover / bohemia / is a brittle / leaf on a / tree', 16). A. D.
Winans, fellow Californian, veteran Haight-Ashbury-ite, and founder
of Second Coming Press and magazine with its outlet for a plenitude
of Beat poets, has readily acknowledged debts across his voluminous
output to Kaufman, Bukowski and Micheline. San Francisco serves
him, and him it, as though paired companions, the idiom in play that
of urban Beat. His collection *San Francisco Poems* (2012) bequeaths
much of this fond but un-blinkered cityscape. Poetry like 'I Kiss the
Feet of Angels', reprinted in *Drowning Like Li Po in River of Wine:
Selected Poems, 1970–2010* (2010), gives early tribute ('In the morn-
ing / the poems rise with the fog / at night they nest / in my eyes', 221).
'Poem for Ginsberg' offers the amused tease of 'I saw the best minds of
my generation . . . naked under their fashion designer clothes'. Other
Beat lines invoke Lewis Carroll for 'Corso the mad hatter' and New
Orleans for 'Kaufman black Messiah / walking Bourbon Street / eat-
ing a golden sardine'.

California also gives context to Jack Hirschman and George
Herms, the one a veteran street poet and activist, the other a collage-
maker and painter. They share a Beat-like resolve in having their
work reflect quotidian life and objects, worlds of time and appetite
beyond the academy or closed art circles. Since first publication with
A Correspondence with Americans (1960) and across more than
forty collections Hirschman, still a Marxist (his many translations
include the poems of Stalin) and like Ferlinghetti a former poet lau-
reate of San Francisco, has championed street poetry, populist voice.
His *Front Lines: Selected Poems* (2002) and *All That's Left* (2008)
embody both his politics and style of verse. George Herms brings
eclectic skills to bear, assemblages, sculptures, drawings and writ-
ings. His public art, as it has been called, give Beat and post-Beat
verse an important elision of both a visual and lexical idiom.

Post-Beat Texts: Fiction

Post-Beat fiction yields no less a diversity. One can start with trans-
Pacific and transatlantic contributions. Maxine Hong Kingston's

Tripmaster Monkey: His Fake Book (1989), with its delineation of
the countercultural 1960s and Frank Chin figure of Wittman Ah Sing
as Chinese American Beat-hipster based on her fellow author Frank
Chin, not only calls upon Chinese rites of passage but does so within
San Francisco and Beat heritage as home turf. Sing seeks to re-embody
Sun Wu Kong as warrior figure and Monkey King, but he does so as
Bay Area peacenik, Chinatown and Berkeley dramatist, above all Beat
activist. Tony Litt's *Beatniks: An English Road Movie* (1997, 2002)
brings an 'England to America' dimension into play, Quixotic 'Beat'
journeying as a species of existential miscue. Wry, understated, very
English-ironic, its clever shadowing of *On the Road* does persuasive
good service, a triumph of how the legacy percolates into but actually
does not quite work under British auspices.[14]

   The novel's story of recently graduated and sexually adventure-
some Mary as narrator, Jack (his real name never revealed) and Neal
(Matthew), each to one degree or another would-be 'hip' Beat aco-
lytes although from the UK's provincial Ampthill and Bedford (not
far from the 'Mid-Beds District Council Offices', 133), gives engag-
ing bent to life imitating art. The 'road' journey, first to Brighton in
Mary's family Vauxhall and then across highway America to Califor-
nia in their 1994 Honda Accord Coupe, delivers engaging invention,
the play of hip and unhip, the loyal but eventually gimcrack belief in
Kerouac as messiah. Pseudo-Zen, tokes of weed, 'yabyum' bed three-
somes, and homoerotics between Jack and Neal, all come into play.
The burial, in East and West Coast America, of urns bearing the ashes
of Neal's cat Koko lightly subverts Beat ritual. The 6 Gallery reading
is invoked in contrast with an ill-attended midweek 'spontaneous'
poetry reading in the local English library.

   'It is the 1960s. It is Friday, 29 July 1966' (6). The date signifies
Bob Dylan's turn to the electric guitar, for Jack the end of history, a
magic marker for the one Beat time as all-time. His account bespeaks
awe, the credo of true believer:

   All this – our poetry – begins back in the 6 Gallery in San Fran-
   cisco in 1955. That was when Allen Ginsberg, the great Ameri-
   can Jew and poet, stood up, a little drunk, shaking at the knees,
   to read out part of his great poem, 'Howl for Carl Solomon'.
   American literature – strike that – WORLD literature was never
   to be the same again. It was the greatest thing ever to hit. There
   were five other poets at the reading: Gary Snyder, Philip Whalen,

Philip Lamantia, Michael McClure, Kenneth Rexroth. Jack Kerouac, who I'm named after, and Neal Cassady, who Neal took his name from – they were both there. This was the moment when poetry and word and voice and breath got their freedom. (60–1)

Charade, however, enters the tally. Jack's secret penchant for arcade video games falls infinitely short of the exhilarations of Kerouac and Cassady. For all the mention of Parker or Coltrane, Neal turns out to be Travolta-style disco fan and dancer. It falls to him to observe 'England is such a small island. You drive to the edge, then all you can do is stop' (136). Yet Mary finds herself saying 'America is a very big and scary country' (262). Their proposed magazine *Bohemia Café* they intend as a vehicle for the abject verse of Otto Lang, Beat-ish fellow traveller found drowning in the river but actually a hospital death of hypothermia. The stretch here to magazines like *Evergreen Review*, *Yugen*, *Beatitude* or *Floating Bear* could not be greater. The one cultural regime, imperfections and all, so stands disarmingly out of kilter with the other.

As they traverse the United States, Brooklyn Bridge to Golden State Bridge, and following *On the Road* from the Chelsea Hotel, through Bear Mountain, Chicago, Denver, and finally to Big Sur, the scales fall. Jack finds he hates the America of road, motels, and fast food, and against writ refuses to pick up a black hitchhiker. When he and Mary engage in petty shoplifting (on one occasion, of shampoo) it is as if to underwrite their piecemeal theft of Beat identity. She discerns, well enough, the fraud when nearing Chicago and can say of Jack 'I wasn't sure if he was gazing into some mythic West or trying not to get carsick' (265). Neal, who has earlier mysteriously disappeared, turns up in San Francisco all hippie and English tree protester against a proposed by-pass ('It's this whole Kerouac road thing, this America myth stuff. You can't live by it in England', 316). The novel's last sentence suitably leaves matters on unexplained terms as to Jack's car and road flight from Neal and Mary in Point Sur ('It was only after we arrived back in San Francisco, after hitch-hiking for over six hours, that we found out what happened', 325). Litt writes with slyness and verve, inside awareness of the appeal of Beatdom but never without shrewdly lowered eye.

When 'Harry met Jay' might best summarise Larry Closs's *Beatitude* (2011), a novel both of gay desire and shared obsession with the writings of Kerouac and Ginsberg.[15] The dalliance of Harry Charity and Jay Bishop, respectively editorial and arts employees of the entertainment weekly *Element*, and Harry's turbulent past love of the out-of-control Matteo, is played out against the Manhattan book-trade, office politics, galleries and parties. The plot, one that also involves Jay's relationship with his one-time girlfriend Zahra, at times distinctly underwhelms. Harry's ache, his love quest, reads all too plaintively. But *Beatitude*, true to its name, makes its claims also as fact-fiction, and in no clearer respect than in how it plaits Beat's lure of adventuring, texts, readings and first editions into the novel's route-way.

Closs's interleafing of iconic Beat artefacts and moments gives needed weight to the story even if, at times, the effect is of disquisition, log-entry. Early into the fray is the Kerouac scroll of *On the Road*, then housed in the Berg Collection in the basement at the New York Public Library, and to which the pair gain tremulous access in 1995 as though it were its Dead Sea predecessor. The 'tag team' (53) of Kerouac and Burroughs, and the Carr–Kammerer affair is copiously annotated. 'Howl' is rhapsodised for 'jaw dropping images' (60). A 'United States of Poetry' party has Harry meeting Bob Holman (162) with a follow-up in the Whitney exhibition 'Beat Culture and the New America, 1950–1965' (173). Ginsberg makes appearances as variously rude brush-off figure, reader of his poetry at the Museum of Modern Art, and warm interviewee when Harry visits him at his 435 East Twelfth Street apartment. Asked what he thinks is his best achievement, his poet's response specifies 'beauty in the language. Kind of massive, ecstatic, poetic oratory' (240). Two Ginsberg poems, unpublished at the time, are offered in the appendix, 'Like Other Guys' ('I should . . . / Stop publishing poems, they chop down trees', 261) and 'Carl Solomon Dream' ('"What's it like in the afterworld?" I ask . . . / He answers, "The first rule is, 'Remember you're dead.' The / second rule is 'Act like you're dead'"', 262). Life enters art directly, a Beat or post-Beat trope if ever there were.

On publication Ali Eskandarian's *Golden Years: An Iranian Beat Punk Novel* (2016) was touted as being 'in thrall to the great American beats' while also having 'visions of Ancient Assyrian futurism'.[16] The latter likely amounts to tease or even marketing, the exoticism of two discrepant worlds Beat-American and Farsee-Iranian joined across time the one into the other. But as this near-autobiographical and culturally savvy novel unfolds its chronicle of

a five-man 'Iranian underground rock band' (30) based in Williams-
burg, Brooklyn, much of it on the road and busy in sex, drugs and
indeed rock and roll, it also throws up a Beat/beatnik holograph of
the age. For these are the 1960s carried into the 2000s ('The Zeros',
161), at once Beat-like backward glance ('I hope to have some mag-
ical visions' says the narrator, 48) and a 'now' of gigs, narcotics
(pot, cocaine, amphetamines, tramadol), drink, groupies, and occa-
sional hard-won love in women like Mana and Allison. The lives of
Koli, Siamak, Dari, Manuchehr and the narrator may well represent
escape from the bequeathed regime of the Shah, the Ayatollah and
the Iran–Iraq War. But to quite what? Iran is in process of becoming
nostalgia, a memory of ancient peoples and foodways like Ghormeh
Sabzi. America offers opportunity, affluence, an endless availability
of women albeit under dire chauvinist rules. But for all the lure of
Manhattan parties, sex, drink and Warhol chic, it can equally drive
the narrator's creative spirit to the edge.

Shoestring city tours come and go, New York, Dallas, Los
Angeles, London, Paris. The registering voice, that of the band's
songwriter and loft-dweller, moves between excess and contempla-
tion of his musicianship under commodity rules. The ready hedon-
ist, he also recognises the danger of becoming an isolate. His taste
for writerly metaphor ('I walk back home through the bazaar of
history', 174) and creative ear as much as eye ('I played Lou Reed's
Berlin until it got too personal', 185) evidently bespeaks the art-
ist. But uncertainty enters. At one point, at the LA shoreline and
as if to declare allegiance, he shouts to the ocean 'Come on, you
big bad sea, you talked to Jack Kerouac, now talk to me!' (216)
to which the sea answers, mirror like, in the name of better wis-
dom. An Afterword by Eskandarian's Dutch colleague Oscar van
Gelderen designates *Golden Years* 'Ali's great Iranian-American
novel' (243), a tribute to the author startlingly shot and killed by
a disaffected band-mate from his group Yellow Dogs in November
2013. The Afterword could also have said the novel adds a new
inflection to Beat's roll-call.

Beat Discourse

Discursive Beat, if so it can be called, throws up adjunct bearings.
A trio serves for the larger round: letter collection, a classic of
New Journalism, a publisher's memoir. First off, *As Ever*, the title
phrase for the Ginsberg–Cassady correspondence and Burroughs's

usual signing-off, does duty for Beat as almost obsessive epistolary round.[17] This shared letter-writing, as often given over to discussion of work-in-progress as to local occasion or voyage, supplies a graph both of individual and cross-referential creative impulse. How consciously each writer was of pitching for history, the more so as Beat became a password, remains guesswork. But the letters constitute their own self-standing repository of authorship, a thesaurus. Fortunately, most have been found diligent editors.

Resources are abundant. *The Letters of Allen Ginsberg* (2008) gives a timeline mirror both of Beat as literary circle and cultural politics. The distance covered reaches from 1940s protest letters to the *New York Times* invoking Woodrow Wilson's idealism, through assiduous correspondence with Kerouac, Burroughs, Corso and Orlovsky, to a late letter to Bill Clinton. Ginsberg's role as Beat stage-manager, even impresario, has no better embodiment. The two-volume *Jack Kerouac: Selected Letters, 1940–1956* (1995) and *Jack Kerouac: Selected Letters, 1957–1969* (1999), edited by the veteran Beat scholar Ann Charters, give witness to Kerouac's irresistibly athletic call to transmuting world into word. Whether a miniature like 'All my life is a foreign country', written to John Clellon Holmes in July 1949, or his excursions into the poetics of spontaneous composition with Cassady, Ginsberg and the rest of the Beat literary fellowship, or business exchanges with his agent Sterling Lord, the letters bespeak authorship as not just a calling but expressly *his* calling.

Burroughs, likewise, infuses his letters with an inerasable idiom, laconic, cracker-barrel, full of un-blinkered watchfulness. Both *The Letters of William Burroughs, 1945–1959* (1993), written overwhelmingly to Ginsberg and Kerouac, and *Rub Out the Words: The Letters of William Burroughs, 1959–1974* (2012), which takes up his life of same-sex desire, drugs, place and publishers, re-emphasise his resistance to perceived viruses of control. The editorial fashioning of *The Yage Letters* (1963), his Amazon Forest exchanges with Ginsberg on the search for the ultimate hallucinogenic (and maybe telepathic) drug, arouses suspicion that this is Beat's own epistolary novel. No full account can overlook Cassady's letters, respectively gathered in *As Ever: The Collected Correspondence of Allen Ginsberg and Neal Cassady, 1944–1966* (1977) and *Neal Cassady, Collected Letters, 1944–1967* (2004), those most of all which deal with his insistence on writing from the existential instant.[18] Ginsberg's 'first thought, best thought' and Kerouac's 'spontaneous prose', if they have sources in Charlie Parker and Jackson Pollock, draw also from the instinctive qualities of authorship in Cassady's letter writing.

Secondly, Hunter Thompson's interview with George Plimpton for the *Paris Review* in 2000 leaves no doubt of countercultural allegiances: 'We were all outside the law: Kerouac, Miller, Burroughs, Ginsberg, Kesey; I didn't have a gauge as to who was the worst outlaw. I just recognized allies: my kind of people.'[19] Nowhere does his 'gonzo' New Journalism more fiercely show its alliance with Beat temperament than in *Fear and Loathing in Las Vegas: A Savage Journey to the Heart of the American Dream* (1971). Ostensibly reportage of the Mint 400 bike race and then the National District Attorney's Association meeting on 'Narcotics and Dangerous Drugs', it furnishes camera-eye black comedy, a compellingly readable war-diary. The terrain is the American Dream as casino glut (6), Las Vegas as 'Freak Kingdom' (83), the Nixon era as 'doomstruck' (178). Thompson shows his roustabout paces throughout, himself in the guise of Raoul Duke, his companion the Chicano tenant lawyer Oscar Zeta Acosta whom he dubs 'the Samoan'. Ralph Steadman's brilliant reptilian line drawing supply the perfect visuals. Booze, cocaine, mescaline, LSD and other drugs, hotel-room trashings, Cadillac and Chevy frenetic driving, the Rolling Stones playing 'Sympathy for the Devil' all operate as counterpoint to the 'dangerous gibberish' of the law and order convention and the Middle America it encodes. It will not do to call Thompson a paid-up Beat enlistee, but the dissident gothic of *Fear and Loathing* undoubtedly belongs in the neighbourhood.

Thirdly, as publisher of Grove Press, and with it *Evergreen Review* begun in 1957, Barney Rosset assumes his deserved place in the Beat chronicle. His stance was invariably bold, greatly honourable. That is not to say *My Life in Publishing and How I Fought Censorship* (2017), his posthumous autobiography, reads other than dutifully.[20] But Rosset rightly can observe 'In many ways Maurice Girodias of Olympia Press was my French counterpart' (207), just as John Calder was in England. His early good-faith promotion of the work of Samuel Beckett and Henry Miller, publication of *The New American Poetry*, and championing of Kerouac and Ginsberg and even more so Burroughs in the face of censorship and court prosecution, singles him out for distinction. Rosset's summary of Beat as generation and accomplishment bears citing:

> I think now of Allen Ginsberg as the organizer of the Beat Generation, the conceptual person who guided the other. Wherever there is a moral battlefield somewhere or other on the planet, say Czechoslovakia or India or Cuba, more often than not Allen Ginsberg showed up, ready to shed light into the darkness, chant Om, bring a sense of beatitude and peace to the scene. William Burroughs was the brain of the Beat Generation; Jack Kerouac, the Beats' shining star, was its heart, and Allen was its soul. This in no way dims the luster of Lawrence Ferlinghetti, or Michael McClure or Gregory Corso or Gary Snyder or so many others. (220–1)

Rosset's role in promoting Beat writing deserves its bouquet. He was intrinsic to making Beat more than Greenwich Village fad or passing entertainment.

Beat Visual Heritage

Beat visual art, not inappropriately, has much come into view, whether the neo-impressionist canvases of Ferlinghetti, the gun-splatter prints of Burroughs, the recovered notebook line-drawings and paintings of Kerouac, or Ted Joans's memorial canvas *Bird Lives* (1955) and Manhattan wall paintings. Video documentary and film abounds, from Peter Whitehead's countercultural document of the Albert Hall Beat poetry reading *Wholly Communion* (1965) to the revisioning of the Ginsberg and Lucien Carr relationship in the feature film *Kill Your Darlings* (2013). In the case of Beat and photography, the bodies of image created across time by Beats themselves and those in which they themselves are the subjects amount to a genuine trove. They number individual portraits and portfolios, gallery displays, wall posters, and even collections of postcards.

'Beat Aperture', a phrase sometimes used in gallery shows of the images, offers the relevant gloss, photographer, image and viewer under intimate contract one with the other. Dissent can easily domesticate into coffee-table chic or pin-up as with Che Guevara or the Black Panthers. Beat shares this in degree, sometimes deliberately and collaboratively. Book-cover shots of Kerouac, Ginsberg in festival beads and kurta, Burroughs at a reading or in commercials have all passed into Beat visual lore. In *Mad to Be Saved: The Beats, the '50s and Film* (1998) David Sterritt observes with well-taken astuteness, 'A pungent visuality often pervades Beat writing and thinking.'[21] Even if his focus emphasises cinema, the point holds for each of the more inclusive ways Beat has entered into remembered sight as well as word.

Early into the fray was Fred McDarrah, lifelong photographer for the *The Village Voice* and who in collections like *The Beat Scene* (1960) and *Kerouac and Friends: A Beat Generation* (1985) captured most of Beat's leading lights – Kerouac on stage with arms outspread, a beaming Ed Sanders, Ginsberg reading. Mellon Tytell's *The Beat Book* (1974) offers camera images that anticipate the forty or more which accompany her husband John Tytell's *Paradise Outlaws: Remembering the Beats* (1999). Tytell's scrupulously professional photographing of Ginsberg, Burroughs, Corso, di Prima and others comes with helpful annotations of the subjects involved and time and circumstance of shooting. Celebrated other collections have taken on classic status. Harold Chapman's of-the-moment yet actually meticulously compositional *The Beat Hotel* (1984) creates a strong memory of rue Gît-le-Cœur as art colony – he was the last to leave the hotel on its change of owners. Larry Keenan's period iconography in *Beat Culture and the New America, 1950–1965*, especially in the exhibition at the Whitney Museum, New York in 1995, imply both opportunistic moment and an instinct for memorialisation. Larry Fink's *The Beats* (2014) contrasts markedly with his well-known 'social graces' and partygoing albums.

Whether or not the photography of Allen Ginsberg and William Burroughs matches the professionals', it comprises a necessary consortium. *Beat Memories: The Photographs of Allen Ginsberg* (2010), drawn from the near 400 left in his estate and based on the exhibition in the National Gallery of Art, Washington, DC, from May to December 2010, underlines the poet's lifelong interest in camera art.[22] A follow-on display took place at Greenwich Village's Grey Gallery, Washington Square East, in 2013.[23] Among the forerunners had been *Photographs: Allen Ginsberg* (1991), with canny essays on the play of lens and eye by both Ginsberg and Corso, and *Snapshot Poetics: A Photographic Memoir of the Beat Generation* (1993). Other previous shows of his work include *Hideous Human Angels* at the Holly Solomon Gallery in New York, *Memory Gardens* at the

Middendorf Gallery, both in 1985, and *Strange Familiar Snapshots* at the Brent Sikkema Fine Art Gallery in New York in 1991. Exhibitions were frequent: in the United States at the Dallas Museum of Art, the Naropa Institute and the Kellas Museum in Lawrence, Kansas; in Europe at galleries in Cologne, the Netherlands and France. In 1988, with the filmmaker Robert Frank, he had taught a joint seminar at the Camera Obscura School of Art in Tel Aviv under the title 'Photographic Poetics'. *Beat Memories*, however, black-and-white images each given his handwritten explanatory gloss, gathers most of his principal work into the one volume.

An opening image has Burroughs, on a Manhattan rooftop, upright in kind with the aerials and posts behind him, and with right hand shading his brow as if looking ahead or into the future. There follows one of Ginsberg's best-known images, a street shot of Neal Cassady with cigarette in hand and arms wrapped around his lover Natalie Jackson in front of a movie-house marquee showing Brando's *The Wild One* and *Tarzan the Ape Man*. Kerouac follows, sideways on, set against a background of wall and fire-escape ladders, his demeanour pensive as he smokes and carries a book in his jacket pocket. Ginsberg himself, young, manicured, with winning full smile and notebook on lap, gazes outward. These make for a preface of sorts to a full menu, from another young Ginsberg in vest and aboard ship through to older Ginsberg scarf-wrapped in front of Maghreb white housing.

Other images supply a virtual Beat mural: Orlovsky strolling at the beach, the photographer Berenice Abbott, with whom and as with Robert Frank and Richard Avedon Ginsberg discussed camera technique, Burroughs gesticulating to Kerouac on a settee (several times over used as a book cover), Carl Solomon cross-legged in his apartment, and Ginsberg, Corso, Ferlinghetti with arms linked in front of City Lights Bookstore. A notable inclusion shows Corso, Burroughs and Paul Bowles in a line-up all holding cameras, with Ian Sommerville just in view, and with a Tangier wall as backdrop and taken when the group touched base with the expatriate Morocco circle of Paul and Jane Bowles. The effect is mirror photography, refractions. Gray Snyder is to be seen in full monk-travelling outfit. Burroughs and Orlovsky feature in various bed-and-body shots, the gay male gaze. A seated Kerouac in 1964, bloated, sad, full of sullen visage, gazes back at the camera. Huncke sits outdoors, ironically the drug and street veteran with Coca Cola in hand. A head-tilted Bob Dylan with jacket around his shoulders poses in Tompkins Square Park. Ginsberg's lens is rarely less than engaging, if the 'snapshot', then also attentive, adept in managing photographic space and measure.

Taking Shots: The Photography of William S. Burroughs (2014) almost inevitably overlaps on occasion with *Beat Memories*, but it carries Burroughs's inerasable own stamp.[24] The title alone gives a classic touch of flair, heroin shot, gun shot, camera shot. Just as in *Naked Lunch* he writes, 'I am a recording instrument . . . I do not presume to impose "story", "plot", "continuity"' (174), so the editors of *Taking Shots* rightly insist that 'His photographs were not made for aesthetic reasons but to focus the viewer – usually himself – on the now' (30). That sparse, in-your-eye, seemingly unmediated immediacy runs throughout, whether the stills of St. Louis houses and landscapes he called 'fugitive', the Tangier sequences, the shots of car and unadorned city streets, his take on Soho building and scaffolds, or his red bedcover sequence. They each take their place alongside the more Beat-connecting images.

These include his self-portraits. Several have him reflexively holding a negative in hand, his gelatin-silver prints. Another catches him gazing intently at the *Book of the Dead* papyrus in the British Museum. Yet another has him posed with two air pistols. His camera looks to the Ginsberg of young manhood, book in hand, pensive, on the roof of Ginsberg's apartment at 206 East 7th Street, New York in 1953. A 1957 shot has Kerouac with face bunched, toughness in his pose. Bryon Gysin is caught painting, bent over his canvas and in shorts and singlet. Harold Norse is to be seen holding a jewel to his eye. Much of Beat compositional relevance are his assemblages, whether imagistic photocollage of *Time* magazine covers interposing image and inked script or fold-over scenes given choice Burroughs titles like 'Real Tea Made Here' and 'The Nova Express'. They might well be thought of as the visual equivalent of one of his narrative cut-ups.

The Beat Goes On

Inter-Beat. Post-Beat. Visual Beat. The threads pull together. How not to think, first, of the historic readings? The 6 Gallery occasion in 1955 has long become archival glamour, Beat's iconic public birthing, the launch of 'Howl'. The Albert Hall reading in London in 1965, *Wholly Communion* as it was called in Peter Whitehead's film of the event, gave international focus not to say controversy to Beat as festival, staging, a rite of excitatory spoken delivery and listening as much as print on the page. *The Beat Generation: Legacy and Celebration* at New York University in May 1994, a six-day reunion to celebrate the half-century since Ginsberg, Kerouac and Burroughs first met, not only culminated in a full-length reading of *On the Road* but featured women's Beat panels, Ed Sanders compeering, Hunter Thompson at the microphone, and readings from Corso, Ferlinghetti, Norse, Micheline, McClure and Jan Kerouac. Under the title *Beat Generation, New York, San Francisco, Paris*, the Centre Pompidou from June to October 2016 gave Beat another European occasion, the French capital as historic Beat nexus and a display case of original publications and their translation, visual and other artwork, readings and lectures. 'The Beat Goes On' supplies the remit for the ninth annual Jazz and Beat Fest sponsored by the John Natsoulas Gallery in October 2016 with its call for 'Beat influenced poems [that] are anti-authoritarian, rhapsodic, jazzy'.

Each of these kinds of main event joins with Beat museum and display centres. As Ferlinghetti rightly acknowledges Naropa Institute, now University, since its founding by Chögyam Rinpoche, Ginsberg, Waldman, di Prima and the composer John Cage, and in whose image Vienna's Schule für Dichtung was created, serves as a major creative arts and archival fulcrum. San Francisco's Beat Museum in Broadway, founded in 2003, and the American Museum of Beat Art (AMBA) based in Alhambra, California, both maintain holdings of cultural record and celebration. The itineraries across America and Europe of the *On the Road* scroll draw ready acolytes, the novel in the one-take original manuscript as muralist icon.

The publication in 2015 of *City Lights Pocket Poets Anthology, 60th Anniversary Edition*, under Lawrence Ferlinghetti's editorial banner, reminds that from the original anthology onward Beat poetry has taken its place alongside an international line-up.[25] This is Ginsberg and fellow Beats inevitably taking centre stage, but in the wider company of names like Cardenal, Brecht, Voznesensky, Mayakovsky, Cortázar, Lowry, Picasso and Pasolini. International Beat, moreover, written from geographies and languages beyond the United States, contributes its own considerable folder. Beat has its expression not just within the Village or North Beach and other countercultural America but across a huge expanse of transnational writing and performance. Juan Felipe Herrera, for one instance, US poet laureate and Chicano activist, unhesitatingly acknowledges the influence of Ginsberg on his own poetry's performative code-switching and measure. Beat authorship beyond the United States – from Mexico to Canada, Europe to Asia, the Maghreb to the Pacific Rim – spans a wide range of writers, languages and cultures that include Michael Horovitz in the UK, Simon Vinkenoog in the Netherlands, Fernanda Pivano in Italy, Elfriede Jelinek in Austria, and Nanao Sakaki in Japan.[26]

Beat, be it the stellar names or those who hold place as inter- or post-Beat, continues to find readerships, not to say listenerships. Journal outlets and associations play a part in keeping discussion alive even if for diehards they carry the taint of academism or pop journalism. *Beat Scene* (1988–) under the editorship of Kevin Ring attracts a wide readership as does *Literary Kicks*, the digital website launched by Levi Asher in 1994. The rise of scholarly groupings like the Beat Studies Association (BSA) in 2004, with both its online *The Beat Review* (2007–12) and subsequent *Journal of Beat Studies* begun in 2011, and the European Beat Studies Network (EBSN) founded in 2010, underscore academic interest.

Canonical Beat. The term bears a perfect contradiction. Beat was always to be thought oppositional, a stance, even a fist, against convention. In one sense it has seized its own legacy, the galaxy of reprints, film adaptations, recordings, videos, photography, song lyrics, and translations of *Howl*, *On the Road* and *Naked Lunch*, in particular. Yet, as the perspectives outlined in this chapter underscore, Beat's legacies have also created their own insistence across literary work, film, music, art and performance. Currents of interest in Beat needless to say have fluctuated. Other countercultural trends that have centred on gender or sexuality or environment or wealth inequality have given notice of its signage. But, to revert back to Ezra Pound's observation, Beat authorship in all its own different manifestations keeps on staying news.

Notes

1. Lawrence Ferlinghetti, Interview, in George Plimpton (ed.), *Beat Writers at Work*, *The Paris Review* Interviews, New York: Modern Library, 1999, 338.

2. Vernon Frazer (ed.), *Selected Poems of Post-Beat Poets* (2008) – Web. The poem earlier printed as a single item in the series *Poems for All*, No. 263, Sacramento, August 2003.

3. Joyce Johnson, 'Art Beat', PBS interview with David Coles, 24 October 2102. The reception of Kerouac has also had its quirks. Official China, through one its main publishing houses in the early 1960s, left no doubt of near-comic ideological contempt for the Beats and Kerouac in particular: 'The main goal of publishing this abridged translation of the "representative work" of the so-called "Beat Generation' is to illustrate for the reader the social phenomenon of the "Beat Generation," and to allow the reader to see the extreme backwardness and reactionary nature of capitalist society, the depths to which American capitalist literature has sunk, and the stinky, corrupt things that are being promoted . . . *On the Road* basically cannot be considered a novel.' Quoted in Lü Shisheng, 'Zai lushang wenben zhi chuanyi de lishi bianqian – dui guonei fanyi xingwei de fansi" (Transformations in the history of translations of *On the Road* – reflections on the process of translation in China), *Foreign Languages and Their Teaching*, 2 (2015), 64–9; 66. I am most grateful to Professor Wendy Larsen of the University of Oregon for this reference

4. Cited in Helen Weaver, *A Memoir of Kerouac and the Fifties*, San Francisco: City Lights Books, 2009, 12.

5. Patti Smith, 'William S. Burroughs: A Man Within', Independent documentary, 2010, dir. Yony Leyser.

6. Selectively these include; Allen Ginsberg, *Journals: Early Fifties Early Sixties*, New York: Grove 1977; *Journals Mid-Fifties, 1954–1958*, New York: HarperCollins, 1995; Jack Kerouac, *Windblown World: The Journals of Jack Kerouac, 1947–1954*, New York: Viking, 2004; and William Burroughs, *Last Words: The Final Journals of William S. Burroughs*, New York: Grove, 2000.

7. John Tytell, *Naked Angels: The Lives and Literature of the Beat Generation*, New York: Grove Press, 1976, 259.

8. Bob Dylan, *Tarantula*, New York: St. Martin's Press, 1966, 1971, 1994.

9. Dylan, *Tarantula*, vi.

10. *The Thing from Another World*, 1951, dir. Howard Hawks, *The Thing*, 1982, dir. John Carpenter.

11. *Selected Poems by Post-Beat Poets* in Chinese translation is available from Shanghai Century Publishing, 2007. The original anthology in English is available in pdf form on the web.

12. The Horowitz *New York Times* obituary appeared 1 January 2004; 'The Fable of the Final Hour', in Seymour Krim (ed.), *The Beats*, New York: Fawcett World Library, 1960, 27–33.

13. Paul Hawkins, 'Charles Plymell: The Benzedrine Highway Interview (Revised)', Online, May 2008.

14. Toby Litt, *Beatniks: An English Road Movie*, London: Secker & Warburg, 1997. London and New York: Marion Boyars, 2002.
15. Larry Closs, *Beatitude*, Bar Harbor: Rebel Satori Press, 2011.
16. Ali Eskandarian, *Golden Years: An Iranian American Beat Novel*, London: Faber & Faber, 2016, cover blurb.
17. Neal Cassady and Allen Ginsberg, *As Ever: The Collected Correspondence of Allen Ginsberg and Neal Cassady*, Berkeley: Creative Arts, 1977.
18. Neal Cassady, *Collected Letters, 1944–1967*, New York: Penguin, 2003.
19. Hunter Thompson, *The Kingdom of Fear: Loathsome Secrets of a Star-Crossed Child in the Final Days of the American Century*, New York: Simon & Shuster, 2003. 51.
20. Barney Rosset, *My Life in Publishing and How I Fought Censorship*, New York: OR Books, 2018.
21. David Sterritt, *Mad to Be Saved: The Beats, The '50s, and Film*, Carbondale: Southern Illinois University Press, 1998, 9. Sterritt usefully summarises this account in 'The Beats and Visual Culture', in Stephen Belletto (ed.), *The Cambridge Companion to the Beats*, Cambridge: Cambridge University Press, 2017, 265–78.
22. *Beat Memories: The Photographs of Allen Ginsberg*, National Gallery of Art, Washington, DC. London, Munich and New York: DelMonico Books/Prestel, 2010.
23. *Photographs: Allen Ginsberg*, Las Vegas and Santa Fe: Twin Palms Press, 1991.
24. Patricia Allmer and John Sears (eds), *Taking Shots: The Photography of William S. Burroughs*, London, Munich and New York: Prestel, 2014.
25. Lawrence Ferlinghetti (ed.), *City Lights Pocket Poets Anthology*, 60th Anniversary Edition, San Francisco: City Lights Books, 2015.
26. For coverage, see A. Robert Lee (ed.), *The Routledge Handbook of International Beat Literature*, New York: Routledge, 2018.

Bibliography

The Major Beats

Allen Ginsberg

Howl and Other Poems, San Francisco: City Lights Books, 1956.

Empty Mirror: Early Poems, New York: Totem Books/Corinth Books, 1961.

Kaddish and Other Poems, 1958–1960, San Francisco: City Lights Books, 1961.

The Yage Letters, with William Burroughs, San Francisco: City Lights Books, 1963.

Reality Sandwiches, 1953–60, San Francisco: City Lights Books, 1963.

Wichita Vortex Sutra, San Francisco: City Lights Books, 1966.

Planet News: 1961–1967, San Francisco: City Lights Books, 1968.

Indian Journals, March 1962–May 1963, New York: Grove Press, 1970.

The Fall of America: Poems of These States, 1965–1971, San Francisco: City Lights Books, 1972.

Allen Verbatim: Lectures on Poetry, Politics, Consciousness, ed. Gordon Ball, New York: McGraw Hill, 1974.

Mind Breaths: Poems, 1972–1977, San Francisco: City Lights Books, 1977.

Plutonian Ode: Poems, 1977–1980, San Francisco: City Lights Books, 1982.

Collected Poems, 1947–1980, New York: Harper & Row, 1984.

Howl: Original Draft Facsimile, ed. Barry Miles, New York: Harper & Row, 1986.

White Shroud: Poems, 1980–1985, New York: Harper & Row, 1986.

Photographs, Santa Fe: Twin Palms, 1991.

Cosmopolitan Greetings: Poems 1986–1992, New York: HarperCollins, 1994.

Selected Poems, 1947–1995, New York: HarperCollins, 1996. Reprinted New York: Penguin Books, 1997, Penguin Classics, 2001.

Death and Fame: Poems, 1993–1995, New York: HarperFlamingo, 1999.

Deliberate Prose: Selected Essays, 1952–1995, ed. Bill Morgan, New York: HarperCollins, 2000.

Howl 50th Anniversary Edition, New York: Harper Perennial, 2006.

The Letters of Allen Ginsberg, ed. Bill Morgan, Philadelphia: Da Capo Press, 2008.

Allen Ginsberg, Wait Till I'm Dead: Uncollected Poems, ed. Bill Morgan, New York: Grove Press, 2016.

Criticism

Baker, Deborah, *A Blue Hand: The Tragicomic, Mind-Altering Odyssey of Allen Ginsberg, a Holy Fool, a Rebel Muse, a Dharma Bum, and His Prickly Bride in India*, New York: Penguin, 2008.

Burns, Glen, *Great Poets Howl: A Study of Allen Ginsberg's Poetry, 1943–1955*, Frankfurt am Main and New York: Peter Lang, 1983.

Caveney, Graham, *Screaming with Joy: The Life of Allen Ginsberg*, New York: Broadway Books, 1999.

Hyde, Lewis (ed.), *On the Poetry of Allen Ginsberg*, Ann Arbor: University of Michigan Press, 1984.

Katz, Eliot, *The Poetry and Politics of Allen Ginsberg*, St Andrews: Beatdom Books, 2015.

Kramer, Jane, *Allen Ginsberg in America*, New York: Random House, 1969.

McNally, Dennis, *Desolate Angel: Jack Kerouac, the Beat Generation and America*, New York: McGraw Hill, 1979.

Merrill, Thomas F., *Allen Ginsberg*, Boston, MA: Twayne, 1988.

Mottram, Eric, *Allen Ginsberg in the Sixties*, Brighton: Unicorn Bookshop, 1972.

Miles, Barry, *Ginsberg: A Biography*, New York: Simon & Schuster, 1989.

—, *Allen Ginsberg: Beat Poet*, London: Virgin, 2010.

Morgan, Bill, *Howl on Trial: The Battle for Free Expression*, San Francisco: City Lights Books, 2007.

—, *I Celebrate Myself: The Somewhat Private Life of Allen Ginsberg*, New York: Penguin, 2007.

—, *The Works of Allen Ginsberg, 1941–1997: A Descriptive Bibliography*, Westport: Greenwood Press, 1995.

Portugés, Paul, *The Visionary Poetics of Allen Ginsberg*, Santa Barbara: Ross-Erikson, 1978.

Raskin, Jonah, *American Scream: Allen Ginsberg's 'Howl' and the Making of the Beat Generation*, Berkeley: University of California Press, 2004.

Sanders, Edward, *The Poetry and Life of Allen Ginsberg: A Narrative Poem*, Woodstock, NY: The Overlook Press, 2000.

Schumacher, Michael, *Dharma Lion: A Critical Biography of Allen Ginsberg*, New York: St. Martin's Press, 1992.

Shinder, Jason (ed.), *The Poem That Changed America: 'Howl' Fifty Years Later*, New York: Farrar, Straus and Giroux, 2006.

Theado, Matt, *Allen Ginsberg*, New York: Oxford University Press, 2012.
Trigilio, Tony, *'Strange Prophecies Anew': Rereading Apocalypse in Blake, H.D., and Ginsberg*, Madison, NJ: Farleigh Dickinson University Press. 2000.
—, *Allen Ginsberg's Buddhist Poetics*, Carbondale: Southern Illinois University Press, 2007.

Jack Kerouac

The Town and the City, New York: Harcourt Brace, 1950.
On the Road, New York: Viking, 1957.
The Dharma Bums, New York: Viking, 1958.
The Subterraneans, New York: Grove Press, 1958.
Doctor Sax: Faust Part Three, New York: Grove Press, 1959.
Maggie Cassidy: A Love Story, New York: Avon, 1959.
Mexico City Blues, New York: Grove Press, 1959.
Lonesome Traveler, New York: McGraw Hill, 1960.
The Scripture of the Golden Eternity, Chevy Chase: Totem Press/Corinth, 1960.
Tristessa, New York: Avon, 1960.
Book of Dreams, San Francisco: City Lights Books, 1961.
Pull My Daisy, New York: Grove Press, 1961.
Big Sur, New York: Farrar, Straus, 1962.
Desolation Angels, New York: Coward-McCann, 1965.
Satori in Paris, New York: Grove Press, 1966.
Vanity of Duluoz: An Adventurous Education, 1935–1946, New York: Coward, 1968.
Pic, New York: Grove Press, 1971.
Scattered Poems, San Francisco: City Lights Books, 1971.
Visions of Cody, New York: McGraw-Hill, 1972.
Pomes All Sizes, San Francisco: City Lights Books, 1992.
Old Angel Midnight, San Francisco: Grey Fox, 1993.
Book of Blues, New York: Penguin, 1995.
The Portable Jack Kerouac, ed. Ann Charters, New York: Viking, 1995.
Jack Kerouac: Selected Letters, 1940–1956, ed. Ann Charters, New York: Viking, 1995.
Book of Haikus, New York: Penguin, 2003.
Windblown World: The Journals of Jack Kerouac, 1947–1954, ed. Douglas Brinkley, New York: Viking, 2004.
Road Novels, 1957–1960: On the Road, The Dharma Bums, The Subterraneans, Tristessa, Lonesome Traveler, New York: Library of America, 2007.
And the Hippos were Boiled in Their Tanks, with William Burroughs, New York: Grove Press, 1945, 2008.

On the Road: The Original Scroll, New York: Penguin Classics, 2008.
The Haunted Life and Other Writings, ed. Todd Tietchen, Boston, MA: Da Capo, 2014.

Criticism

Amburn, Ellis, Subterranean Kerouac: The Hidden Life of Jack Kerouac, New York: St. Martin's Press, 1998.
Amram, David, Offbeat: Collaborating with Kerouac, New York: Thunder's Mouth, 2002.
Beaulieu, Victor-Lévy, Jack Kerouac: essai poulet, Éditions du Jour, 1972; English translation: Jack Kerouac: A Chicken Essay, trans. Sheila Fischmann, Toronto: Coach House, 1975.
Charters, Ann, A Bibliography of the Works of Jack Kerouac, New York: Phoenix, 1973.
—, Kerouac: A Biography, San Francisco: Straight Arrow Books, 1973.
Clark, Tom, Jack Kerouac, New York: Harcourt Brace Jovanovich, 1984.
Donaldson, Scott (ed.), On the Road: Text and Criticism, New York: Viking, 1979.
Ellis, R. J., Liar! Liar! Jack Kerouac, Novelist, London: Greenwich Exchange, 1999.
French, Warren, Jack Kerouac: Novelist of the Beat Generation, Boston, MA: Twayne, 1986.
García-Robles, Jorge, At the End of the Road: Jack Kerouac in Mexico, trans. Daniel C. Schechter, Minneapolis: University of Minnesota Press, 2014.
Geis, Deborah (ed.), Beat Drama: Playwright and Performances of the 'Howl' Generation, London: Bloomsbury, 2016.
Gifford, Barry, and Lee, Lawrence, Jack's Book: An Oral Biography of Jack Kerouac, New York: St. Martin's Press, 1978.
Hipkiss, Robert A., Jack Kerouac: Prophet of the New Romanticism, Lawrence: The Regents Press of Kansas, 1976.
Holmes, John Clellon, Gone in October: Last Reflections on Jack Kerouac, Hailey: Limberlost Press, 1985.
Holladay, Hilary, and Holton, Robert (eds), What's Your Road Man? Critical Essays on Jack Kerouac's On the Road, Carbondale: University of Southern Illinois Press, 2009.
Holton, Robert, On the Road: Kerouac's Ragged American Journey, New York: Twayne, 1999.
Hrebeniak, Michael, Action Writing: Jack Kerouac's Wild Form, Carbondale: Southern Illinois University Press, 2006.
Hunt, Tim, Kerouac's Crooked Road: Development of a Fiction, Hamden: Archon, 1981.

—, *The Textuality of Soulwork: Jack Kerouac's Quest for Spontaneous Prose*, Ann Arbor: University of Michigan Press, 2014.

Jarvis, Charles E., *Visions of Kerouac: A Biography*, Lowell: Ithaca Press, 1974.

Johnson, Joyce, *The Voice is All: The Lonely Victory of Jack Kerouac*, New York: Viking, 2012.

Jones, James T., *A Map of Mexico City Blues*, Carbondale: University of Southern Illinois Press, 2010.

—, *Jack Kerouac's Duluoz Legend: The Mythic Form of an Autobiographical Fiction*, Carbondale: Southern Illinois University Press, 1999.

—, *Use My Name: Jack Kerouac's Forgotten Families*, Toronto: ECW Press, 1999.

Mahler, Paul, *Kerouac: The Definitive Biography*, New York: Taylor Trade, 2004.

Maher, Paul (ed.), *Empty Phantoms: Interviews and Encounters with Jack Kerouac*, New York: Thunder's Mouth Press, 2005.

McNally, Dennis, *Desolate Angel: Jack Kerouac, the Beats, and America*, New York: Random House, 1979.

Melehy, Hassan, *Kerouac: Language, Poetics, and Territory*, New York and London: Bloomsbury Academic, 2016.

Miles, Barry, *Jack Kerouac: King of the Beats*, New York: Henry Holt, 1998.

Nicosia, Gerald, *Memory Babe: A Critical Biography of Jack Kerouac*, Berkeley: University of California Press, 1994.

Poteet, Maurice, *Textes de l'exode*, Montreal: Guérin Littérature, 1987.

Ring, Kevin, *All Day Looking for His Hat . . .: Essays on Jack Kerouac and Other Stories*, Ziri: Editions Baes, 2014.

Swartz, Omar, *The View from On the Road: The Rhetorical Vision of Jack Kerouac*, Carbondale: Southern Illinois University Press, 1999.

Theado, Matt, *Understanding Jack Kerouac*, Columbia: University of South Carolina Press, 2000.

Turner, Steve, *Angel-Headed Hipster*, London: Bloomsbury, 1996.

Weaver, Helen, *The Awakener: A Memoir of Kerouac and the Fifties*, San Francisco: City Lights, 2009.

Weinreich, Regina, *The Spontaneous Poetics of Jack Kerouac: A Study of the Fiction*, Carbondale: Southern Illinois University Press, 1987.

William Burroughs

Junky, New York: Ace, 1953.

Naked Lunch, Paris: Olympia Press, 1959.

The Soft Machine, Paris: Olympia Press, 1961.

The Ticket That Exploded, Paris: Olympia Press, 1962.

The Yage Letters, with Allen Ginsberg, San Francisco: City Lights Books, 1963.

Nova Express, New York: Grove Press, 1964.

The Job: Interviews with William Burroughs, ed. Daniel Odier, London: Jonathan Cape, 1970.
The Wild Boys: A Book of the Dead, New York: Grove Press, 1971.
Exterminator!, New York: Seaver/Viking, 1973.
Kentucky Ham, New York: E. Dutton, 1973.
Port of Saints, London: Covent Garden, 1973.
The Last Words of Dutch Schultz, New York: Viking, 1975.
The Third Mind, with Brion Gysin, New York: Viking, 1978.
Ah Pook is Here and Other Texts, London: Calder, 1979.
Cities of the Red Night, New York: Holt, Rinehart & Winston, 1981.
A William Burroughs Reader, ed. John Calder, London: Pan, 1982.
The Place of Dead Roads, New York: Holt, Rinehart & Winston, 1983.
The Burroughs File, San Francisco: City Lights Books, 1984.
The Adding Machine: Selected Essays, New York: Seaver Books; London: Calder, 1985.
Queer, New York: Viking, 1985.
The Western Lands, New York: Viking/Penguin, 1987.
Interzone, New York: Viking/Penguin, 1989.
The Cat Inside, New York: Viking, 1992.
The Letters of William S. Burroughs, 1945–1959, ed. Oliver Harris, New York Viking/Penguin, 1993.
My Education: A Book of Dreams, New York: Viking, 1995.
Word Virus: The William Burroughs Reader, ed. James Grauerholz and Ira Silverberg, New York: Grove Press/Atlantic, 1998.
Last Words: The Final Journals of William S. Burroughs, New York: Grove Press, 2000.
Taking Shots: The Photography of William S. Burroughs, ed. Patricia Allmer and John Sears, Munich: Prestel, 2014.

Criticism

Ansen, Alan, *William Burroughs: An Essay*, Sudbury: Water Row, 1986.
Bolton, Michael Sean, *Mosaic of Juxtaposition: William S. Burroughs's Narrative Revolution*, Amsterdam: Rodopi, 2014.
Caveny, Graham, *Gentleman Junkie: The Life and Legacy of William S. Burroughs*, Boston, MA: Little, Brown, 1998.
Gensmer, Synne, and Fallows, Colin (eds), *The Art of William S. Burroughs: Cut-Ups, Cut-Ins, Cut-Outs*, Vienna: Moderne Kunst Nürnberg, 2012.
Harris, Oliver, *William Burroughs and the Secret of Fascination*, Carbondale: Southern Illinois University Press, 2003.
Johnson, Rob, *The Last Years of William Burroughs: Beats in South Texas*, College Station: Texas A&M University Press, 2006.
Lydenberg, Robin, *Word Cultures: Radical Theory and Practice in William S. Burroughs's Fiction*, Urbana: University of Illinois Press, 1987.

Miles, Barry, *William Burroughs: El Hombre Invisible*, New York: Hyperion, 1993.
—, *Call Me Burroughs: A Life*, New York: Twelve Books,, 2014.
—, *William S. Burroughs*, London: Weidenfeld & Nicholson, 2014.
Morgan, Ted, *Literary Outlaw: The Life and Times of William Burroughs*, New York: Holt, 1988.
Mottram, Eric, *William Burroughs: The Algebra of Need*, Buffalo: Intrepid Press, 1971; London: Boyars, 1977.
Murphy, Timothy, *Wising Up the Marks: The Amodern William Burroughs*, Berkeley: University of California Press, 1997.
Russell, Jamie, *Queer Burroughs*, New York: Palgrave, 2001.
Schneiderman, David, and Walsh, Philip, *Retaking the Universe: Williams S. Burroughs in the Age of Civilization*, London: Pluto, 2004.
Skerl, Jennie, *William S. Burroughs*, Boston, MA: Twayne, 1985.
Skerl, Jennie, and Lydenberg, Robin (eds), *William Burroughs at the Front: Critical Reception, 1959–1989*, Carbondale: Southern Illinois University Press, 1991.
Sobieszek, Robert A., *Ports of Entry: William S. Burroughs and the Arts*, Los Angeles County Museum of Art: Thames & Hudson, 1996.
Weidner, Chad, *The Green Ghost: William Burroughs and the Ecological Mind*, Carbondale: Southern Illinois University Press, 2016.

Gregory Corso

The Vestal Lady on Brattle, and Other Poems, Cambridge, MA: R. Brukenfeld, 1955.
Gasoline, San Francisco: City Lights Books, 1958.
Happy Birthday of Death, New York: New Directions, 1960.
The American Express, Paris: Olympia Press, 1961.
Long Live Man, New York: New Directions, 1962.
Elegiac Feelings American, New York: New Directions, 1970.
Herald of the Autochthonic Spirit, New York: New Directions, 1981.
Mindfield: New and Selected Poems, New York: Thunder's Mouth, 1989.
An Accidental Autobiography: The Selected Letters of Gregory Corso, ed. Bill Morgan, New York: New Directions, 2003.

Criticism

Olson, Kirby, *Gregory Corso: Doubting Thomist*, Carbondale: Southern Illinois University Press, 2002.
Skau, Michael, '*A Clown in a Grave': Complexities and Tensions in the Works of Gregory Corso*, Carbondale: University of Southern Illinois Press, 1999.

Stevenson, Gregory, *Exiled Angel: A Study of the Works of Gregory Corso*, London: Hearing Eye, 1989.

Lawrence Ferlinghetti

Pictures of the Gone World, San Francisco: City Lights Books, 1955.
A Coney Island of the Mind, New York: New Directions, 1958.
Her, New York: New Directions, 1960.
The Secret Meaning of Things, New York: New Directions, 1969.
Tyrannus Nix?, New York: New Directions, 1969.
Back Roads to Far Places, New York: New Directions, 1971.
Open Eye, Open Heart, New York: New Directions, 1973.
Who are We Now?, San Francisco: City Lights Books, 1976.
Landscapes of Living and Dying, New York: New Directions, 1979.
A Trip to Italy and France, New York: New Directions, 1980.
Endless Life: Selected Poems, New York: New Directions, 1984.
Over All the Obscene Boundaries: European Poems and Transitions, New York: New Directions, 1985.
Love in the Days of Rage, New York: Dutton, 1988.
These are My Rivers: New and Selected Poems, 1955–1993, New York: New Directions, 1993.
A Far Rockaway of the Heart, New York: New Directions, 1997.
How to Paint Sunlight: Lyric Poems and Others, 1997–2000, New York: New Directions, 2000.
San Francisco Poems, San Francisco: City Lights Books, 2001.
Life Studies, Life Stories, San Francisco: City Lights Books, 2003.
Americus: Part 1, New York: New Directions, 2004.
Poetry as Insurgent Art, New York: New Directions, 2007.
Time of Useful Consciousness, Americus Book 11, New York: New Directions, 2012.
I Greet You at the Beginning of a Great Career: The Selected Correspondence of Lawrence Ferlinghetti and Allen Ginsberg, 1955–1997, San Francisco: City Lights Books, 2015.
Writing across the Landscape: Travel Journals, 1960–2013, ed. Giada Diano and Matthew Gleeson, New York: Liveright, 2015.

Criticism

Morgan, Bill, *Lawrence Ferlinghetti: A Comprehensive Bibliography*, New York: Garland Publishing, 1982.
Silesky, Barry, *Ferlinghetti, The Artist in His Time*, New York: Warner Books, 1990.
Smith, Larry, *Lawrence Ferlinghetti: Poet-at-Large*, Carbondale: Southern Illinois University Press, 1990.

Selected Beat Authorships

Bonnie Bremser/Brenda Frazer

Troia: Mexican Memoirs, New York: Croton Press, 1969.
For Love of Ray, London: London Magazine Editions, 1971.

Ray Bremser

Poems of Madness, New York: Paper Book Gallery, 1965.
Angel, New York: Tomkins Square Press, 1967.
Drive Suite, San Francisco: Nova Broadcast Press, 1968.
Black is Black Blues, Buffalo: Intrepid Press, 1971.
Blowing Mouth/The Jazz Poems, 1965–1970, Cherry Valley: Cherry Valley Editions, 1978.
Born Again, Santa Barbara: Am Here Books, 1985.
The Conquerors, Cherry Valley: Cherry Valley Editions, 1989.

Carolyn Cassady

Heart Beat: My Life with Jack & Neal, Berkeley: Creative Arts, 1976.
Off The Road: My Years with Cassady, Kerouac, and Ginsberg, New York: William Morrow, 1990.

Neal Cassady

The First Third and Other Writings, San Francisco: City Lights Books, 1981.
Neal Cassady: Collected Letters, 1944–1967, ed. David Moore, New York: Penguin, 2004.

Criticism

Plummer, William, *The Holy Goof: A Biography of Neal Cassady*, New York: Paragon House, 1981.
Sandison, David, and Vickers, Graham, *Neal Cassady: The Fast Life of a Beat Hero*, Chicago: Chicago Review Press, 2006.

Andy Clausen

Without Doubt, Berkeley: Zeitgeist Press, 1990.
Trek to the Top of the World, Berkeley: Zeitgeist Press, 1996.
Fortieth Century Man: Selected Verse, 1996–1966, New York: Autonomedia, 1997.
Ginsberg, Corso, and Me, Pressure Press, 2009.

From the Beat, Pressure Press, 2012.
Home of the Blues: More Selected Poems, Boulder: Museum of American Poetics Publications, 2013.

Elise Cowen

Elise Cowen: Poems and Fragments, ed. Tony Trigilio, Boise: Ahsahta Press, 2014.

Diane di Prima

This Kind of Bird Flies Backwards, New York: Totem Press, 1958.
Dinners and Nightmares, New York: Corinth Books, 1961.
Earthsong: Poems, 1957–1959, New York: Poets Press, 1968.
Memoirs of a Beatnik, New York: Olympia Press, 1969.
Revolutionary Letters, San Francisco: City Lights Books, 1971.
Loba, Part 1, Santa Barbara: Capra Press, 1973.
Selected Poems, 1958–1975, Plainfield: North Atlantic Books, 1975.
Loba as Eve, New York: Phoenix Book Shop, 1975.
Loba, Part II, Point Reyes: Eidolon Editions, 1977.
Loba: Parts I–VIII, Berkeley: Wingbow Press, 1978.
Pieces of a Song: Selected Poems, San Francisco: City Lights Books, 1990.
Loba, New York: Penguin, 1998.
Recollections of My Life as a Woman, New York: Viking, 2001.
The Poetry Deal, San Francisco: City Lights Books, 2014.

Bob Dylan

Chronicles, Volume 1, New York: Simon & Schuster, 2004.
Writings and Drawings, New York: Random House, 1973.
Tarantula, New York: Macmillan, 1971.

Criticism

Corcoran, Neil (ed.), *Do You Mr. Jones? Bob Dylan with the Poets and the Professors*, London: Chatto & Windus, 2002.
Ricks, Christopher, *Dylan's Visions of Sin*, New York: Viking/Penguin, 2003.

William Everson (Brother Antoninus)

Earth Poetry: Selected Essays & Interviews of William Everson, ed. Lee Bartlett, Berkeley: Oyez, 1980.
Dark God of Eros: A William Everson Reader, ed. Albert Gelpi, Berkeley: Heyday Books, 2003.

Criticism

Bartlett, Lee, *William Everson: The Life of Brother Antoninus*, New York: New Directions, 1988.
Brophy, Robert (ed.), *William Everson: Remembrances and Tributes*, Long Beach: The Robinson Jeffers Newsletter, 1995.

John Clellon Holmes

Go, New York: Scribners, 1952.
The Horn, New York: Random House, 1958.
Get Home Free, New York: Dutton, 1964.
Nothing More to Declare, New York: Dutton, 1967.
Displaced Person: The Travel Essays, Selected Essays, Volume I, Fayetteville: University of Arkansas Press, 1987.
Representative Men: The Biographical Essays, Selected Essays, Volume II, Fayetteville: University of Arkansas Press, 1988.
Passionate Opinions: The Cultural Essays, Selected Essays, Volume III, Fayetteville: University of Arkansas Press, 1988.
Night Music: Selected Poems, Fayetteville: University of Arkansas Press, 1989.

Criticism

Charters, Ann, and Charters, Samuel, *Brother Souls: John Clellon Holmes, Jack Kerouac and the Beat Generation*, Jackson: University Press of Mississippi, 2010.

Herbert Huncke

Huncke's Journal, New York: Poet's Press, 1965.
The Evening Sun Turned Crimson, Cherry Valley: Cherry Valley Editions, 1980.
Guilty of Everything: The Autobiography of Herbert Huncke, Madras, NY: Manhuman Press, 1987, New York: Paragon House, 1990.
The Herbert Huncke Reader, ed. Benjamin G. Schafer, New York: William Morrow, 1997.

Criticism

Holladay, Hilary, *Herbert Huncke: The Times Square Hustler Who Inspired Jack Kerouac and the Beat Generation*, Tucson: Schaffner Press, 2015.

Ted Joans

Jazz Poems, New York: Rhino Press, 1959.
All of Ted Joans and No More, New York: Excelsior, 1961.
The Hipsters, New York: Corinth, 1961.
Black Pow-Wow: Jazz Poems, New York: Hill & Wang, 1969.
Afrodisia: New Poems, New York: Hill & Wang, 1970.
A Black Manifesto in Jazz Poetry and Prose, London: Calder & Boyars, 1971.
Teducation: Selected Poems, Minneapolis: Coffee House Press, 1999.

Joyce Johnson

Come and Join the Dance, New York: Atheneum, 1962.
Bad Connections, New York: Putnam, 1978.
Minor Characters: A Young Woman's Coming of Age in the Beat Orbit of Jack Kerouac, New York: Penguin, 1983.
In the Night Café, New York: Dutton, 1989.
What Lisa Knew: The Truth and Lies of the Steinberg Case, New York: Putnam, 1990.
Door Wide Open: A Beat Love Affair in Letters, 1957–1958, New York: Viking, 2000.
Missing Men: A Memoir, New York: Penguin, 2005.
The Voice is All: The Lonely Victory of Jack Kerouac, New York: Penguin, 2012.

Hettie Jones

How I Became Hettie Jones, New York: Dutton, 1990.
Drive: Poems, New York: Hanging Loose Press, 1998.
All Told, New York: Hanging Loose Press, 2003.
Love H: The Letters of Hettie Jones and Helene Dorn, Durham, NC: Duke University Press, 2016.

LeRoi Jones /Amiri Baraka

Preface to a Twenty Volume Suicide Note, New York: Token Press/Corinth, 1961.
Cuba Libre, New York: Fair Plays for Cuba Committee, 1961.
Blues People: Negro Music in White America, New York: William Morrow, 1963.
Dutchman and The Slave: Two Plays, New York: William Morrow, 1964.
The Dead Lecturer, New York: Grove Press, 1964.

The System of Dante's Hell, New York: Grove Press, 1965.
Home: Social Essays, New York: William Morrow, 1966.
Black Art, Newark: Jihad, 1967.
Slave Ship: A One Act Play, Newark: Jihad, 1967.
The Baptism and The Toilet, New York: Grove Press, 1967.
Tales, New York: Grove Press, 1967.
Black Magic: Sabotage; Target Study; Black Art; Collected Poetry, 1961–1967, New York: Bobbs-Merrill, 1969.
It's Nation Time, Chicago: Third World Press, 1970.
Selected Poetry of Amiri Baraka/LeRoi Jones, New York: William Morrow, 1979.
Daggers and Javelins, Essays, 1974–1979, New York: William Morrow, 1984.
The Autobiography of LeRoi Jones, New York: Freundlich Books, 1984.
The LeRoi Jones/Amiri Baraka Reader, ed. William Harris, New York: Thunder Mouth's Press, 1991.
Transbluesency: The Selected Poems of Amiri Baraka/LeRoi Jones, New York: Marsilio Publishers, 1995.
Someone Blew Up America & Other Poems, Philipsburg: House of Nehesi Publishers, 2003.
The Book of the Monk, Candia: John LeBow, 2005.
S.O.S.: Poems, 1961–2013, ed. Paul Vengelisti, New York: Grove Press, 2015.

Criticism

Benston, Kimberley W., *Baraka: The Renegade and The Mask*, New Haven: Yale University Press, 1975.
Brown, Lloyd W., *Amiri Baraka*, Boston, MA: Twayne, 1980.
Harris, William J., *The Poetry and Poetics of Amiri Baraka: The Jazz Aesthetic*, Columbia: University of Missouri Press, 1985.
Hudson, Theodore, *From LeRoi Jones to Amiri Baraka*, Durham, NC: Duke University Press, 1973.
Sollors, Werner, *Amiri Baraka/LeRoi Jones: the Quest for a 'Populist Modernism'*, New York: Columbia University Press, 1978.

Lenore Kandel

The Love Book, San Francisco: Stolen Paper Editions, 1966.
Word Alchemy, New York: Grove Press, 1967.

Criticism

Wolf, Leonard, *Voices from the Love Generation*, Boston, MA: Little, Brown, 1968.

Bob Kaufman

Abomunist Manifesto, San Francisco: City Lights Books, 1959.
Does the Secret Mind Whisper?, San Francisco: City Lights Books, 1959.
Second April, San Francisco: City Lights Books, 1961.
Solitudes Crowded with Loneliness, New York: New Directions, 1965.
Golden Sardine, San Francisco: City Lights Books, 1967.
The Ancient Rain: Poems, 1956–1978, New York: New Directions, 1981.
Cranial Guitar, ed. Gerald Nicosia, Minneapolis: Coffee House Press, 1996.

Edie Kerouac Parker

You'll Be Okay: My Life with Jack Kerouac, San Francisco: City Lights Books, 2007.

Jan Kerouac

Baby Drive, New York: St. Martin's Press, 1981.
Train Song, New York: Henry Holt, 1988.

Joan Haverty Kerouac

Nobody's Wife: The Smart Aleck and the King of the Beats, California: Creative Arts Book Company, 2000.

Ken Kesey

One Flew over the Cuckoo's Nest, New York: Viking, 1962.
Sometime a Great Notion, New York: Viking, 1964.
Kesey's Garage Sale, New York: Viking, 1973.
Demon Box, New York: Viking, 1986.
Sailor Song, New York: Viking, 1992.
Last Go Round, New York: Viking, 1994.
Kesey's Jail Journal, New York: Viking, 2003.

Criticism

Leeds, Barry, *Ken Kesey*, New York: Unger, 1981.
Porter, Gilbert M., *The Art of Grit: Ken Kesey's Fiction*, Columbia: University of Missouri Press, 1982.

Tuli Kupferberg

Birth magazine (ed.), 3 issues, 1958.
Beating, New York: Birth Press, 1959.
Snow Job, New York: Birth Press, 1959.
3000000000 . . . Beatniks; or The War against the Beat, New York: Birth Press, 1961.
1001 Ways to Live without Working, New York: Birth Press, 1961.
1001 Ways to Beat the Draft, New York: Grove Press, 1967.
1000 Ways to Make Love, New York: Grove Press, 1969.
Kill for Peace, York: Strolling Dog Press, 1987.
Kill for Peace, Again, New York: Strolling Dog Press, 1987.
I Hate Poems about Poems about Poems, Santa Cruz: We Press, 1994.
Teach Yourself Fucking, Brooklyn: Autonomedia, 2000.

Joanne Kyger

The Tapestry and the Web, San Francisco: Four Season Foundation, 1965.
Joanne, Bolinas: Angel Hair Press, 1970.
Places to Go, Los Angeles: Black Sparrow Press, 1970.
Desecheo Notebook, Berkeley: Arif Press, 1971.
Trip Out & Fall Back, Berkeley: Arif Press, 1974.
The Wonderful Focus of You, Calais: Z. Press, 1980.
The Japan and India Journals, 1960–1964, Bolinas: Timbouctou Books, 1981.
Mexico Blonde, Bolinas: Evergreen Press, 1981.
Up My Coast, Point Reyes: Floating Island Books, 1981.
Going On: Selected Poems, 1958–1980, New York: Dutton, 1983.
The Dharma Committee, Bolinas: Smithereens Press, 1986.
Just Space: Poems, 1979–1989, Santa Rosa: Black Sparrow Press, 1991.
As Ever: Selected Poems, New York: Penguin, 2002.
About Now: Collected Poems, National Poetry Foundation, 2007.
On Time: Poems, 2005–2014, San Francisco: City Lights Books, 2015.

Philip Lamantia

Erotic Poems, Berkeley: Bern Porter Books, 1946.
Ekstasis, San Francisco: Auerhahn Press, 1959.
Destroyed Works, San Francisco: Auerhahn Press, 1962.
Touch of the Marvelous, Berkeley: Oyez, 1966.
Selected Poems, 1943–1966, San Francisco: City Lights Books, 1967.
The Blood of the Air, San Francisco: City Lights Books, 1970.
Becoming Visible, San Francisco: City Lights Books, 1981.
Meadowlark West, San Francisco: City Lights Books, 1986.
Bed of Sphinxes, City Lights Books, 1997.

The Collected Poems of Philip Lamantia, Berkeley: University of California Press, 2013.

Criticism

Frattali, Steven, *Hypodermic Light: The Poetry of Philip Lamantia and the Question of Surrealism*, New York: Peter Lang, 2005.

Joanna McClure

Wolf Eyes, San Francisco: Bearthm Press, 1974.
Eulogy, Berkeley: Arif Press, 1977.
Extended Love Poem, Berkeley: Arif Press, 1978.
Hard Edge, Minneapolis: Coffee House Press, 1987.
Catching Light: Collected Poems of Joanna McClure, Berkeley: North Atlantic Books, 2013.

Michael McClure

Passage, Big Sur: Jonathan Williams, 1956.
For Artaud, New York: Totem Press, 1959.
Hymns to St. Geryon and Other Poems, San Francisco: Auerhahn Press, 1959.
Dark Brown, San Francisco: Auerhahn Press, 1961.
The New Book/A Book of Torture, New York: Grove Press, 1961.
Meat Science Essays, New York: Grove Press, 1963.
The Beard, Berkeley: Oyez, 1965.
Poisoned Wheat, San Francisco: Oyez, 1965.
Freewheelin' Frank, New York: Grove Press, 1967.
Ghost Trantras, San Francisco: Four Seasons Press, 1969.
The Sermons of Jean Harlow and the Curses of Bill the Kid, San Francisco: Four Seasons Foundation, 1969.
Star, New York: Grove Press, 1970.
A Fist-Full (1956–1957), Los Angeles: Black Sparrow Press, 1974.
Jaguar Skies, New York: New Directions, 1975.
Scratching the Beat Surface: Essays on New Vision from Blake to Kerouac, San Francisco: North Point, 1982.
Selected Poems, New York: New Directions, 1986.
Simple Eyes and Other Poems, New York: New Directions, 1994.
Huge Dreams: San Francisco and Beat Poems, New York: Penguin, 1999.
Rain Mirror, New York: New Directions, 1999.
Plum Stones: Cartoons of No Heaven, Oakland: O Books, 2002.
Mysteriosos and Other Poems, New York: New Directions, 2010.

Of Indigo and Safron: New and Selected Poems, Berkeley: University of California Press, 2010.
Mephistos and Other Poems, San Francisco: City Lights Books, 2016.

Criticism

Bartlett, Lee, *The Sun is But a Morning Star: Studies in West Coast Poetry and Poetics*, Albuquerque: University of New Mexico Press, 1989.
Phillips, Rod, *Michael McClure*, Western Writers Series 159, Boise: Boise State University Press, 2003.

Martin Matz

In the Seasons of My Eye: Selected Writings, 1953–2001, ed. Romy Ashby, New York: Panther Books, 2005.

David Meltzer

Arrows: Selected Poetry, 1957–1992, Santa Rosa: Black Sparrow Press, 1994.
Beat Thing, Albuquerque: La Alameda Press, 2004.

Jack Micheline

River of Red Wine and Other Poems, New York: Troubadour Press, 1958.
I Kiss Angels, New York: Interim Press, 1962.
In the Bronx and Other Stories, New York: Sam Hooker, 1965.
Poems of Dr. Innisfree, San Francisco: Beatitude Press, 1975.
Street of Lost Fools, Mastic: Street Press, 1975.
Yellow Horn, San Francisco: Golden Mountain Press, 1975.
Last house in America, San Francisco: Second Coming Press, 1976.
North of Manhattan: Collected Poems, Ballads and Songs, 1954–1975, San Francisco: Manroot Press, 1976.
Purple Submarine, Greenlight Press, 1976.
Skinny Dynamite, San Francisco: Second Coming Press, 1980.
67 Poems for Downtrodden Saints, San Francisco: FMSBW, 1999.

Criticism

Bennett, John (ed.), *Ragged Lion: A Tribute to Jack Micheline*, Brooklyn/Ellensberg: The Smith Publishers and Vagabond Press, 1999.
Kaufman, Alan (ed.), *The Outlaw Bible of American Poetry*, New York: Thunder's Mouth Press, 1999.

Harold Norse

Hotel Nirvana: Selected Poems, 1953–1973, San Francisco: City Lights Books, 1974.
Beat Hotel, German trans. Carl Weissner, Augsburg: MaroVerlag, 1975; English original first published: San Diego: Atticus Press, 1983.
Carnivorous Saint: Gay Poems, 1941–1946, San Francisco: Sunshine Press, 1977.
Memoirs of a Bastard Angel: A Fifty-Year Literary and Erotic Odyssey, New York: Thunder's Mouth Press, 1989.
In the Hub of the Fiery Force: Collected Poems of Harold Norse, 1934–2003, New York: Thunder Mouth's Press, 2003.

Peter Orlovsky

Clean Asshole Poems & Smiling Vegetable Songs: Poems, 1957–1977, San Francisco: City Lights Books, 1978.
Writing Poems is a Saintly Things, Sacramento: Irregular Press, 2001.
Peter Orlovsky, A Life in Words: Intimate Chronicles of a Beat Writer, with Bill Morgan, Boulder: Paradigm Publishers, 2014; New York: Routledge, 2015.

Irving Rosenthal

Sheeper, New York: Grove Press, 1967.

Albert Saijo

Trip Trap: Haiku Along the Road from San Francisco to New York, 1959, with Jack Kerouac and Lew Welch, Bolinas: Grey Fox Press, 1973.
—, *Outspeaks: A Rhapsody*, Honolulu: Bamboo Ride Press, 1997.

Ed Sanders

Poem from Jail, San Francisco: City Lights Books, 1963.
Peace Eye, Cleveland: Frontier Press, 1966.
Tales of Beatnik Glory, vol. 1, New York: Stonehill, 1975.
Investigative Poetry, San Francisco: City lights Books, 1976.
Thirsting for Peace in a Raging Century: Selected Poems, 1961–1985, Minneapolis: Coffee House Press, 1987.
Tales of Beatnik Glory, vols 1 and 2, New York: Citadel Underground, 1990.
The Fugs Second Album, Liner Notes, Fugs Records, 1993.
1968: A History in Verse, Santa Rosa: Black Sparrow Press, 1997.

America: A History in Verse, Santa Rosa: Black Sparrow Press, 2000.

Tales of Beatnik Glory, vols 1–4, Cambridge, MA: Da Capo Press, 2004.

Let's Not Keep Fighting the Trojan War: New and Selected Poems, 1986–2009, Minneapolis: Coffee House Press, 2009.

Fug You: An Informal History of the Peace Eye Bookstore, Fuck You Press, the Fugs, and Counterculture in the Lower East Side, Cambridge, MA: Da Capo Press, 2011.

Patti Smith

Just Kids: From Brooklyn to the Chelsea Hotel, A Life of Art and Friendship, New York: HarperCollins, 2010.

Gary Snyder

Myths & Texts, New York: New Directions, 1960.

The Back Country, New York: New Directions, 1968.

Regarding Wave, New York: New Directions, 1970.

Turtle Island, New York: New Directions, 1974.

The Old Ways, San Francisco: City Lights Books, 1977.

Axe Handles, San Francisco: North Point Press, 1983.

Left Out in the Rain: New Poems, 1947–1986, San Francisco: North Point Press, 1986.

Riprap and Cold Mountain Poems, San Francisco: North Point Press, 1990.

Mountains and Rivers without End, Washington, DC: Counterpoint, 1996.

A Place in Space: Ethics, Aesthetics, and Watersheds, Washington, DC: Counterpoint, 1995.

The Gary Snyder Reader: Prose, Poetry, and Translations, 1952–1998, ed. Gary Snyder, Washington, DC: Counterpoint, 1999.

Look Out: A Selection of Writings, New York: New Directions, 2002.

Back on the Fire: Essays, Emeryville: Shoemaker & Hoard, 2005.

Danger on Peaks, Washington, DC: Shoemaker & Hoard, 2005.

The Selected Letters of Gary Snyder and Allen Ginsberg, 1956–1991, Berkeley: Counterpoint, 2009.

This Present Moment: New Poems, Berkeley: Counterpoint, 2015.

The Great Clod: Notes and Memoirs on Nature and History in East Asia, Berkeley: Counterpoint, 2016.

Criticism

Davidson, Michael, *The San Francisco Renaissance: Poetics and Community at Mid-Century*, New York, Cambridge University Press, 1989.

Dean, Tim, *Gary Snyder and the American Unconscious: Inhabiting the Ground*, New York: St. Martin's Press, 1991.

Gonnerman, Mark, *A Sense of the Whole: Reading Gary Snyder's Mountains and Cities Without End*, New York: Counterpoint, 2015.

Gray, Timothy, *Gary Snyder and the Pacific Rim: Creating Countercultural Community*, Iowa City: University Press of Iowa, 2006.

Halper, Jon (ed.), *Gary Snyder: Dimensions of a Life*, San Francisco: Sierra Club Books, 1991.

McNeil, Katherine, *Gary Snyder: A Bibliography*, New York: The Phoenix Bookshop,, 1983.

Molesworth, Charles, *Gary Snyder's Vision: Poetry and The Real Work*, Columbia: University of Missouri Press, 1983.

Murphy, Patrick D., *A Place for Wayfaring: The Poetry and Prose of Gary Snyder*, Corvallis: University of Oregon Press, 2000.

—, *Understanding Gary Snyder*, Columbia: University of South Carolina Press, 1992.

— (ed.), *Critical Essays on Gary Snyder*, Boston, MA: G. K. Hall, 1990.

Schuler, Robert, *Journeys towards the Original Mind: The Long Poems of Gary Snyder*, New York: Peter Lang, 1994.

Streuding, Bob, *Gary Snyder*, Boston, MA: Twayne, 1976.

Suiter, John, *Poets on the Peaks: Gary Snyder, Philip Whalen & Jack Kerouac in the North Cascades*, Washington, DC: Counterpoint, 2002.

White, Kenneth, *The Tribal Dharma: An Essay on the Work of Gary Snyder*, Dyfed: Unicorn, 1975.

Barbara Pabst Solomon

The Beat of Life, New York: J. B. Lippincott, 1960.

Carl Solomon

Mishaps Perhaps, San Francisco: City Lights Books, 1966.

More Mishaps, San Francisco: City Lights Books, 1968.

Emergency Messages: An Autobiographical Miscellany by Carl Solomon, ed. John Tytell, New York: Paragon House, 1989.

A. B. Spellman

The Beautiful Days, New York: The Poets Press, 1965.

Four Lives in the Bebop Business, New York: Pantheon Books, 1966.

Things I Must Have Known, Minneapolis: Coffee House Press, 2008.

Jack Spicer

The Collected Books of Jack Spicer, ed. Robin Blaser, Santa Rosa: Black
  Sparrow Press, 1975.
The House That Jack Built: The Collected Lectures of Jack Spicer, Middle-
  town: Wesleyan University Press, 1998.
My Vocabulary Did This to Me: The Collected Poetry of Jack Spicer, ed.
  Peter Gizzi and Kevin Killian, Middletown: Wesleyan University Press,
  2008.

Criticism

Ellingham, Lewis, and Killian, Kevin, *Poet be Like God: Jack Spicer and
  the San Francisco Renaissance*, Hanover: University Press of New
  Hampshire, 1998.
Vincent, John Emil (ed.), *After Spicer: Critical Essays*, Middletown: Wes-
  leyan University Press, 2011.

Janine Pommy Vega

Poems to Fernando, San Francisco: City Lights Books, 1968.
Journal of a Hermit, Cherry Valley: Cherry Valley Editions, 1974.
Morning Passage, New York: Telephone Books, 1976.
Tracking the Serpent: Journeys to Four Continents, San Francisco: City
  Lights, 1997.
Mad Dogs of Trieste: New & Selected Poems, Santa Rosa: Black Sparrow
  Press, 2000.
The Green Piano, Boston, MA: Black Sparrow Books, 2005.

Anne Waldman

Baby Breakdown, Indianapolis: Bobbs-Merrill, 1970.
Giant Night, New York: Corinth Books, 1970.
Spin-Off, Bolinas: Big Sky, 1972.
Fast Speaking Woman and Other Chants, San Francisco: City Lights
  Books, 1975.
Helping the Dreamer: New and Selected Poems, 1966–1988, Minneapolis:
  Coffee House Press, 1989.
Iovis: All is Full of Love, Minneapolis: Coffee House Press, 1993.
Kill or Cure, New York: Penguin, 1994.
Iovis 11, Minneapolis: Coffee House Press, 1997.
Marriage: A Sentence, New York: Penguin, 2000.

Vow to Poetry: Essays, Interviews, and Manifestos, Minneapolis: Coffee House Press, 2001.
Outrider: Essays, Poems, Interviews, Albuquerque: La Alameda Press, 2006.
The Iovis Trilogy: Colors in the Mechanism of Concealment, Minneapolis: Coffee House Press, 2011.

Helen Weaver

The Daisy Sutra: Conversations with My Dog, Woodstock: Buddha Rock Press, 2001.
The Awakener: A Memoir of Kerouac and the Fifties, San Francisco: City Lights Books, 2009.

ruth weiss

One More Step West is the Sea, San Francisco: Ellis Press, 1958.
Gallery of Women, San Francisco; Adler Press, 1959.
South Pacific, San Francisco: Adler Press, 1959.
The Brink (16mm film), 1961; San Francisco: Videocassette, 1986.
Light and Other Poems, San Francisco: Pieces & Pieces Foundation, 1976.
Desert Journal, Boston, MA: Good Gay Poets, 1977.
Single Out, Mill Valley: D'Aurora Press, 1978.
For These Women of the Beat, San Francisco: 3300 Press, 1997.
A New View of the Matter, Prague: Mata, 1999.
Full Circle: Ein Kreis vollendet sich, Vienna: Edition Exil, 2002.
Africa, Berkeley: The Bancroft Library Press, 2003.
White Is All Colors: Weiss ist alle Farben, Donau: Edition Thanhäuser, 2004.
No Dancing Aloud/Lautes Tanzen nicht erlaubt, Vienna: Edition Exil, 2006.
Can't Stop the Beat: The Life and Works of a Beat Poet, San Francisco: Divine Arts, 2011.
A Fool's Journey: Poems & Stories/Die Reise des Narren: Gedichte & Erzählungen, Vienna: Edition Exil, 2012.

Lew Welch

Wobbly Rock, San Francisco: Auerhahn, 1960.
On, Out, Berkeley: Oyez, 1965.
Hermit Poems, San Francisco: Four Seasons Foundation, 1965.
Courses, San Francisco: Dace Haselwood, 1968.
Ring of Bone, Bolinas: Grey Fox Press, 1973.

Trip Trap: Haiku along the Road from San Francisco to New York, 1959, with Jack Kerouac and Albert Saijo, Bolinas: Grey Fox Press, 1973.
How I Work as a Poet, Bolinas: Grey Fox Press, 1977.
I, Leo: An Unfinished Novel, Bolinas: Grey Fox Press, 1977.

Criticism

Phillips, Rod, *'Forest Beatniks' and 'Urban Thoreaus': Jack Kerouac, Gary Snyder, Lew Welch, and Michael McClure,* New York: Peter Lang, 2000.
Saroyan, Aram, *Genesis Angels: The Saga of Lew Welch and the Beat Generation,* New York: William Morrow, 1979.

Philip Whalen

Like I Say, New York, New York: Totem Press/Corinth Books, 1960.
Memoirs of an Interglacial Age, San Francisco: Auerhahn Press, 1960.
Self-Portrait from Another Direction, San Francisco: Auerhahn Press, 1960.
Highgrade: Doodles, Poems, San Francisco: Coyote's Journal, 1966.
Scenes of Life at the Capital, San Francisco: Maya Quarto Ten, 1970.
Severance Pay: Poems, 1967–1969, San Francisco: Four Seasons Foundation, 1970.
The Kindness of Strangers: Poems, 1967–1974, Bolinas: Four Seasons Foundation, 1976.
Decompressions: Selected Poems, Bolinas: Grey Fox Press, 1977.
Enough Said: Poems, 1974–1979, San Francisco: Grey Fox Press, 1980.
Heavy Breathing: Poems, 1967–1980, San Francisco: Four Seasons Foundation, 1983.
Canoeing up Cabarga Creek: Buddhist Poems, 1955–1986, Berkeley: Parallax Press, 1996.

Criticism

Schneider, David, *Crowded by Beauty: The Life and Zen of Poet Philip Whalen,* Berkeley: The University of California Press, 2015.
Suiter, John, *Poets on the Peaks: Gary Snyder, Philip Whalen & Jack Kerouac,* Washington, DC: Counterpoint, 2002.

Selected International Beat Writings

Cremer, Jan, *I, Jan Cremer,* New York: Shorecraft, 1965.
Ellis, Royston, *The Big Beat Scene,* London: Four Square, 1961.

Horovitz, Michael (ed.), *Children of Albion: Poetry of the Underground*, Harmondsworth: Penguin, 1969.

Litt, Toby, *Beatniks: An English Road Movie*, London: Secker and Warburg, 1997.

Mitchell, Adrian, *Come on Everybody: Poem,s 1953–2008*, Hexham: Bloodaxe Books, 2003.

Nunes, João Carlos Raposo, *Todo O Voo, Que Termina) Neste Corpo*, Edições Távola Redonda, 1976.

Nuttall, Jeff, *Bomb Culture*, London: McGibbon and Kee, 1968.

Sakaki, Nanao, *Break the Mirror: The Poems of Nanao Sakaki*, Noblesboro, MN: Blackberry, 1987.

Shiraishi, Kazuko, *Seinaru Inja Kisetsu/Seasons of Sacred Lust*, New York: New Directions, 1970.

—, *Let's Eat Stars*, Noblesboro, MN: Blackberry, 1977.

Trocchi, Alexander, *Cain's Book*, New York: Grove Press, 1960.

Vinkenoog, Simon, *Hoogseizoen/High Season*, Amsterdam: De Bezige Bij, 1962.

Voznesensky, Andrei, *Dogalypse: San Francisco Poetry Reading*, San Francisco: City Lights Books, 1972.

Wondratschek, Wolf, *Menschen. Orte. Fäuste*, Zurich: Diogenes, 1987.

Beat Anthologies

Allen, Donald (ed.), *The New American Poetry*, New York: Grove, 1960.

Baro, Gene (ed.), *'Beat' Poets*, London: Studio Vista, 1969.

Beatitude Anthology, San Francisco: City Lights Books, 1960.

Carroll, Paul (ed.), *The Young American Poets*, Chicago: Follett Publishing Company, 1968.

Charters, Ann (ed.), *The Portable Beat Reader*, New York: Penguin, 1992.

— (ed.), *Beat Down to Your Soul: What Was the Beat Generation?*, New York: Penguin, 2001.

Ciuraru, Carmela (ed.), *Beat Poets*, New York: Alfred A. Knopf, 2002.

Feldman, Gene, and Gartenberg, Max (eds), *The Beat Generation and the Angry Young Men*, New York: Citadel Press, 1958.

Ferlinghetti, Lawrence (ed.), *City Lights Anthology*, San Francisco: City Lights Books, 1974.

Fisher, Stanley (ed.), *Beat Coast East: An Anthology of Rebellion*, New York: Excelsior Press, 1960.

George-Warren, Holly (ed.), *The Rolling Stone Book of the Beats: The Beat Generation and American Culture*, New York: Hyperion Press, 1999.

Grace, Nancy M., and Johnson, Ronna C. (eds), *Breaking the Rule of Cool: Interviewing and Reading Women Beat Writers*, Jackson: University of Mississippi Press, 2004.

Hollo Anselm (ed.), *Red Cats*, San Francisco: City Lights Books, 1962.
Honan, Park (ed.), *The Beats: An Anthology of 'Beat' Writing*, London: J. M. Dent & Sons, 1987.
Jones LeRoi (ed.), *The Moderns: An Anthology of New Writing*, New York: Corinth Books, 1963.
Kherdian, David (ed.), *Beat Voices: An Anthology of Beat Poetry*, New York: Beech Tree Books, 1996.
Knight, Arthur, and Knight, Kit (eds), *The Beat Vision: A Primary Source Book*, New York: Paragon, 1987.
Knight, Brenda (ed.), *Women of the Beat Generation: The Writers, Artists, and Muses at the Heart of a Revolution*, Berkeley: Conari Press, 1996.
Krim, Seymour (ed.), *The Beats*, Greenwich, Connecticut: Fawcett Publications, 1960.
Micheline, Jack (ed.), *Six American Poets*, New York: Harvard Book Company, 1964.
Mofford, Juliet (ed.), *The Beat Generation*, Carlisle, MA; Discovery Enterprises, 1970, 1998.
Parkinson, Thomas (ed.), *A Casebook on the Beat*, New York: Thomas Y. Crowell, 1961.
Peabody, Richard (ed.), *A Different Beat: Writings by Women of the Beat Generation*, London: Serpent's Tail, 1997.
Penguin Modern Poets 5, *Gregory Corso, Lawrence Ferlinghetti, Allen Ginsberg*, Harmondsworth: Penguin, 1963.
Plimpton, George (ed.), *Beat Writers at Work: The Paris Review*, New York: Modern Library, 1998.
Schulman, Howard (ed.), *Pa'Lante: Poetry Polity Prose of a New World*, New York: League of Militant Poets, 1962.
Waldman, Anne (ed.), *The Beat Book: Poems and Fictions of the Beat Generation*, Boston, MA: Shambhala Publications, 1996.
Waldman, Anne, and Wright, Laura (eds), *Beats at Naropa: An Anthology*, Minneapolis: Coffee House Press, 2009.
Waldman, Anne, and Webb, Marilyn (eds), *Talking Poetics: Annals of the Jack Kerouac School of Disembodied Poetics*, Boulder: Shambhala, 1978.
Wholly Communion: International Poetry at the Royal Albert Hall, dir. Peter Whitehead, Lorrimer Films, 1965.
Wilentz, Elias (ed.), *The Beat Scene*, New York: Corinth Books, 1960.

Selected Screen Materials

The Beat Generation (1959), dir. Charles F. Hass.
A Bucket of Blood (1959), dir. Roger Corman.
'Jack Kerouac: The King of the Beats' (1959), *The Steve Allen Show*, NBC.

Pull My Daisy (1959), dir. Robert Frank and Alfred Leslie.
Beat Girl (1960), dir. Edmond T. Gréville.
The Subterraneans (1960), dir. Ranald MacDougall.
The Brink (1961), script/dir. ruth weiss.
Flaming Creatures (1963), dir. Jack Smith.
Towers Open Fire (1963), dir. Anthony Balch, screenplay William Burroughs.
Wholly Communion (1965), dir. Peter Whitehead.
Heart Beat (1980), dir. John Byrum.
Burroughs: The Movie (1983), dir. Howard Brookner.
Kerouac: The Movie (1985), dir. John Antonelli.
What Happened to Kerouac? (1986), dir. Richard Lerner and Lewis MacAdams.
The Beat Generation: An American Dream (1987), dir. Janet Forman.
Naked Lunch (1991), dir. David Cronenberg.
William S. Burroughs: Commissioner of Sewers (1991), dir. Klaus Maeck.
The Life and Times of Allen Ginsberg (1993), dir. Jerry Aronson.
The NY Beat Generation Show (1995), dir. Mitch Corber.
The Coney Island of Lawrence Ferlinghetti (1996), dir. Christopher Felver.
Original Beats: A Film on Herbert Huncke and Gregory Corso (1996), dir. François Bernardi.
A Poet on the Lower East Side: A Docu-diary on Allen Ginsberg (1997), dir. Gyula Gazdag.
The Last Time I Committed Suicide (1997), dir. Stephen T. Kay.
Diane di Prima: Beat Legend (1998), dir. Mitch Corber.
The Source: A Film of the Beat Generation (1999), dir. Chuck Workman.
Beat (2000), dir. Gary Walkow.
No Direction Home: Bob Dylan (2005), dir. Martin Scorsese.
Neal Cassady (2007), dir. Noah Buschel.
Rebel Roar: The Sound of Michael McClure (2008), dir. Kurt Hemmer.
West Coast Beat & Beyond (2008), dir. Christopher Felver.
Corso: The Last Beat (2009), dir. Gustave Reininger.
Howl (2010), dir. Rob Epstein and Jeffrey Friedman.
William Burroughs: A Man Within (2010), dir. Yony Leyser.
Wow! Ted Joans Lives (2010), dir. Kurt Hemmer and Tom Knoff.
Love Always, Carolyn: A Film about Kerouac, Cassady and Me (2011), dir. Malin Korkeasalo and Maria Ramström.
The Poetry Deal: A Film with Diane di Prima (2011), dir. Melanie La Rosa.
The Beat Hotel (2012), dir. Alan Govenar.
On the Road (2012), dir. Walter Salles and Sam Riley.
Big Sur (2013), dir. Michael Polish.
Ferlinghetti: The Rebirth of Wonder (2013), dir. Christopher Felver.
Kill Your Darling (2013), dir. John Krokidas.

Secondary Scholarship

Selected Books

Adler, Edwards, and Mindich, Bernards (eds), *Beat Art: Visual Works by or about the Beat Generation*, New York: New York School of Education, 1994.

Allen, Donald, and Tallman, Warren, *The Poetics of the New American Poetry*, New York: Grove Press, 1973.

Ash, Mel, *Beat Spirit: The Way of the Beat Writer as a Living Experience*, New York: Penguin Putnam, 1997.

Asher, Levi (ed.), *Beats in Time: A Literary Generation's Legacy*, New York: Literary Kicks, 2011.

Bartlett, Jeffery, *One Vast Page: Essays on the Beat Writers, Their Books, and My Life, 1950–1980*, Berkeley: J. Bartlett, 1991.

Bartlett, Lee (ed.), *The Beats: Essays in Criticism*, Jefferson: McFarland, 1981.

Beckett, Larry, *Beat Poetry*, St Andrews: Beatdom, 2012.

Belletto, Stephen, *The Cambridge Companion to the Beats*, New York: Cambridge University Press, 2017.

Bockris, Victor, *Beat Punks*, Boston, MA: Da Capo, 1998.

Brossard, Chandler (ed.), *The Scene before You: A New Approach to American Culture*, New York: Rinehart & Co, 1955.

Briggs, Robert, *Ruined Time: The 1950s and The Beat*, Scappoose: RBA Publishing, 2006.

Burns, Jim, *Rebels, Beats and Poets*, Penniless Publications, 2015.

Campbell, James, *This is the Beat Generation: New York–San Francisco–Paris*, Berkeley: University of California Press, 1999.

Carden, Mary, *Women Writers of the Beat Era: Autobiography and Intertextuality*, Charlottesville: University of Virginia Press, 2018.

Carr, Roy, *The Hip: Hipsters, Jazz and the Beat Generation*, London: Faber, 1986.

Charters, Ann, *Beats and Company: A Portrait of a Literary Generation*, Garden City: Doubleday, 1986.

— (ed.), *The Beats: Literary Bohemians in Postwar America*, Dictionary of Literary Biography, vol. 16, Detroit: Gale Research Co., 1983.

Cherkovski, Neeli, *Whitman's Wild Children*, Venice: Lapis Press, 1988.

Clay, Steven, and Philips, Rodney, *A Secret Location on the Lower East Side: Adventures in Writing, 1960–1980*, New York: The New York Public Library and Granary Books, 1989.

Cook, Bruce, *The Beat Generation: The Tumultuous '50s Movement and Impact on Today*, New York: Scribner's, 1971.

Cottrell, Robert C., *Sex, Drugs, and Rock 'n' Roll: The Rise of America's 1960s Counterculture*, Lanham: Rowman & Littlefield, 2015.

Damon, Maria, *The Dark End of the Street*, Minneapolis: Minnesota University Press, 1993.

Davidson, Michael, *The San Francisco Poetry Renaissance: Poetics and Community at Mid-Century*, Cambridge: Cambridge University Press, 1989.

Edwards, Brian, *Morocco Bound: Disorienting America's Maghreb, from Casablanca to the Marrakech*, Durham, NC: Duke University Press, 2005.

Elkholy, Sharyn (ed.), *The Philosophy of the Beats*, Lexington: The University Press of Kentucky, 2012.

Fazzino, Jimmy, *World Beats: Beat Generation Writing and the Worldling of U.S. Writing*, Dartmouth: University Press of New England, 2016.

Forsgren, Frida, and Prince, Michael J. (eds), *Out of the Shadows: Beat Women are Not Beaten Women*, Kristiansand: Portal Books, 2015.

Foster, Edward Halsey, *Understanding the Beats*, Columbia: University of South Carolina Press, 1992.

Gair, Christopher, *The Beat Generation: A Beginner's Guide*, Oxford: Oneworld, 2008.

Geis, Deborah R. (ed.), *Beat Drama: Playwrights and Performances of the 'Howl' Generation*, London: Bloomsbury, 2016.

Grace, Nancy M., *Jack Kerouac and the Literary Imagination*, New York: Palgrave, 2007.

Grace, Nancy M., and Skerl, Jennie (eds), *The Transnational Beat Generation*, New York: Palgrave, 2012.

Hemmer, Kurt (ed.), *Encyclopedia of Beat Literature*, New York: Facts on File, 2007.

Halberstam, David, *The Fifties*, New York: Villard Books, 1993.

Harris, Oliver, and Mackay, Polina (eds), *Global Beat Studies*, special issue of *Comparative Literature and Culture*, 18:5 (2016), available online https://docs.lib.purdue.edu/clcweb

Hickey, Morgan, *Bohemian Register: An Annotated Bibliography of the Beat Literary Movement*, Metuchen, NJ: Scarecrow Press, 1990.

Horemans, Rudi (ed.), *Beat Indeed!*, Antwerp: EXA, 1985.

Knight, Brenda, *Women of the Beat Generation*, San Francisco: Conari Books, 1996.

Lardas, John, *The Bop Apocalypse: The Religious Visions of Kerouac, Ginsberg, and Burroughs*, Urbana: University of Illinois Press, 2001.

Lawler, William, *The Beat Generation: A Bibliographic Teaching Guide*, Lanham: Scarecrow Press, 1998.

— (ed.), *Beat Culture, Icons, Lifestyles, and Impact*, Santa Barbara: ABC-CLIO, 2005.

Lee, A. Robert (ed.), *The Beat Generation Writers*, London: Pluto Press, 1996.

—, *Designs of Blackness: Mappings in the Literature and Culture of Afro-America*, London: Pluto Press, 1998.

—, *Modern American Counter Writing: Beats, Outriders, Ethnics*, New York: Routledge, 2010.

— (ed.), *The Routledge Handbook of International Beat Literature*, New York: Routledge, 2018.

Lipton, Lawrence, *The Holy Barbarians*, New York: Messner, 1959.

McDarrah, Fred W., *Kerouac and Friends: A Beat Generation Album*, New York: William Morrow, 1986.

McDarrah, Fred W., and McDarrah, Gloria, *Beat Generation: Glory Days in Greenwich Village*, New York: Schirmer Books, 1996.

Marler, Regina, *Queer Beats: How the Beats Turned on America*, Berkeley: Cleis Press, 2004.

Martinez, Manuel Luis, *Countering the Counterculture: Rereading Postwar American Dissent from Jack Kerouac to Tomás Rivera*, Madison: University of Wisconsin Press, 2003.

Maynard, John A., *Venice West: The Beat Generation in Southern California*, New Brunswick, NJ: Rutgers University Press, 1991.

Miles, Barry, *The Beat Hotel: Ginsberg, Burroughs, and Corso in Paris, 1958–1963*, New York: Grove Press, 2000.

Miller, Douglas T., and Nowak, Marion, *The Fifties: The Way We Really Were*, New York: Doubleday, 1977.

Minnen, Cornelis A. van, Bent, Jaap van der, and Elteren, Mel van (eds), *Beat Culture: The 1950s and Beyond*, Amsterdam: VU University Press, 1999.

Morgan, Bill, *The Beat Generation in New York: A Walking Tour of Jack Kerouac's City*, San Francisco: City Lights Books, 1997.

—, *The Beat Generation in San Francisco: A Literary Tour*, San Francisco: City Lights Books, 2003.

—, *The Typewriter is Holy: The Complete, Uncensored History of the Beat Generation*, New York: Free Press, 2010.

—, *Beat Atlas: A Guide to the Beat Generation in America*, San Francisco: City Lights Books, 2011.

—, *The Beats Abroad: A Global Guide to the Beat Generation*, San Francisco: City Lights Books, 2015.

—, *The Beats Abroad: A Global Guide to the Beat Generation*, San Francisco: City Lights Books, 2016.

—, *The Best Minds of My Generation: A Literary History of the Beats*, New York: Grove Press, 2017.

Mortenson, Erik, *Capturing The Beat Moment: Cultural Politics and the Poetics of Presence*, Carbondale: Southern Illinois University Press, 2010.

Myrsiades, Kostas (ed.), *The Beat Generation: Critical Essays*, New York: Peter Lang, 2002.

Neville, Richard, *Hippie, Hippie Shake: The Dreams, the Trips, the Trials, the Love-ins, the Screw-ups . . . The Sixties*, London: Bloomsbury, 1995.

Newhouse, Thomas, *The Beat Generation and the Popular Novel in the United States, 1945–1970*, Jefferson: MacFarland, 2000.

Pantano, Patricia A., *Women of the Beat Generation, Joyce Johnson, Diane di Prima, and Carolyn Cassady: Female Agency in Transitional Times*, Ann Arbor: ProQuest, 2010.

Pekar, Harvey, *The Beats: A Graphic History*, San Francisco: City Lights Books, 2009.

Phillips, Lisa (ed.), *Beat Culture and the New America, 1958–1965*, New York: Whitney Museum of American Art/Flammarion, 1996.

Podhoretz, Norman, *Doings and Undoings: The Fifties and After in American Writing*, New York: Farrar, Straus and Company, 1964.

Polsky, Ned, *Beats, Hustlers, and Others*, New York: Doubleday, 1967.

Prince, Michael, *Adapting the Beat Poets: Burroughs, Ginsberg and Kerouac on Screen*, Lanham: Rowman & Littlefield, 2016.

Rosen, Ralph, and Murnaghan, Sheila, *The Hip Sublime: Beat Writers and the Classical Tradition*, Columbus: Ohio State University Press, 2017.

Sargent, Jack, *Naked Lens: An Illustrated History of Beat Cinema*, London: Creation Books, 1997.

Skerl, Jennie (ed.), *Reconstructing the Beats*, New York: Palgrave, 2000.

— (ed.), *Teaching Beat Literature*, special issue of *College Literature*, 27:1 (Winter 2000).

Stefanelli, Maria Anita (ed.), *City Lights: Pocket Poets and Pocket Books*, Rome: Ila Palma, Mazzone Editori, 2004.

Sterritt, David, *Mad to be Saved: The Beats, the '50s, and Film*, Carbondale: Southern Illinois University Press, 1998.

—, *Screening the Beats: Media Culture and the Beat Sensibility*, Carbondale: Southern Illinois University Press, 2004.

—, *The Beats: A Very Short Introduction*, New York: Oxford University Press, 2013.

Stevenson, Gregory, *The Daybreak Boys: Essays on the Literature of the Beat Generation*, Carbondale: Southern Illinois University Press, 1990.

—, *Pilgrims to Elsewhere: Reflections on Writings by Jack Kerouac, Allen Ginsberg, Gregory Corso, Bob Kaufman and Other*, Roskilde: Eyecorner Press, 2013.

Strausbaugh, Joseph, *The Village: 400 Years of Beats and Bohemians, Radicals and Rogues, A History of Greenwich Village*, New York: Ecco/HarperCollins, 2013.

Sukenick, Ronald, *Down and In: Life in the Underground*, New York: Collier, 1987.

Tietchen, Todd F., *The Cubalogues: Beat Writers in Revolutionary Cuba*, Gaineville: University Press of Florida, 2010.

Tonkinson, Carol (ed.), *Big Sky Mind: Buddhism and the Beat Generation*, New York: Riverhead, 1995.

Theado, Matt (ed.), *The Beats: A Literary Reference*, New York: Carroll & Graff, 2001.

Tyrell, John, *Naked Angels: The Lives and the Literature of the Beat Generation*, New York: McGraw-Hill, 1976.

—, *Paradise Outlaws: Remembering the Beats*, New York: William Morrow, 1999.

—, *The Beat Interviews*, Beatdom Books, 2014.

—, *Writing Beat and Other Occasions of Literary Mayhem*, Nashville: Vanderbilt University Press, 2014.

—, *Beat Transnationalism*, Beatdom Books, 2017.

Varner, Paul, *Historical Dictionary of the Beat Movement*, Lanham: Scarecrow Press, 2012.

Warner, Simon, *Text and Drugs and Rock 'n' Roll: The Beats and Rock Culture*, London: Bloomsbury, 2013.

Watson, Steven, *The Birth of the Beat Generation: Visionaries, Rebels, and Hipsters, 1944–1960*, New York: Pantheon Books, 1995.

Weldman, Rich, *The Beat Generation FAQ*, Milwaukee: Beatback Books, 2015.

Whaley, Preston, *Blows Like a Horn: Beat Writing, Jazz, Style, and Markets in the Transformation of US Culture*, Cambridge, MA: Harvard University Press, 2004.

Whaley-Bridge, John, *The Emergence of Buddhist American Literature*, Albany: SUNY Press, 2009.

Wilentz, Elias, *The Beat Scene*, New York: Corinth, 1960.

Wilentz, Sean, *Bob Dylan in America*, New York: Doubleday, 2010.

Selected Critical Essays

Bennett, Robert, 'Deconstructing and Reconstructing the Beats: New Directions in Beat Studies', *College Literature*, 32.2 (2005), 177–84,

Breslin, James, 'The Origins of "Howl" and "Kaddish"', *Iowa Review*, 8:2 (1977), 82–108.

Charters, Ann, 'Beat Poetry and the San Francisco Renaissance', in *The Columbia History of American Poetry*, ed. Jay Parini, New York: Columbia University Press, 1993, 581–604.

Codrescu, Andrei, 'Who's Afraid of Anne Waldman?', *Mississippi Review*, 31:3 (2003), 35–57.

Foley, Jack, 'A Second Coming: *A Coney Island of the Mind* 50th Anniversary Edition', *Contemporary Poetry Review*, 2008, online.

Fox, Robert Eliot, 'Ted Joans and the Breach of the African American Canon', *MELUS* (Fall–Winter 2004), 41–58.

Friedman, Amy L., 'Being Here As Hard as I Could: The Beat Generation Women Writers', *Discourses*, 20 (1998), 229–44

Hemmer, Kurt, 'The Prostitute Speaks: Brenda Frazer's *Troia: Mexican Memoirs*', *Paradoxa* 18 (2003), 99–117.

Hunt, Tim, 'Blow as Deep as You Want to Blow': Time, Textuality, and Jack Kerouac's Development of Spontaneous Prose', *Journal of Beat Studies*, 1 (2012), 349–63.

Kern, Robert, 'Mountains and Rivers are Us: Gary Snyder and the Nature of the Nature of Nature', special issue of *College Literature*, 27:1 (Winter 2000), ed. Jennie Skerl, 119–38.

Lee, A. Robert, 'Beat Contenders: Jack Micheline, Ed Sanders, Tuli Kupferberg', in *Global Beat Studies*, special issue of *Comparative Literature and Culture*, 18:5 (2016), ed. Oliver Harris and Polina Mackay, available online https://docs.lib.purdue.edu/clcweb

Millstein, Gilbert, 'Books of the Times', *New York Times*, 5 September 1957.

Perloff, Marjorie, 'A Lion in Our Living Room: Reading Allen Ginsberg in the Eighties', *Poetic License: Essays on Modernist and Postmodern Lyric*, Evanston: Northwestern University Press, 1990, 199–230.

Tallman, Warren, 'Kerouac's Sound', *The Tamarack Review*, 11 (1959), 58–74.

Index

Peter Orlovsky, a Life in Words: Intimate Chronicles of a Beat Writer, 111
'Another Day', 112
'Dear Allen: Ship Will Land Jan 23, 1958 –', 112
'Frirst Poem', 112
'How I Write Poetry & Who I Learned From', 112
'Jerked Off', 112
'Leper's Cry', 112–13
'Out at Sea', 112
'Peter's Jealous of Allen', 112
'Poems from Subway to Work', 112
'Writing Poems Is a Saintly Thing', 112

Parker, Charlie, 6, 152, 159, 164, 175, 187
Partisan Review, 18, 44, 135
Pasolini, Pier Paolo, 192
Patchen, Kenneth, 18, 178
Peace Eye Bookstore/ Ed Sanders, 116
Pélieu, Claude, 180
Peters, Nancy, 17, 22
Picasso, Pablo, 192
Pivano, Fernanda, 193
Plath, Sylvia, 2
Plymell, Charles, 180
Apocalypse Rose, 180
Incognito Sum, 180
The Last of the Moccasins, 180
Pocket Books Poets Series, 10, 39, 166
Podhoretz, Norman, 18
Pollock, Jackson, 132, 153, 187
Pop, Iggy and the Stooges, 13
Port Huron Statement, The, 30
Pound, Ezra, 15, 141, 193
Prescott, Orville, 64
Presley, Elvis, 27
Propper, Dan, 179
For Kerouac in Heaven, 180
'The Fable of the Final Art', 179–80
Proust, Marcel, 66, 67
Pull My Daisy, 23

Ramones, The, 13
Rauschenberg, Robert, 26
Reed, Ishmael, 16
Reed, Lou, 13, 27
Rexroth, Kenneth, 2, 17, 22, 146

Rimbaud, Arthur, 20, 112
Une saison en enfer, 20
'Le Bateau ivre', 20
Rinpoche, Chögyam Trungpa, 34, 192
Rogers, Randall K., 12
Rolling Stones, The, 27
Rollins, Sonny, 120
Rosenberg, Julius and Ethel, 29
Rosenthal, Irving, 24
Rosset, 'Barney' (Barnet), 23, 187–8
My Life in Publishing and How I Fought Censorship, 187–8
Rothko, Mark, 153
Rubin, Jerry, 12
DO IT! Scenarios of the Revolution, 12

St. Mark's Poetry Project, 130, 144
Sakaki, Nanao, 110, 193
Break The Mirror, 110
Let's Eat Stars, 110
Sampas, Stella, 21, 66, 78
San Francisco Renaissance, 2, 17, 25
Sanders, Ed, 11, 30, 39–40, 116–19, 120, 127, 189
1968: A History in Verse, 118
America: A History in Verse, 118
The Family: The Story of Charles Manson's Dune Buggy Attack Battalion, 117
Fuck You! A Magazine of the Arts, 117
Fug You: An Informal Memoir of the Peace Eye Book Store, the Fuck You Press & Counterculture in the Lower East Side, 117
Investigative Poetry, 117
Let's Not Keep Fighting the Trojan War: New and Selected Poems, 1986–2009, 40, 117, 119
Poems from Jail, 116
Poems or New Orleans, 118
The Poetry and Life of Allen Ginsberg: A Narrative Poem, 118
Tales of Beatnik Glory, 116
Thirsting for Peace in a Raging Century: New and Selected Poems, 1961–1985, 117–18
Woodstock Journal, 118
'Ode to a Generation' 119